THE TEACHER.

MORAL INFLUENCES

EMPLOYED IN

THE INSTRUCTION AND GOVERNMENT

OF

THE YOUNG.

A NEW AND REVISED EDITION.

BY JACOB ABBOTT.

With Engravings.

NEW YORK:
HARPER & BROTHERS, PUBLISHER
FRANKLIN SQUARE.
1873.

PREFACE.

THIS book is intended to detail, in a familiar and practical manner, a system of arrangements for the organization and management of a school, based on the employment, so far as is practicable, of *Moral Influences*, as a means of effecting the objects in view. Its design is, not to bring forward new theories or new plans, but to develop and explain, and to carry out to their practical applications such principles as, among all skillful and experienced teachers, are generally admitted and acted upon. Of course it is not designed for the skillful and experienced themselves, but it is intended to embody what they already know, and to present it in a practical form for the use of those who are beginning the work, and who wish to avail themselves of the experience which others have acquired.

Although moral influences are the chief foundations on which the power of the teacher over the minds and hearts of his pupils is, according to this treatise, to rest, still it must not be imagined that the system here recommended is one of persuasion. It is a system of authority—supreme and unlimited authority—a point essential in all plans for the supervision of the young;

but it is authority secured and maintained as far as possible by moral measures. There will be no dispute about the propriety of making the most of this class of means. Whatever difference of opinion there may be on the question whether physical force is necessary at all, every one will agree that, if ever employed, it must be only as a last resort, and that no teacher ought to make war upon the body, unless it is proved that he can not conquer through the medium of the mind.

In regard to the anecdotes and narratives which are very freely introduced to illustrate principles in this work, the writer ought to state that, though they are all substantially true—that is, all except those which are expressly introduced as mere suppositions, he has not hesitated to alter very freely, for obvious reasons, the unimportant circumstances connected with them. He has endeavored thus to destroy the personality of the narratives without injuring or altering their moral effect.

From the very nature of our employment, and of the circumstances under which the preparation for it must be made, it is plain that, of the many thousands who are in the United States annually entering the work, a very large majority must depend for all their knowledge of the art, except what they acquire from their own observation and experience, on what they can obtain from books. It is desirable that the class of works from which such knowledge can be obtained should be increased. Some excellent and highly useful specimens have already appeared, and very many more would be eagerly read by teachers, if properly prepared. It is essential, however, that they should be written by experienced teachers, who have for some years been actively engaged and specially interested in the work; that they should be written in a very practical and familiar style, and that they should exhibit principles which are unquestionably true, and generally admitted by good teachers, and not the new theories peculiar to the writer himself. In a word, utility and practical effect should be the only aim.

CONTENTS.

CHAPTER I.

INTEREST IN TEACHING.

CHAPTER II.

GENERAL ARRANGEMENTS.

CHAPTER III.

INSTRUCTION.

CHAPTER IV.

MORAL DISCIPLINE.

CHAPTER VII.

SCHEMING.

CHAPTER VIII.

REPORTS OF CASES.

CHAPTER IX.

THE TEACHER'S FIRST DAY.

THE TEACHER.

CHAPTER I.

INTEREST IN TEACHING.

A MOST singular contrariety of opinion prevails in the community in regard to the *pleasantness* of the business of teaching. Some teachers go to their daily task merely upon compulsion; they regard it as intolerable drudgery. Others love the work: they hover around the school-room as long as they can, and never cease to think, and seldom to talk, of their delightful labors.

Unfortunately, there are too many of the former class, and the first object which, in this work, I shall attempt to accomplish, is to show my readers, especially those who have been accustomed to look upon the business of teaching as a weary and heartless toil, how it happens that it is, in any case, so pleasant. The human mind is always essentially the same. That which is tedious and joyless to one, will be so to another, if pursued in the same way, and under the same circumstances. And teaching, if it is pleasant, animating, and exciting to one, may be so to all.

I am met, however, at the outset, in my effort to show why it is that teaching is ever a pleasant work, by the want of a name for a certain faculty or capacity of the human mind, through which most of the enjoyment of teaching finds its avenue. Every mind is so constituted as to take a positive pleasure in the exercise of ingenuity in adapting means to an end, and in watching the operation of them—in accomplishing by the intervention of instruments what we could not accomplish without—in devising (when we see an object to be effected which is too great for our *direct* and *immediate* power) and setting at work some *instrumentality* which may be sufficient to accomplish it.

It is said that when the steam-engine was first put into

operation, such was the imperfection of the machinery, that a boy was necessarily stationed at it to open and shut alternately the cock by which the steam was now admitted and now shut out from the cylinder. One such boy, after patiently doing his work for many days, contrived to connect this stop-cock with some of the moving parts of the engine by a wire, in such a manner that the engine itself did the work which had been intrusted to him; and after seeing that the whole business would go regularly forward, he left the wire in charge, and went away to play.

Such is the story. Now if it is true, how much pleasure the boy must have experienced in devising and witnessing the successful operation of his scheme. I do not mean the pleasure of relieving himself from a dull and wearisome duty; I do not mean the pleasure of anticipated play; but I mean the strong interest he must have taken in *contriving and executing his plan*. When, wearied out with his dull, monotonous work, he first noticed those movements of the machinery which he thought adapted to his purpose, and the plan flashed into his mind, how must his eye have brightened, and how quick must the weary listlessness of his employment have vanished. While he was maturing his plan and carrying it into execution—while adjusting his wires, fitting them to the exact length and to the exact position—and especially when, at last, he began to watch the first successful operation of his contrivance, he must have enjoyed a pleasure which very few even of the joyous sports of childhood could have supplied.

It is not, however, exactly the pleasure of exercising *ingenuity in contrivance* that I refer to here; for the teacher has not, after all, a great deal of absolute *contriving* to do, or, rather, his *principal business* is not contriving. The greatest and most permanent source of pleasure to the boy, in such a case as I have described, is his feeling that he is accomplishing a great effect by a slight effort of his own; the feeling of *power;* acting through the *intervention of instrumentality,* so as to multiply his power. So great would be this satisfaction, that he would almost wish to have some other similar work assigned him, that he might have another opportunity to contrive some plan for its easy accomplishment.

Looking at an object to be accomplished, or an evil to be remedied, then studying its nature and extent, and devising and executing some means for effecting the purpose desired, is, in all cases, a source of pleasure; especially when, by the process, we bring to view or into operation new powers, or powers heretofore hidden, whether they are our own powers, or those of objects upon which we act. Experimenting has a sort of magical fascination for all. Some do not like the trouble of making preparations, but all are eager to see the results. Contrive a new machine, and every body will be interested to witness or to hear of its operation. Develop any heretofore unknown properties of matter, or secure some new useful effect from laws which men have not hitherto employed for their purposes, and the interest of all around you will be excited to observe your results; and, especially, you will yourself take a deep and permanent pleasure in guiding and controlling the power you have thus obtained.

This is peculiarly the case with experiments upon mind, or experiments for producing effects through the medium of voluntary acts of others, making it necessary that the contriver should take into consideration the laws of mind in forming his plans. To illustrate this by rather a childish case: I once knew a boy who was employed by his father to remove all the loose small stones, which, from the peculiar nature of the ground, had accumulated in the road before the house. The boy was set at work by his father to take them up, and throw them over into the pasture across the way. He soon got tired of picking up the stones one by one, and so he sat down upon the bank to try to devise some better means of accomplishing his work. He at length conceived and adopted the following plan: He set up in the pasture a narrow board for a target, or, as boys would call it, a mark, and then, collecting all the boys of the neighborhood, he proposed to them an amusement which boys are always ready for—firing at a mark. The stones in the road furnished the ammunition, and, of course, in a very short time the road was cleared; the boys working for the accomplishment of their leader's task, when they supposed they were only finding amusement for themselves.

Here, now, is experimenting upon the mind—the production of useful effect with rapidity and ease by the intervention of proper instrumentality—the conversion, by means of a little knowledge of human nature, of that which would have otherwise been dull and fatiguing labor into a most animating sport, giving pleasure to twenty instead of tedious labor to one. Now the contrivance and execution of such plans is a source of positive pleasure. It is always pleasant to bring even the properties and powers of matter into requisition to promote our designs; but there is a far higher pleasure in controlling, and guiding, and moulding to our purpose the movements of mind.

It is this which gives interest to the plans and operation of human governments. Governments can, in fact, do little by actual force. Nearly all the power that is held, even by the most despotic executive, must be based on an adroit management of the principles of human nature, so as to lead men voluntarily to co-operate with the leader in his plans. Even an army could not be got into battle, in many cases, without a most ingenious arrangement, by means of which half a dozen men can drive, literally drive, as many thousands into the very face of danger and death. The difficulty of leading men to battle must have been, for a long time, a very perplexing one to generals. It was at last removed by the very simple expedient of creating a greater danger behind than there is before. Without ingenuity of contrivance like this, turning one principle of human nature against another, and making it for the momentary interest of men to act in a given way, no government could stand.

I know of nothing which illustrates more perfectly the way by which a knowledge of human nature is to be turned to account in managing human minds than a plan which was adopted for clearing the galleries of the British House of Commons many years ago, before the present Houses of Parliament were built. There was then, as now, a gallery appropriated to spectators, and it was customary to require these visitors to retire when a vote was to be taken or private business was to be transacted. When the officer in attendance was ordered to clear the gallery, it was sometimes found to be a very troublesome and slow operation; for those who first went out remained obstinately as close to the doors as possible, so as to secure the opportunity to come in again first when the doors should be re-opened. The consequence was, there was so great an accumulation around the doors outside, that it was almost impossible for the crowd to get out. The whole difficulty arose from the eager desire of every one to remain as near as possible to the door, *through which they were to come back again.* Notwithstanding the utmost efforts of the officers, fifteen minutes were sometimes consumed in effecting the object, when the order was given that the spectators should retire.

The whole difficulty was removed by a very simple plan. One door only was opened when the crowd was to retire, and they were then admitted, when the gallery was opened again, through *the other.* The consequence was, that as soon as the order was given to clear the galleries, every one fled as fast as possible through the open door around to the one which was closed, so as to be ready to enter first, when that, in its turn, should be opened. This was usually in a few minutes, as the purpose for which the spectators were ordered to retire was in most cases simply to allow time for taking a vote.

Here it will be seen that, by the operation of a very simple plan, the very eagerness of the crowd to get back as soon as possible, which had been the *sole cause of the difficulty*, was turned to account most effectually to the removal of it. Before, the first that went out were so eager to return, that they crowded around the door of egress in such a manner as to prevent others going out; but by this simple plan of ejecting them by one door and admitting them by another, that very eagerness made them clear the passage at once, and caused every one to hurry away into the lobby the moment the command was given.

The planner of this scheme must have taken great pleasure in witnessing its successful operation; though the officer who should go steadily on, endeavoring to remove the reluctant throng by dint of mere driving, might well have found his task unpleasant. But the exercise of ingenuity in studying the nature of the difficulty with which a man has to contend, and bringing in some antagonist principle of human nature to remove it, or, if not an antagonist principle, a similar principle, operating, by a peculiar arrangement of circumstances, in an antagonist manner, is always pleasant. From this source a large share of the enjoyment which men find in the active pursuits of life has its origin.

The teacher has the whole field which this subject opens fully before him. He has human nature to deal with most directly. His whole work is one of experimenting upon mind; and the mind which is before him to be the subject of his operation is exactly in the state to be most easily and pleasantly operated upon. The reason now why some teachers find their work delightful, and some find it wearisomeness and tedium itself, is that some do and some do not take this view of the nature of it. One instructor is like the engine-boy, turning, without cessation or change, his everlasting stop-cock, in the same ceaseless, mechanical, and monotonous routine. Another is like the little workman in his brighter moments, arranging his invention, and watching with delight the successful and easy accomplishment of his wishes by means of it. One is like the officer, driving by vociferations, and threats, and demonstrations of violence, the spectators from the galleries. The other like the shrewd contriver, who converts the very desire to return, which was the sole cause of the difficulty, to a most successful and efficient means of its removal.

These principles show how teaching may, in some cases, be a delightful employment, while in others its tasteless dullness is interrupted by nothing but its perplexities and cares. The school-room is in reality a little empire of mind. If the one who presides in it sees it in its true light; studies the nature and tendency of the minds which he has to control; adapts his plans and his measures to the laws of human nature, and endeavors to accomplish his purposes for them, not by mere labor and force, but by ingenuity and enterprise, he will take pleasure in administering his little government. He will watch, with care and interest, the operation of the moral and intellectual causes which he sets in operation, and find, as he accomplishes his various objects with increasing facility and power, that he will derive a greater and greater pleasure from his work.

Now when a teacher thus looks upon his school as a field in which he is to exercise skill, and ingenuity, and enterprise; when he studies the laws of human nature, and the character of those minds upon which he has to act; when he explores deliberately the nature of the field which he has to cultivate, and of the objects which he wishes to accomplish, and applies means judiciously and skillfully adapted to the object, he must necessarily take a strong interest in his work. But when, on the other hand, he goes to his employment only to perform a certain regular round of daily toil, undertaking nothing and anticipating nothing but this dull and unchangeable routine, and when he looks upon his pupils mere-

ly as passive objects of his labors, whom he is to treat with simple indifference while they obey his commands, and to whom he is only to apply reproaches and punishment when they do wrong, such a teacher never can take pleasure in the school. Weariness and dullness must reign in both master and scholars when things, as he imagines, are going right, and mutual anger and crimination when they go wrong.

Scholars never can be successfully instructed by the power of any dull mechanical routine, nor can they be properly governed by the blind, naked strength of the master; such means must fail of the accomplishment of the purposes designed, and consequently the teacher who tries such a course must have constantly upon his mind the discouraging, disheartening burden of unsuccessful and almost useless labor. He is continually uneasy, dissatisfied, and filled with anxious cares, and sources of vexation and perplexity continually arise. He attempts to remove evils by waging against them a useless and most vexatious warfare of threatening and punishment; and he is trying continually *to drive*, when he might know that neither the intellect nor the heart are capable of being driven.

I will simply state one case, to illustrate what I mean by the difference between blind force and active ingenuity and enterprise in the management of school. I once knew the teacher of a school who made it his custom to have writing attended to in the afternoon. The school was in the country, and it was the old times when quills, instead of steel pens, were universally used. The boys were accustomed to take their places at the appointed hour, and each one would set up his pen in the front of his desk for the teacher to come and mend them. The teacher would accordingly pass around the school-room, mending the pens, from desk to desk, thus enabling the boys, in succession, to begin their task. Of course, each boy, before the teacher came to his desk, was necessarily idle, and, almost necessarily, in mischief. Day after day the teacher went through this regular routine. He sauntered slowly and listlessly through the aisles, and among the benches of the room, wherever he saw the signal of a pen. He paid, of course, very little attention to the writing, now and then reproving, with an impatient tone, some extraordinary instance of carelessness, or leaving his work to suppress some rising disorder. Ordinarily, however, he seemed to be lost in vacancy of thought, dreaming, perhaps, of other scenes, or inwardly repining at the eternal monotony and tedium of a teacher's life. His boys took no interest in their work, and of course made no progress. They were sometimes unnecessarily idle, and sometimes mischievous, but never usefully or pleasantly employed, for the whole hour was passed before the pens could all be brought down. Wasted time, blotted books, and fretted tempers were all the results which the system produced.

The same teacher afterward acted on a very different principle. He looked over the field, and said to himself, "What are the objects which I wish to accomplish in this writing exercise, and how can I best accomplish them? I wish to obtain the greatest possible amount of industrious and careful practice in writing. The first thing evidently is to save the wasted time." He accordingly made preparation for mending the pens at a previous hour, so that all should be ready, at the appointed time, to commence the work together. This could be done quite as conveniently when the boys were engaged in studying, by requesting them to put out their pens at an appointed and *previous* time. He sat at his table, and the pens of a whole bench were brought to him, and, after being carefully mended, were returned, to be in readiness for the writing hour. Thus the first difficulty, the loss of time, was obviated.

"I must make them *industrious* while they write," was his next thought. After thinking of a variety of methods, he determined to try the following: he required all to begin together at the top of the page, and write the same line, in a hand of the same size. They were all required to begin together, he himself beginning at the same time, and writing about as fast as he thought they ought to write in order to secure the highest improvement. When he had finished his line, he ascertained how many had preceded him and how many were behind. He requested the first to write slower, and the others faster; and by this means, after a few trials, he secured uniform, regular, systematic, and industrious employment throughout the school. Probably there were, at first, difficulties in the operation of the plan, which he had to devise ways and means to surmount; but what I mean to present particularly to the reader is, that he was *interested in his experiments.* While sitting in his desk, giving his command to *begin* line after line, and noticing the unbroken silence, and attention, and interest which prevailed (for each boy was interested to see how nearly with the master he could finish his work), while presiding over such a scene he must have been interested. He must have been pleased with the exercise of his almost military command, and to witness how effectually order and industry, and excited and pleased attention, had taken the place of listless idleness and mutual dissatisfaction.

After a few days, he appointed one of the older and more judicious scholars to give the word for beginning and ending the lines, and he sat surveying the scene, or walking from desk to desk, noticing faults, and considering what plans he could form for securing more and more fully the end he had in view. He found that the great object of interest and attention among the boys was to come out right, and that less pains were taken with the formation of the letters than there ought to be to secure the most rapid improvement.

But how shall he secure greater pains? By stern commands and threats? By going from desk to desk, scolding one, rapping the knuckles of another, and holding up to ridicule a third, making examples of such individuals as may chance to attract his special attention? No; he has learned that he is operating upon a little empire of mind, and that he is not to endeavor to drive them as a man drives a herd, by mere peremptory command or half angry blows. He must study the nature of the effect that he is to produce, and of the materials upon which he is to work, and adopt, after mature deliberation, a plan to accomplish his purpose founded upon the principles which ought always to regulate the action of mind upon mind, and adapted to produce the *intellectual effect* which he wishes to accomplish.

In the case supposed, the teacher concluded to appeal to emulation. While I describe the measure he adopted, let it be remembered that I am now only approving of the resort to ingenuity and invention, and the employment of moral and intellectual means for the accomplishment of his purposes, and not of the measures themselves. I am not sure the plan I am going to describe is a wise one; but I am sure that the teacher, while trying it, must *have been interested in his intellectual experiment.* His business, while pursued in such a way, could not have been a mere dull and uninteresting routine.

He purchased, for three cents apiece, two long lead pencils—an article of great value in the opinion of the boys of country schools—and he offered them, as prizes, to the boy who would write most carefully; not to the one who should write *best,* but to the one whose book should exhibit most appearance of *effort* and *care* for a week. After announcing his plan, he watched with strong interest its operation. He walked round the room while the writing was in progress, to observe the effect of his measure. He did not reprove those who were writing carelessly; he simply noticed who and how many they were. He did not commend those who were evidently making effort; he noticed who and how many they were, that he might understand how far, and upon what sort of minds, his experiment was successful, and where it failed. He was taking a lesson in human nature—human nature as it exhibits itself in boys—and was preparing to operate more and more powerfully by future plans.

The lesson which he learned by the experiment was this, that one or two prizes will not influence the majority of a large school. A few of the boys seemed to think that the pencils were possibly within their reach, and *they* made vigorous efforts to secure them; but the rest wrote on as before. Thinking it certain that they should be surpassed by the others, they gave up the contest at once in despair.

The obvious remedy was to *multiply* his prizes, so as to bring one of them within the reach of all. He reflected, too, that the real prize, in such a case, is not the value of the pencil, but the *honor of the victory;* and as the honor of the victory might as well be coupled with an object of less, as well as with one of greater value, the next week he divided his two pencils into quarters, and offered to his pupils eight prizes instead of two. He offered one to every five scholars, as they sat on their benches, and every boy then saw that a reward would certainly come within five of him. His chance, accordingly, instead of being one in twenty, became one in five.

Now is it possible for a teacher, after having philosophized upon the nature of the minds upon which he is operating, and surveyed the field, and ingeniously formed a plan, which plan he hopes will, through his own intrinsic power, produce certain effects—is it possible for him, when he comes, for the first day, to witness its operations, to come without feeling a strong interest in the result? It is not possible. After having formed such a plan, and made such arrangements, he will look forward almost with impatience to the next writing-hour. He wishes to see whether he has estimated the mental capacities and tendencies of his little community aright; and when the time comes, and he surveys the scene, and observes the operation of his measure, and sees many more are reached by it than were influenced before, he feels a strong gratification, and it is a gratification which is founded upon the noblest principles of our nature. He is tracing, on a most interesting field, the operation of cause and effect. From being the mere drudge, who drives, without intelligence or thought, a score or two of boys to their daily tasks, he rises to the rank of an intellectual philosopher, exploring the laws and successfully controlling the tendencies of mind.

It will be observed, too, that all the time this teacher was performing these experiments, and watching with intense interest the results, his pupils were going on undisturbed in their pursuits. The exercises in writing were not interrupted or deranged. This is a point of fundamental importance; for, if what I should say on the subject of exercising ingenuity and contrivance in teaching should be the means, in any case, of leading a teacher to break in upon the regular duties of his school, and destroy the steady uniformity with which the great objects of such an institution should be pursued, my remarks had better never have been written. There may be variety in methods and plan, but, through all this variety, the school, and every individual pupil of it, must go steadily forward in the acquisition of that knowledge which is of greatest importance in the business of future life. In other words, the variations and changes admitted by the teacher ought to be mainly confined to the modes of accomplishing those permanent objects to which all the exercises and arrangements of the school ought steadily to aim. More on this subject, however, in another chapter.

I will mention one other circumstance, which will help to explain the difference in interest and pleasure with which teachers engage in their work. I mean the different views they take *of the offenses of their pupils*. One class of teachers seem never to make it a part of their calculation that their pupils will do wrong, and when any misconduct occurs they are discontented and irritated, and look and act as if some unexpected occurrence had broken in upon their plans. Others understand and consider all this beforehand. They seem to think a little, before they go into their school, what sort of beings boys and girls are, and any ordinary case of youthful delinquency or dullness does not surprise them. I do not mean that they treat such cases with indifference or neglect, but that they *expect* them, and *are prepared for them*. Such a teacher knows that boys and girls are the *materials* he has to work upon, and he takes care to make himself acquainted with these materials, *just as they are*. The other class, however, do not seem to know at all what sort of beings they have to deal with, or, if they know, do not *consider*. They expect from them what is not to be obtained, and then are disappointed and vexed at the failure. It is as if a carpenter should attempt to support an entablature by pillars of wood too small and weak for the weight, and then go on, from week to week, suffering anxiety and irritation as he sees them swelling and splitting under the burden, and finding fault *with the wood* instead of taking it to himself; or as if a plowman were to attempt to work a hard and stony piece of

ground with a poor team and a small plow, and then, when overcome by the difficulties of the task, should vent his vexation and anger in laying the blame on the ground instead of on the inadequate and insufficient instrumentality which he had provided for subduing it.

It is, of course, one essential part of a man's duty, in engaging in any undertaking, whether it will lead him to act upon matter or upon mind, to become first well acquainted with the circumstances of the case, the materials he is to act upon, and the means which he may reasonably expect to have at his command. If he underrates his difficulties, or overrates the power of his means of overcoming them, it is his mistake—a mistake for which *he* is fully responsible. Whatever may be the nature of the effect which he aims at accomplishing, he ought fully to understand it, and to appreciate justly the difficulties which lie in the way.

Teachers, however, very often overlook this. A man comes home from his school at night perplexed and irritated by the petty misconduct which he has witnessed, and been trying to check. He does not, however, look forward and endeavor to prevent the occasions of such misconduct, adapting his measures to the nature of the material upon which he has to operate, but he stands, like the carpenter at his columns, making himself miserable in looking at it after it occurs, and wondering what to do.

"Sir," we might say to him, "what is the matter?"

"Why, I have such boys I can do nothing with them. Were it not for *their misconduct*, I might have a very good school."

"Were it not for their misconduct? Why, is there any peculiar depravity in them which you could not have foreseen?"

"No; I suppose they are pretty much like all other boys," he replies, despairingly; "they are all hair-brained and unmanageable. The plans I have formed for my school would be excellent if my boys would only behave properly."

"Excellent plans," might we not reply, "and yet not adapted to the materials upon which they are to operate! No. It is your business to know what sort of beings boys are, and to make your calculations accordingly."

Two teachers may therefore manage their schools in totally different ways, so that one of them may necessarily find the business a dull, mechanical routine, except as it is occasionally varied by perplexity and irritation, and the other a prosperous and happy employment. The one goes on mechanically the same, and depends for his power on violence, or on threats and demonstrations of violence. The other brings all his ingenuity and enterprise into the field to accomplish a steady purpose by means ever varying, and depends for his power on his knowledge of human nature, and on the adroit adaptation of plans to her fixed and uniform tendencies.

I am very sorry, however, to be obliged to say that probably the latter class of teachers are decidedly in the minority. To practice the art in such a way as to make it an agreeable employment is difficult, and it requires much knowledge of human nature, much attention and skill. And, after all, there are some circumstances necessarily attending the work which constitute a heavy drawback on the pleasures which it might otherwise afford. The almost universal impression that the business of teaching is attended with peculiar trials and difficulties proves this.

There must be some cause for an impression so general. It is not right to call it a prejudice, for, although a single individual may conceive a prejudice, whole communities very seldom do; unless in some case which is presented at once to the whole, so that, looking at it through a common medium, all judge wrong together. But the general opinion in regard to teaching is composed of a vast number of *separate* and *independent* judgments, and there must be some good ground for the universal result.

It is best, therefore, if there are any real and peculiar sources of trial and difficulty in this pursuit, that they should be distinctly known and acknowledged at the outset. Count the cost before going to war. It is even better policy to overrate than to underrate it. Let us see, then, what the real difficulties of teaching are.

It is not, however, as is generally supposed, *the confinement.* A teacher is confined, it is true, but not more than men of other professions and employments; not more than a merchant, and probably not as much. A physician is confined in a different way, but more closely than a teacher: he can never leave home: he knows generally no vacation, and nothing but accidental rest.

The lawyer is confined as much. It is true there are not throughout the year exact hours which he must keep, but, considering the imperious demands of his business, his personal liberty is probably restrained as much by it as that of the teacher. So with all the other professions. Although the nature of the confinement may vary, it amounts to about the same in all. On the other hand, the teacher enjoys, in reference to this subject of confinement, an advantage which scarcely any other class of men does or can enjoy. I mean vacations. A man in any other business may *force* himself away from it for a time, but the cares and anxieties of his business will follow him wherever he goes. It seems to be reserved for the teacher to enjoy alone the periodical luxury of a *real and entire release from business and care*. On the whole, as to confinement, it seems to me that the teacher has little ground of complaint.

There are, however, some real and serious difficulties which always have, and, it is to be feared, always will, cluster around this employment; and which must, for a long time, at least, lead most men to desire some other employment for the business of life. There may perhaps be some who, by their peculiar skill, can overcome or avoid them, and perhaps the science of teaching may, at some future day, be so far improved that all may avoid them. As I describe them, however, now, most of the teachers into whose hands this treatise may fall will probably find that their own experience corresponds, in this respect, with mine.

1. The first great difficulty which the teacher feels is a sort of *moral responsibility for the conduct of others*. If his pupils do wrong, he feels almost personal responsibility for it. As he walks out some afternoon, wearied with his labors, and endeavoring to forget, for a little time, all his cares, he comes upon a group of boys in rude and noisy quarrels, or engaged

in mischief of some sort, and his heart sinks within him. It is hard enough for any one to witness their bad conduct with a spirit unruffled and undisturbed, but for their teacher it is perhaps impossible. He feels *responsible;* in fact, he is responsible. If his scholars are disorderly, or negligent, or idle, or quarrelsome, he feels *condemned himself* almost as if he were himself the actual transgressor.

This difficulty is, in a great degree, peculiar to a teacher. A physician is called upon to prescribe for a patient; he examines the case, and writes his prescription. When this is done his duty is ended; and whether the patient obeys the prescription and lives, or neglects it and dies, the physician feels exonerated from all responsibility. He may, and in some cases does, feel *anxious concern*, and may regret the infatuation by which, in some unhappy case, a valuable life may be hazarded or destroyed. But he feels no *moral responsibility* for another's guilt.

It is so with all the other employments in life. They do, indeed, often bring men into collision with other men. But, though sometimes vexed and irritated by the conduct of a neighbor, a client, or a patient, they feel not half the bitterness of the solicitude and anxiety which come to the teacher through the criminality of his pupil. In ordinary cases he not only feels responsible for efforts, but for their results; and when, notwithstanding all his efforts, his pupils will do wrong, his spirit sinks with an intensity of anxious despondency which none but a teacher can understand.

This feeling of something very like *moral accountability for the guilt of other persons* is a continual burden. The teacher in the presence of the pupil never is free from it. It links him to them by a bond which perhaps he ought not to sunder, and which he can not sunder if he would. And sometimes, when those committed to his charge are idle, or faithless, or unprincipled, it wears away his spirits and his health together. I think there is nothing analogous to this moral connection between teacher and pupil unless it be in the case of a parent and child. And here, on account of the comparative smallness of the number under the parent's care, the evil is so much diminished that it is easily borne.

2. The second great difficulty of the teacher's employments is *the immense multiplicity of the objects of his attention and care* during the time he is employed in his business. His scholars are individuals, and notwithstanding all that the most systematic can do in the way of classification, they must be attended to in a great measure as individuals. A merchant keeps his commodities together, and looks upon a cargo composed of ten thousand articles, and worth a hundred thousand dollars, as one; he speaks of it as one; and there is, in many cases, no more perplexity in planning its destination than if it were a single box of raisins. A lawyer may have a great many important cases, but he has only one at a time; that is, he *attends* to but one at a time. The one may be intricate, involving many facts, and requiring to be examined in many aspects and relations. But he looks at but few of these facts and regards but few of these relations at a time. The points which demand his attention come one after another in regular succession. His mind may thus be kept calm. He avoids confusion and perplexity. But no skill or classification will turn the poor teacher's hundred scholars into one, or enable him, except to a very limited extent, and for a very limited purpose, to regard them as one. He has a distinct and, in many respects, a different work to do for every one of the crowd before him. Difficulties must be explained in detail, questions must be answered one by one, and each scholar's own conduct must be considered by itself. His work is thus made up of a thousand minute particulars, which are all crowding upon his attention at once, and which he can not group together, or combine, or simplify. He must, by some means or other, attend to them in all their distracting individuality. And,

in a large and complicated school, the endless multiplicity and variety of objects of attention and care impose a task under which few intellects can long stand.

I have said that this endless multiplicity and variety can not be reduced and simplified by classification. I mean, of course, that this can be done only to a very limited extent compared with what may be effected in the other pursuits of mankind. Were it not for the art of classification and system, no school could have more than ten scholars, as I intend hereafter to show. The great reliance of the teacher is upon this art, to reduce to some tolerable order what would otherwise be the inextricable confusion of his business. He *must be systematic*. He must classify and arrange; but, after he has done all that he can, he must still expect that his daily business will continue to consist of a vast multitude of minute particulars, from one to another of which the mind must turn with a rapidity which few of the other employments of life ever demand.

These are the essential sources of difficulty with which the teacher has to contend; but, as I shall endeavor to show in succeeding chapters, though they can not be entirely removed, they can be so far mitigated by the appropriate means as to render the employment a happy one. I have thought it best, however, as this work will doubtless be read by many who, when they read it, are yet to begin their labors, to describe frankly and fully to them the difficulties which beset the path they are about to enter. "The wisdom of the prudent is to understand his way." It is often wisdom to understand it beforehand.

CHAPTER II.

GENERAL ARRANGEMENTS.

HE distraction and perplexity of the teacher's life are, as was explained in the last chapter, almost proverbial. There are other pressing and exhausting pursuits, which wear away the spirit by the ceaseless care which they impose, or perplex and bewilder the intellect by the multiplicity and intricacy of their details; but the business of teaching, by a pre-eminence not very enviable, stands, almost by common consent, at the head of the catalogue.

I have already alluded to this subject in the preceding chapter, and probably the majority of actual teachers will admit the truth of the view there presented. Some will, however, doubtless say that they do not find the business of teaching so perplexing and exhausting an employment. They take things calmly. They do one thing at a time, and that without useless solicitude and anxiety. So that teaching, with them, though it has, indeed, its solicitudes and cares, as every other responsible employment must necessarily have, is, after all, a calm and quiet pursuit, which they follow from month to month, and from year to year, without any extraordinary agitations, or any unusual burdens of anxiety and care.

There are, indeed, such cases, but they are exceptions, and unquestionably a considerable majority, especially of those who are beginners in the work, find it such as I have described. I think it need not be so, or, rather, I think the evil may be avoided to *a very great degree*. In this chapter I shall endeavor to show how order may be produced out of that almost inextricable mass of confusion into which so many teachers, on commencing their labors, find themselves plunged.

The objects, then, to be aimed at in the general arrangements of schools are twofold:

1. That the teacher may be left uninterrupted, to attend to one thing at a time.

2. That the individual scholars may have constant employment, and such an amount and such kinds of study as shall be suited to the circumstances and capacities of each.

I shall examine each in their order.

1. The following are the principal things which, in a vast number of schools, are all the time pressing upon the teacher; or, rather, they are the things which must every where press upon the teacher, except so far as, by the skill of his arrangements, he contrives to remove them.

1. Giving leave to whisper or to leave seats.
2. Distributing and changing pens.
3. Answering questions in regard to studies.
4. Hearing recitations.
5. Watching the behavior of the scholars.
6. Administering reproof and punishment for offenses as they occur.

A pretty large number of objects of attention and care, one would say, to be pressing upon the mind of the teacher at one and the same time—and *all the time* too! Hundreds and hundreds of teachers in every part of our country, there is no doubt, have all these crowding upon them from morning to night, with no cessation, except perhaps some accidental and momentary respite. During the winter months, while the principal common schools in our country are in operation, it is sad to reflect how many teachers come home every evening with bewildered and aching heads, having been vainly trying all the day to do six things at a time, while He who made the human mind has determined that it shall do but one. How many become discouraged and disheartened by what they consider the unavoidable trials of a teacher's life, and give up in despair, just because their faculties will not sustain a six-fold task. There are multitudes who, in early life, attempted teaching, and, after having been worried, almost to distraction, by the simultaneous pressure of these multifarious cares, gave up the employment in disgust, and now unceasingly wonder how any body can like teaching. I know multitudes of persons to whom the above description will exactly apply.

I once heard a teacher who had been very successful, even in large schools, say that he could hear two classes recite, mend pens, and watch his school all at the same time, and that without any distraction of mind or any unusual fatigue. Of course the recitations in such a case must be from memory. There are very few minds, however, which can thus perform triple or quadruple work, and probably none which can safely be tasked so severely. For my part, I can do but one thing at a time; and I have no question that the true policy for all is to learn not *to do every thing at once,* but so to classify and arrange their work that *they shall have but one thing at once to do.* Instead of vainly attempting to attend simultaneously to a dozen things, they should so plan their work that only *one* will demand attention.

Let us, then, examine the various particulars above mentioned in succession, and see how each can be disposed of, so as not to be a constant source of interruption and derangement.

1. *Whispering* and *leaving seats.* In regard to this subject

there are very different methods now in practice in different schools. In some, especially in very small schools, the teacher allows the pupils to act according to their own discretion. They whisper and leave their seats whenever they think it necessary. This plan may possibly be admissible in a very small school, that is, in one of ten or twelve pupils. I am convinced, however, that it is a very bad plan even here. No vigilant watch which it is possible for any teacher to exert will prevent a vast amount of mere talk entirely foreign to the business of the school. I tried this plan very thoroughly, with high ideas of the dependence which might be placed upon conscience and a sense of duty, if these principles are properly brought out to action in an effort to sustain the system. I was told by distinguished teachers that it would not be found to answer. But predictions of failure in such cases only prompt to greater exertions, and I persevered. But I was forced at last to give up the point, and adopt another plan. My pupils would make resolutions enough; they understood their duty well enough. They were allowed to leave their seats and whisper to their companions whenever, *in their honest judgment, it was necessary for the prosecution of their studies.* I knew that it sometimes would be necessary, and I was desirous to adopt this plan to save myself the constant interruption of hearing and replying to requests. But it would not do. Whenever, from time to time, I called them to account, I found that a large majority, according to their own confession, were in the habit of holding daily and deliberate communication with each other on subjects entirely foreign to the business of the school. A more experienced teacher would have predicted this result; but I had very high ideas of the power of cultivated conscience, and, in fact, still have. But then, like most other persons who become possessed of a good idea, I could not be satisfied without carrying it to an extreme.

Still it is necessary, in ordinary schools, to give pupils

sometimes the opportunity to whisper and leave seats.* Cases occur where this is unavoidable. It can not, therefore, be forbidden altogether. How, then, you will ask, can the teacher regulate this practice, so as to prevent the evils which will otherwise flow from it, without being continually interrupted by the request for permission?

By a very simple method. *Appropriate particular times at which all this business is to be done*, and *forbid it altogether* at every other time. It is well, on other accounts, to give the pupils of a school a little respite, at least every hour; and if this is done, an intermission of study for two minutes each time will be sufficient. During this time *general* permission should be given for the pupils to speak to each other, or to leave their seats, provided they do nothing at such a time to disturb the studies of others. This plan I have myself very thoroughly tested, and no arrangement which I ever made operated for so long a time so uninterruptedly and so entirely to my satisfaction as this. It of course will require some little time, and no little firmness, to establish the new order of things where a school has been accustomed to another course; but where this is once done, I know no one plan so simple and so easily put into execution which will do so much toward relieving the teacher of the distraction and perplexity of his pursuits.

In making the change, however, it is of fundamental importance that the pupils should themselves be interested in it. Their co-operation, or, rather, the co-operation of the majority, which it is very easy to obtain, is absolutely essential to success. I say this is very easily obtained. Let us suppose that some teacher, who has been accustomed to require his pupils to ask and obtain permission every time they wish to speak to a companion, is induced by these remarks to introduce this plan. He says, accordingly, to his school,

* There are some large and peculiarly-organized schools in cities and large towns to which this remark may perhaps not apply.

"You know that you are now accustomed to ask me whenever you wish to obtain permission to whisper to a companion or to leave your seats; now I have been thinking of a plan which will be better for both you and me. By our present plan you are sometimes obliged to wait before I can attend to your request. Sometimes I think it is unnecessary, and deny you, when perhaps I was mistaken, and it was really necessary. At other times, I think it very probable that when it is quite desirable for you to leave your seat you do not ask, because you think you may not obtain permission, and you do not wish to ask and be refused. Do you, or not, experience these inconveniences from our present plans?"

The pupils would undoubtedly answer in the affirmative.

"I myself experience great inconvenience too. I am very frequently interrupted when busily engaged, and it also occupies a great portion of my time and attention to consider and answer your requests for permission to speak to one another and to leave your seats. It requires as much mental effort to consider and decide whether I ought to allow a pupil to leave his seat, as it would to determine a much more important question; therefore I do not like our present plan, and I have another to propose."

The pupils are now all attention to know what the new plan is. It will always be of great advantage to the school for the teacher to propose his new plans from time to time to his pupils in such a way as this. It interests them in the improvement of the school, exercises their judgment, establishes a common feeling between teacher and pupil, and in many other ways assists very much in promoting the welfare of the school.

"My plan," continues the teacher, "is this: to allow you all, besides the recess, a short time, two or three minutes perhaps, every hour" (or every half hour, according to the character of the school, the age of the pupils, or other circumstances, to be judged of by the teacher), "during which you may all whisper or leave your seats *without* asking permission."

Instead of deciding the question of the *frequency* of this general permission, the teacher may, if he pleases, leave it to the pupils to decide. It is often useful to leave the decision of such a question to them. On this subject, however, I shall speak in another place. It is only necessary here to say that *this* point may be safely left to them, since the time is so small which is to be thus appropriated. Even if they vote to have the general permission to whisper every half hour, it will make but eight minutes in the forenoon. There being six half hours in the forenoon, and one of them ending at the close of school, and another at the recess, only *four* of these *rests*, as a military man would call them, would be necessary; and four, of two minutes each, would make eight minutes. If the teacher thinks that evil would result from the interruption of the studies so often, he may offer the pupils *three* minutes rest every *hour* instead of *two* minutes every *half hour*, and let them take their choice; or he may decide the case altogether himself.

Such a change, from *particular permission on individual requests* to *general permission* at *stated times*, would unquestionably be popular in every school, if the teacher managed the business properly. And by presenting it as an object of common interest, an arrangement proposed for the common convenience of teacher and pupils, the latter may be much interested in carrying the plan into effect. We must not rely, however, entirely upon their *interest in it.* All that we can expect from such an effort to interest them, as I have described and recommended, is to get a majority on our side, so that we may have only a small minority to deal with by other measures. Still, *we must calculate on having this minority, and form our plans accordingly*, or we shall be greatly disappointed. I shall, however, in another place, speak of this principle of interesting the pupils in our plans for the purpose of securing a majority in our favor, and explain the methods by which the minority is then to be governed. I only mean here to say that, by such means, the teacher may easily interest a large proportion of the scholars in carrying his plans into effect, and that he must expect to be prepared with other measures for those who will not be governed by these.

You can not reasonably expect, however, that, immediately after having explained your plan, it will at once go into full and complete operation. Even those who are firmly determined to keep the rule will, from inadvertence, for a day or two, make communication with each other. They must be *trained*, not by threatening and punishment, but by your good-humored assistance, to their new duties. When I first adopted this plan in my school, something like the following proceedings took place.

"Do you suppose that you will perfectly keep this rule from this time?"

"No, sir," was the answer.

"I suppose you will not. Some, I am afraid, may not really be determined to keep it, and others will forget. Now I wish that every one of you would keep an exact account to-day of all the instances in which you speak to another person, or leave your seat, out of the regular times, and be prepared to report them at the close of the school. Of course, there will be no punishment; but it will very much assist you to watch yourselves, if you expect to make a report at the end of the forenoon. Do you like this plan?"

"Yes, sir," was the answer; and all seemed to enter into it with spirit.

In order to mark more definitely the times for communication, I wrote, in large letters, on a piece of pasteboard, "STUDY HOURS," and making a hole over the centre of it, I hung it upon a nail over my desk. At the close of each half hour a little bell was to be struck, and this card was to be taken down. When it was up, they were, on no occasion whatever (except some such extraordinary occurrence as sickness, or my sending one of them on a message to another, or something clearly out of the common course) to speak to each other; but were to wait, whatever they wanted, until the *Study Card*, as they called it, was taken down.

"Suppose now," said I, "that a young lady has come into school, and has accidentally left her book in the entry— the book from which she is to study during the first half hour of the school. She sits near the door, and she might, in a moment, slip out and obtain it. If she does not, she must spend the half hour in idleness, and be unprepared in her lesson. What is it her duty to do?"

"To go," "Not to go," answered the scholars, simultaneously.

"It would be her duty *not* to go; but I suppose it will be very difficult for me to convince you of it.

"The reason is this," I continued; "if the one case I have supposed were the *only* one which would be likely to occur, it would undoubtedly be better for her to go; but if it is understood that in such cases the rule may be dispensed with, that understanding will tend very much to cause such cases to occur. Scholars will differ in regard to the degree of inconvenience which they must submit to rather than break the rule. They will gradually do it on slighter and slighter occasions, until at last the rule will be disregarded entirely. We must therefore draw a *precise line*, and individuals must submit to a little inconvenience sometimes to promote the general good."

At the close of the day I requested all in the school to rise. While they were standing, I called them to account in the following manner:

"Now it is very probable that some have, from inadvertence or from design, omitted to keep an account of the number of transgressions of the rule which they have committed during the day; others, perhaps, do not wish to make a report of themselves. Now as this is a common and voluntary effort, I wish to have none render assistance who do not, of their own accord, desire to do so. All those, therefore, who are not able to make a report, from not having been correct in keeping it, and all those who are unwilling to report themselves, may sit."

A very small number hesitatingly took their seats.

"I am afraid that all do not sit who really wish not to report themselves. Now I am honest in saying I wish you to do just as you please. If a great majority of the school really wish to assist me in accomplishing the object, why, of course, I am glad; still, I shall not call upon any for such assistance unless it is freely and voluntarily rendered."

One or two more took their seats while these things were saying. Among such there would generally be some who would refuse to have any thing to do with the measure simply from a desire to thwart and impede the plans of the teacher. If so, it is best to take no notice of them. If the teacher can contrive to obtain a great majority upon his side, so as to let them see that any opposition which they can raise is of no consequence and is not even noticed, they will soon be ashamed of it.

The reports, then, of those who remained standing were called for; first, those who had whispered only once were requested to sit, then those who had whispered more than once and less than five times, and so on, until at last all were down. In such a case the pupils might, if thought expedient, again be requested to rise for the purpose of asking some other questions with reference to ascertaining whether they had spoken most in the former or latter part of the forenoon. The number who had spoken inadvertently, and the number who had done it by design, might be ascertained. These inquiries accustom the pupils to render honest and faithful accounts of themselves. They become, by such means, familiarized to the practice, and by means of it the teacher can many times receive most important assistance.

In all this, however, the teacher should speak in a pleasant tone, and maintain a pleasant and cheerful air. The acknowledgments should be considered by the pupils not as confessions of guilt for which they are to be rebuked or punished, but as voluntary and free reports of the result of *an experiment* in which all were interested.

Some will have been dishonest in their reports: to diminish the number of these, the teacher may say, after the report is concluded,

"We will drop the subject here to-day. To-morrow we will make another effort, when we shall be more successful. I have taken your reports as you have offered them without any inquiry, because I had no doubt that a great majority of this school would be honest at all hazards. They would not, I am confident, make a false report even if, by a true one, they were to bring upon themselves punishment; so that I think I may have confidence that nearly all these reports have been faithful. Still it is very probable that among so large a number some may have made a report which, they are now aware, was not perfectly fair and honest. I do not wish to know who they are; if there are any such cases, I only wish to say to the rest how much pleasanter it is for you that you have been honest and open. The business is now all ended; you have done your duty; and, though you reported a little larger number than you would if you had been disposed to conceal your faults, yet you go away from school with a quiet conscience. On the other hand, how miserable must any boy feel, if he has any nobleness of mind whatever, to go away from school to-day thinking that he has not been honest; that he has been trying to conceal his faults, and thus to obtain a credit which he did not justly deserve. Always be honest, let the consequence be what it may."

The reader will understand that the object of such measures is simply *to secure as large a majority as possible* to make *voluntary* efforts to observe the rule. I do not expect that by such measures *universal* obedience can be exacted. The teacher must follow up the plan after a few days by other measures for those pupils who will not yield to such inducements as these. Upon this subject, however, I shall speak more particularly at a future time.

In my own school it required two or three weeks to exclude whispering and communication by signs. The period necessary to effect the revolution will be longer or shorter, according to the circumstances of the school and the dexterity of the teacher; and, after all, the teacher must not hope *entirely* to exclude it. Approximation to excellence is all that we can expect; for unprincipled and deceiving characters will perhaps always be found, and no system whatever can prevent their existence. Proper treatment may indeed be the means of their reformation, but before this process has arrived at a successful result, others similar in character will have entered the school, so that the teacher can never expect perfection in the operation of any of his plans.

I found so much relief from the change which this plan introduced, that I soon took measures for rendering it permanent; and though I am not much in favor of efforts to bring all teachers and all schools to the same plans, this principle of *whispering at limited and prescribed times alone* seems to me well suited to universal adoption.

The following simple apparatus has been used in several schools where this principle has been adopted. A drawing and description of it is inserted here, as by this means some teachers, who may like to try the course here recommended, may be saved the time and trouble of contriving something of the kind themselves.

The figure *a a a a* on the next page is a board about 18 inches by 12, to which the other parts of the apparatus are to be attached, and which is to be secured to the wall at the height of about 8 feet, and *b c d c* is a plate of tin or brass, 8 inches by 12, of the form represented in the drawing. At *c c*, the lower extremities of the parts at the sides, the metal is bent round, so as to clasp a wire which runs from *c* to *c*, the ends of which wire are bent at right angles, and run into the board. The plate will consequently turn on this axis as on a hinge. At the top of the plate, *d*, a small projection of the tin turns inward, and to this one end of the cord, *m m*, is attached. This cord passes back from *d* to a small pulley at the upper part of the board, and at the lower end of it a tassel, loaded so as to be an exact counterpoise to the card, is attached. By raising the tassel, the plate will of course fall over forward till it is stopped by the part *b* striking the board, when it will be in a horizontal position. On the other hand, by pulling down the tassel, the plate will be raised and drawn upward against the board, so as to present its convex surface, with the words STUDY HOURS upon it, distinctly to the school. In the drawing it is represented in an inclined position, being not quite drawn up, that the parts might more easily be seen. At *d* there is a small projection of the tin upward, which touches the clapper of the bell suspended above every time the plate passes up or down, and thus gives notice of its motions.

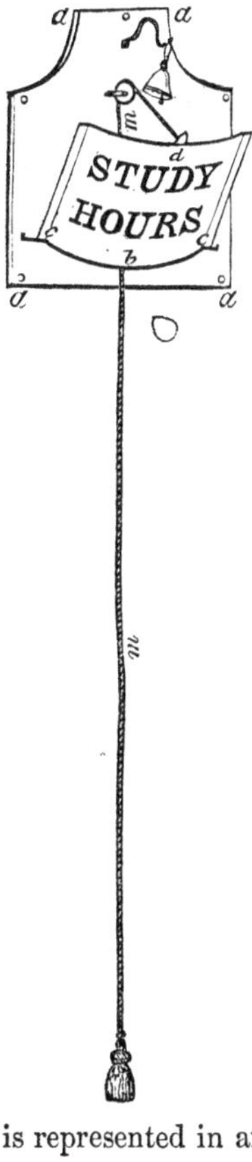

Of course the construction may be varied very much, and it may be more or less expensive, according to the wishes of the teacher. In the first apparatus of this kind which I used, the plate was simply a card of pasteboard, from which the machine took its name. This was cut out with a penknife, and, after being covered with marble-paper, a strip of white paper was pasted along the middle with the inscription upon it. The wire *c c*, and a similar one at the top of the plate, were passed through a perforation in the pasteboard, and then passed into the board. Instead of a pulley, the cord, which was a piece of twine, was passed through a little staple made of wire and driven into the board. The whole was made in one or two recesses in school, with such tools and materials as I could then command. The bell was a common table bell, with a wire passing through the handle. The whole was attached to such a piece of pine board as I could get on the occasion. This coarse contrivance was, for more than a year, the grand regulator of all the movements of the school.

I afterward caused one to be made in a better manner. The plate was of tin, gilded, the border and the letters of the inscription being black. A parlor bell-rope was carried over a brass pulley, and then passed downward in a groove made in the mahogany board to which the card was attached.

A little reflection will, however, show the teacher that the form and construction of the apparatus for marking the times of study and of rest may be greatly varied. The chief point is simply to secure the *principle* of whispering at definite and limited times, and at those alone. If such an arrangement is adopted, and carried faithfully into effect, it will be found to relieve the teacher of more than half of the confusion and perplexity which would otherwise be his hourly lot. I have detailed thus particularly the method to be pursued in carrying this principle into effect, because I am convinced of its importance, and the incalculable assistance which such an arrangement will afford to the teacher in all his plans. Of course, I would not be understood to recommend its adoption in those cases where teachers, from their own experience, have devised and adopted *other* plans which accomplish as effectually the same purpose. All that I mean is to insist upon the absolute necessity of *some* plan, to remove this very common source of interruption and confusion, and I recommend this mode where a better is not known.

2. The second of the sources of interruption, as I have enumerated them, is the distribution of pens and of stationery. This business ought, if possible, to have a specific time assigned to it. Scholars are, in general, far too particular in regard to their pens. The teacher ought to explain to them that, in the transaction of the ordinary business of life, they can not always have exactly such a pen as they would like. They must learn to write with various kinds of pens, and when furnished with one that the teacher himself would consider suitable to write a letter to a friend with, he must be content. They should understand that the *form* of the letters is what is important in learning to write, not the smoothness and clearness of the hair lines; and that though writing looks better when executed with a perfect pen, a person may *learn* to write nearly as well with one which is not absolutely perfect. So certain is this, though often overlooked, that a person would perhaps learn faster with chalk, upon a black board, than with the best goose-quill ever sharpened.

I do not make these remarks to show that it is of no consequence whether scholars have good or bad pens, but only that this subject deserves very much less of the time and attention of the teacher than it usually receives. When the scholars are allowed, as they very often are, to come when they please to change their pens, breaking in upon any business—interrupting any classes—perplexing and embarrassing the teacher, however he may be employed, there is a very serious obstruction to the progress of the scholars, which is by no means repaid by the improvement in this branch.

To guard against these evils, a regular and well-considered system should be adopted for the distribution of pens and stationery, and when adopted it should be strictly and steadily adhered to.

3. Answering questions about studies. A teacher who does not adopt some system in regard to this subject will be always at the mercy of his scholars. One boy will want to know how to parse a word, another where the lesson is, another to have a sum explained, and a fourth will wish to show his work to see if it is right. The teacher does not like to discourage such inquiries. Each one, as it comes up, seems necessary; each one, too, is answered in a moment; but the endless number and the continual repetition of them consume his time and exhaust his patience.

There is another view of the subject which ought to be taken. Perhaps it would not be far from the truth to estimate the average number of scholars in the schools in our country at fifty. At any rate, this will be near enough for our present purpose. There are three hours in each session, according to the usual arrangement, making one hundred and eighty minutes, which, divided among fifty, give about three minutes and a half to each individual. If the reader has, in his own school, a greater or a less number, he can easily correct the above calculation, so as to adapt it to his own case, and ascertain the portion which may justly be appropriated to each pupil. It will probably vary from two to four minutes. Now a period of four minutes slips away very fast while a man is looking over perplexing figures on a slate, and if he exceeds that time at all in individual attention to any one scholar, he is doing injustice to his other pupils. I do not mean that a man is to confine himself rigidly to the principle suggested by this calculation of cautiously appropriating no more time to any one of his pupils than such a calculation would assign to each, but simply that this is a point which should be kept in view, and should have a very strong influence in deciding how far it is right to devote attention exclusively to individuals. It seems to me that it shows very clearly that one ought to teach his pupils, as much as possible, *in masses*, and as little as possible by private attention to individual cases.

The following directions will help the teacher to carry these principles into effect. When you assign a lesson, glance over it yourself, and consider what difficulties are likely to arise. You know the progress which your pupils have made, and can easily anticipate their difficulties. Tell them all together, in the class, what their difficulties will be, and how they may surmount them. Give them directions how they are to act in the emergencies which will be likely to occur. This simple step will remove a vast number of the questions which would otherwise become occasions for interrupting you. With regard to other difficulties, which can not be foreseen and guarded against, direct the pupils to bring them to the class at the next recitation. Half a dozen of the class might, and very probably would, meet with the same difficulty. If they bring this difficulty to you one by one, you have to explain it over and over again, whereas, when it is brought to the class, one explanation answers for all.

As to all questions about the lesson—where it is, what it is, and how long it is—never answer them. Require each pupil to remember for himself, and if he was absent when the lesson was assigned, let him ask his class-mate in a rest.

You *may* refuse to give particular individuals the private assistance they ask for in such a way as to discourage and irritate them, but this is by no means necessary. It can be done in such a manner that the pupil will see the propriety of it, and acquiesce pleasantly in it.

A child comes to you, for example, and says,

"Will you tell me, sir, where the next lesson is?"

"Were you not in the class at the time?"

"Yes, sir; but I have forgotten."

"Well, I have forgotten too. I have a great many classes to hear, and, of course, a great many lessons to assign, and

I never remember them. It is not necessary for me to remember."

"May I speak to one of the class to ask about it?"

"You can not speak, you know, till the Study Card is down; you may then."

"But I want to get my lesson now."

"I don't know what you will do, then. I am sorry you don't remember.

"Besides," continues the teacher, looking pleasantly, however, while he says it, "if I knew, I think I ought not to tell you."

"Why, sir?"

"Because, you know, I have said I wish the scholars to remember where the lessons are, and not come to me. You know it would be very unwise for me, after assigning a lesson once for all in the class, to spend my time here at my desk in assigning it over again to each individual one by one. Now if I should tell *you* where the lesson is now, I should have to tell others, and thus should adopt a practice which I have condemned."

Take another case. You assign to a class of little girls a subject of composition, requesting them to copy their writing upon a sheet of paper, leaving a margin an inch wide at the top, and one of half an inch at the sides and bottom. The class take their seats, and, after a short time, one of them comes to you, saying she does not know how long an inch is.

"Don't you know any thing about it?"

"No, sir, not much."

"Should you think *that* is more or less than an inch?" (pointing to a space on a piece of paper much too large).

"More."

"Then you know something about it. Now I did not tell you to make the margins *exactly* an inch and half an inch, but only as near as you could judge.

"Would *that* be about right?" asks the girl, showing a distance.

"I must not tell you, because, you know, I never in such cases help individuals; if that is as near as you can get it, you may make it so."

It may be well, after assigning a lesson to a class, to say that all those who do not distinctly understand what they have to do may remain after the class have taken their seats, and ask: the task may then be distinctly assigned again, and the difficulties, so far as they can be foreseen, explained.

By such means these sources of interruption and difficulty may, like the others, be almost entirely removed. Perhaps not altogether, for many cases may occur where the teacher may choose to give a particular class permission to come to him for help. Such permission, however, ought never to be given unless it is absolutely necessary, and should never be allowed to be taken unless it is distinctly given.

4. Hearing recitations. I am aware that many attempt to do something else at the same time that they are hearing a recitation, and there may perhaps be some individuals who can succeed in this. If the exercise to which the teacher is attending consists merely in listening to the reciting word for word some passage committed to memory, it can be done. I hope, however, to show in a future chapter that there are other and far higher objects which every teacher ought to have in view in his recitations, and he who understands these objects, and aims at accomplishing them—who endeavors to *instruct* his class, to enlarge and elevate their ideas, to awaken a deep and paramount interest in the subject which they are examining, will find that his time must be his own, and his attention uninterrupted while he is presiding at a class. All the other exercises and arrangements of the school are, in fact, preparatory and subsidiary to this. Here, that is, in the classes, the real business of teaching is to be done. Here the teacher comes in contact with his scholars mind with

mind, and here, consequently, he must be uninterrupted and undisturbed. I shall speak more particularly on this subject hereafter under the head of instruction; all I wish to secure in this place is that the teacher should make such arrangements that he can devote his exclusive attention to his classes while he is actually engaged with them.

Each recitation, too, should have its specified time, which should be adhered to with rigid accuracy. If any thing like the plan I have suggested for allowing rests of a minute or two every half hour should be adopted, it will mark off the forenoon into parts which ought to be precisely and carefully observed. I was formerly accustomed to think that I could not limit the time for my recitations without great inconvenience, and occasionally allowed one exercise to encroach upon the succeeding, and this upon the next, and thus sometimes the last was excluded altogether. But such a lax and irregular method of procedure is ruinous to the discipline of a school. On perceiving it at last, I put the bell into the hands of a pupil, commissioning her to ring regularly, having myself fixed the times, saying that I would show my pupils that I could be confined myself to system as well as they. At first I experienced a little inconvenience; but this soon disappeared, and at last the hours and half hours of our artificial division entirely superseded, in the school-room, the divisions of the clock face. I found, too, that it exerted an extremely favorable influence upon the scholars in respect to their willingness to submit readily to the necessary restrictions imposed upon them in school, to show them that the teacher was subject to law as well as they.

But, in order that I may be specific and definite, I will draw up a plan for the regular division of time, for a common school, not to be *adopted*, but to be *imitated;* that is, I do not recommend exactly this plan, but that some plan, precise and specific, should be determined upon, and exhibited to the school by a diagram like the following:

FORENOON.

IX. X. XI. XII.

READING.		WRITING.	R.	G.	ARITHMETIC.	

AFTERNOON.

II. III. IV. V.

GEOGRAPHY.		WRITING.	R.	G.	GRAMMAR.	

A drawing on a large sheet, made by some of the older scholars (for a teacher should never do any thing of this kind which his scholars can do for him), should be made and pasted up to view, the names of the classes being inserted in the columns under their respective heads. At the double lines at ten and three, there might be a rest of two minutes, an officer appointed for the purpose ringing a bell at each of the periods marked on the plan, and making the signal for the *rest*, whatever signal might be determined upon. It is a good plan to have the bell *touched* five minutes before each half hour expires, and then exactly at its close. The first bell would notify the teacher or teachers, if there are more than one in the school, that the time for their respective recitations is drawing to a close. At the second bell the new classes should take their places without waiting to be called for. The scholars will thus see that the arrangements of the school are based upon system, to which the teacher himself conforms, and not subjected to his own varying will. They will thus not only go on more regularly, but they will themselves yield more easily and pleasantly to the necessary arrangements.

The fact is, children love system and regularity. Each

one is sometimes a little uneasy under the restraint which it imposes upon him individually, but they all love to see its operation upon others, and they are generally very willing to submit to its laws, if the rest of the community are required to submit too. They show this in their love of military parade; what allures them is chiefly the *order* of it; and even a little child creeping upon the floor will be pleased when he gets his playthings in a row. A teacher may turn this principle to most useful account in forming his plans for his school, in observing that the teacher is governed by them too as well as they.

It will be seen by reference to the foregoing plan that I have marked the time for the recesses by the letter R. at the top. Immediately after them, both in the forenoon and in the afternoon, twenty minutes are left, marked G., the initial standing for general exercise. They are intended to denote periods during which all the scholars are in their seats, with their work laid aside, ready to attend to whatever the teacher may desire to bring before the whole school. There are so many occasions on which it is necessary to address the whole school, that it is very desirable to appropriate a particular time for it. In most of the best schools I believe this plan is adopted. I will mention some of the subjects which would come up at such a time.

1. There are some studies which can be advantageously attended to by the whole school together, such as Punctuation, and, to some extent, Spelling.

2. Cases of discipline which it is necessary to bring before the whole school ought to come up at a regularly-appointed time. By attending to them here, there will be a greater importance attached to them. Whatever the teacher does will seem to be more deliberate, and, in fact, *will be* more deliberate.

3. General remarks, bringing up classes of faults which prevail; also general directions, which may at any time be

needed; and, in fact, any business relating to the general arrangements of the school.

4. Familiar lectures from the teacher on various subjects. These lectures, though necessarily brief and quite familiar in their form, may still be very exact and thorough in respect to the knowledge conveyed. When they are upon scientific subjects they may sometimes be illustrated by experiments,

more or less imposing, according to the ingenuity of the teacher, the capacity of the older scholars to assist him in the preparations, or the means and facilities at his command.*

* In some of the larger institutions of the country the teacher will have convenient apparatus at his disposal, and a room specially adapted to the purpose of experiments. The engraving represents a room at the Spingler Institute at New York. But let not the teacher suppose that these special facilities are essential to enable him to give instruction to his pupils in such a way. I have known a much larger balloon than the one represented in the engraving to be constructed by the teacher and pupils of a common country school from directions in Rees's Cyclopedia, and sent up in the open air. The aeronaut that accompanied it was a hen—poor thing!

The design of such lectures should be to extend the *general knowledge* of the pupils in regard to those subjects on which they will need information in their progress through life. In regard to each of these particulars I shall speak more particularly hereafter, in the chapters to which they respectively belong. My only object here is to show, in the general arrangements of the school, how a place is to be found for them. My practice has been to have two periods of short duration, each day, appropriated to these objects: the first to the *business of the school*, and the second to such studies or lectures as could be most profitably attended to at such a time.

We come now to one of the most important subjects which present themselves to the teacher's attention in settling the principles upon which he shall govern his school. I mean the degree of influence which the boys themselves shall have in the management of its affairs. Shall the government of school be a *monarchy* or a *republic?* To this question, after much inquiry and many experiments, I answer, a monarchy; an absolute, unlimited monarchy; the teacher possessing exclusive power as far as the pupils are concerned, though strictly responsible to the committee or to the trustees under whom he holds his office.

While, however, it is thus distinctly understood that the power of the teacher is supreme, that all the power rests in him, and that he alone is responsible for its exercise, there ought to be a very free and continual *delegation* of power to the pupils. As much business as possible should be committed to them. They should be interested as much as possible in the affairs of the school, and led to take an active part in carrying them forward; though they should, all the time, distinctly understand that it is only *delegated* power which they exercise, and that the teacher can, at any time, revoke what he has granted, and alter or annul at pleasure any of their decisions. By this plan we have the responsibility resting where it ought to rest, and yet the boys are trained to business, and led to take an active interest in the welfare of the school. Trust is reposed in them, which may be greater or less, as they are able to bear. All the good effects of reposing trust and confidence, and committing the management of important business to the pupils will be secured, without the dangers which would result from the entire surrender of the management of the institution into their hands.

There have been, in several cases, experiments made with reference to ascertaining how far a government strictly republican would be admissible in a school. A very fair experiment of this kind was made some years since at the Gardiner Lyceum, in Maine. At the time of its establishment, nothing was said of the mode of government which it was intended to adopt. For some time the attention of the instructors was occupied in arranging the course of study, and attending to the other concerns of the institution; and, in the infant state of the Lyceum, few cases of discipline occurred, and no regular system of government was necessary.

Before long, however, complaints were made that the students at the Lyceum were guilty of breaking windows in an old building used as a town-house. The principal called the students together, mentioned the reports, and said that he did not know, and did not wish to know who were the guilty individuals. It was necessary, however, that the thing should be examined into, and that restitution should be made, and, relying on their faithfulness and ability, he should leave them to manage the business alone. For this purpose, he nominated one of the students as judge, some others as jurymen, and appointed the other officers necessary in the same manner. He told them that, in order to give them time to make a thorough investigation, they were excused from farther exercises during the day.

The principal then left them, and they entered on the

trial. The result was that they discovered the guilty individuals, ascertained the amount of mischief done by each, and sent to the selectmen a message, by which they agreed to pay a sum equal to three times the value of the injury sustained.

The students were soon after informed that this mode of bringing offenders to justice would hereafter be always pursued, and arrangements were made for organizing a *regular republican government* among the young men. By this government all laws which related to the internal police of the institution were to be made, all officers were appointed, and all criminal cases were to be tried. The students finding the part of a judge too difficult for them to sustain, one of the professors was appointed to hold that office, and, for similar reasons, another of the professors was made president of the legislative assembly. The principal was the executive, with power to *pardon*, but not to *sentence*, or even *accuse*.

Some time after this a student was indicted for profane swearing; he was tried, convicted, and punished. After this he evinced a strong hostility to the government. He made great exertions to bring it into contempt, and when the next trial came on, he endeavored to persuade the witnesses that giving evidence was dishonorable, and he so far succeeded that the defendant was acquitted for want of evidence, when it was generally understood that there was proof of his guilt, which would have been satisfactory if it could have been brought forward. For some time after this the prospect was rather unfavorable, though many of the students themselves opposed with great earnestness these efforts, and were much alarmed lest they should lose their free government through the perverseness of one of their number. The attorney general, at this juncture, conceived the idea of indicting the individual alluded to for an attempt to overturn the government. He obtained the approbation of the principal, and the grand jury found a bill. The court, as the case was so important, invited some of the trustees, who were in town, to attend the trial. The parent of the defendant was also informed of the circumstances and requested to be present, and he accordingly attended. The prisoner was tried, found guilty, and sentenced, if I mistake not, to expulsion. At his earnest request, however, to be permitted to remain in the Lyceum and redeem his character, he was pardoned and restored, and from that time he became perfectly exemplary in his conduct and character. After this occurrence the system went on in successful operation for some time.

The legislative power was vested in the hands of a general committee, consisting of eight or ten, chosen by the students from their own number. They met about once a week to transact such business as appointing officers, making and repealing regulations, and inquiring into the state of the Lyceum. The instructors had a negative upon all their proceedings, but no direct and positive power. They could pardon, but they could assign no punishments, nor make laws inflicting any.

Now such a plan as this may succeed for a short time, and under very favorable circumstances; and the circumstance which it is chiefly important should be favorable is, that the man who is called to preside over such an association should possess such talents of *generalship* that he can really manage the institution *himself*, while the power is *nominally* and *apparently* in the hands of the boys. Should this not be the case, or should the teacher, from any cause, lose his personal influence in the school, so that the institution should really be surrendered into the hands of the pupils, things must be on a very unstable footing. And, accordingly, where such a plan has been adopted, it has, I believe, in every instance, been ultimately abandoned.

Real self-government is an experiment sufficiently hazardous among men, though Providence, in making a daily supply of food necessary for every human being, has imposed a most powerful check upon the tendency to anarchy and confusion. Let the populace of Paris or of London materially interrupt the order and break in upon the arrangements of the community, and in eight-and-forty hours nearly the whole of the mighty mass will be in the hands of the devourer, hunger, and they will be soon brought to submission. On the other hand, a month's anarchy and confusion in a college or an academy would be delight to half the students, or else times have greatly changed since I was within college walls.

Although it is thus evident that the important concerns of a literary institution can not be safely committed into the hands of the students, very great benefits will result from calling upon them to act upon and to decide questions relative to the school within such limits and under such restrictions as are safe and proper. Such a practice will assist the teacher very much if he manages it with any degree of dexterity; for it will interest his pupils in the success of the school, and secure, to a very considerable extent, their co-operation in the government of it. It will teach them self-control and self-government, and will accustom them to submit to the majority—that lesson which, of all others, it is important for a republican to learn.

In endeavoring to interest the pupils of a school in the work of co-operating with the teacher in its administration, no little dexterity will be necessary at the outset. In all probability, the formal announcement of this principle, and the endeavor to introduce it by a sudden revolution, would totally fail. Boys, like men, must be gradually prepared for power, and they must exercise it only so far as they are prepared. This, however, can very easily be done. The teacher should say nothing of his general design, but, when some suitable opportunity presents, he should endeavor to lead his pupils to co-operate with him in some particular instance.

For example, let us suppose that he has been accustomed to distribute the writing-books with his own hand when the writing-hour arrives, and that he concludes to delegate this simple business first to his scholars. He accordingly states to them, just before the writing exercise of the day on which he proposes the experiment, as follows:

"I have thought that time will be saved if you will help me distribute the books, and I will accordingly appoint four distributors, one for each division of the seats, who may come to me and receive the books, and distribute them each to his own division. Are you willing to adopt this plan?"

The boys answer "Yes, sir," and the teacher then looks carefully around the room, and selects four pleasant and popular boys—boys who he knows would gladly assist him, and who would, at the same time, be agreeable to their school-mates. This latter point is necessary in order to secure the popularity and success of the plan.

Unless the boys are very different from any I have ever met with, they will be pleased with the duty thus assigned them. They will learn system and regularity by being taught to perform this simple duty in a proper manner. After a week, the teacher may consider their term of service as having expired, and thanking them in public for the assistance they have rendered him, he may ask the scholars if they are willing to continue the plan, and if the vote is in favor of it, as it unquestionably would be, each boy probably hoping that he should be appointed to the office, the teacher may nominate four others, including, perhaps, upon the list, some boy popular among his companions, but whom he has suspected to be not very friendly to himself or the school. I think the most scrupulous statesman would not object to securing influence by conferring office in such a case. If difficulties arise from the operation of such a measure, the plan can easily be modified to avoid or correct them. If it is successful, it may be continued, and the principle may be extended, so as in the end to affect very considerably all the arrangements and the whole management of the school.

Or, let us imagine the following scene to have been the commencement of the introduction of the principle of limited self-government into a school.

The preceptor of an academy was sitting at his desk, at the close of school, while the pupils were putting up their books and leaving the room. A boy came in with angry looks, and, with his hat in his hands bruised and dusty, advanced to the master's desk, and complained that one of his companions had thrown down his hat upon the floor, and had almost spoiled it.

The teacher looked calmly at the mischief, and then asked how it happened.

"I don't know, sir. I hung it on my nail, and he pulled it down."

"I wish you would ask him to come here," said the teacher. "Ask him pleasantly."

The accused soon came in, and the two boys stood together before the master.

"There seems to be some difficulty between you boys about a nail to hang your hats upon. I suppose each of you think it is your own nail."

"Yes, sir," said both the boys.

"It will be more convenient for me to talk with you about this to-morrow than to-night, if you are willing to wait. Besides, we can examine it more calmly then. But if we put it off till then, you must not talk about it in the mean time, blaming one another, and keeping up the irritation that you feel. Are you both willing to leave it just where it is till to-morrow, and try to forget all about it till then? I expect I shall find you both a little to blame."

The boys rather reluctantly consented. The next day the master heard the case, and settled it so far as it related to the two boys. It was easily settled in the morning, for they had had time to get calm, and were, after sleeping away their anger, rather ashamed of the whole affair, and very desirous to have it forgotten.

That day, when the hour for the transaction of general business came, the teacher stated to the school that it was necessary to take some measures to provide each boy with a nail for his hat. In order to show that it was necessary, he related the circumstances of the quarrel which had occurred the day before. He did this, not with such an air and manner as to convey the impression that his object was to find fault with the boys, or to expose their misconduct, but to show the necessity of doing something to remedy the evil which had been the cause of so unpleasant an occurrence. Still, though he said nothing in the way of reproof or reprehension, and did not name the boys, but merely gave a cool and impartial narrative of the facts, the effect, very evidently, was to bring such quarrels into discredit. A calm review of misconduct, after the excitement has gone by, will do more to bring it into disgrace than the most violent invectives and reproaches directed against the individuals guilty of it at the time.

"Now, boys," continued the master, "will you assist me in making arrangements to prevent the recurrence of all temptations of this kind hereafter? It is plain that every boy ought to have a nail appropriated expressly to his use. The first thing to be done is to ascertain whether there are enough for all. I should like, therefore, to have two committees appointed: one to count and report the number of nails in the entry, and also how much room there is for more; the other to ascertain the number of scholars in school. They can count all who are here, and, by observing the vacant desks, they can ascertain the number absent. When this investigation is made, I will tell you what to do next."

The boys seemed pleased with the plan, and the committees were appointed, two members on each. The master took care to give the quarrelers some share in the work, apparently forgetting, from this time, the unpleasant occurrence which had brought up the subject.

When the boys came to inform him of the result of their inquiries, he asked them to make a little memorandum of it in writing, as he might forget the numbers, he said, before the time came for reading them. The boys brought him, presently, a rough scrap of paper, with the figures marked upon it. He told them he should forget which was the number of nails, and which the number of scholars, unless they wrote it down.

"It is the custom among men," said he, "to make out their report, in such a case, fully, so that it would explain itself; and I should like to have you, if you are willing, make out yours a little more distinctly."

Accordingly, after a little additional explanation, the boys made another attempt, and presently returned with something like the following:

"The committee for counting the nails report as follows:

Number of nails..................35

Room for more...................15."

The other report was very similar, though somewhat rudely written and expressed, and both were perfectly satisfactory to the preceptor, as he plainly showed by the manner in which he received them.

I need not finish the description of this case by narrating particularly the reading of the reports, the appointment of a committee to assign the nails, and to paste up the names of the scholars, one to each. The work, in such a case, might be done in recesses, and out of school hours; and though, at first, the teacher will find that it is as much trouble to accomplish business in this way as it would be to attend to it directly himself, yet, after a very little experience, he will find that his pupils will acquire dexterity and readiness, and will be able to render him very material assistance in the accomplishment of his plans.

This, however—the assistance rendered to the teacher—is not the main object of the adoption of such measures as this. The main design is to interest the pupils in the management and the welfare of the school—to identify them, as it were, with it. And such measures as the above will accomplish this object; and every teacher who will try the experiment, and carry it into effect with any tolerable degree of skill, will find that it will, in a short time, change the whole aspect of the school in regard to the feelings subsisting between himself and his pupils.

Each teacher who tries such an experiment will find himself insensibly repeating it, and after a time he may have quite a number of officers and committees who are intrusted with various departments of business. He will have a secretary, chosen by ballot by the scholars, to keep a record of all the important transactions in the school for each day. At first he will dictate to the secretary, thus directing him precisely what to say, or even writing it for him, and then merely requiring him to copy it into the book provided for the purpose. Afterward he will give the pupil less and less assistance, till he can keep the record properly himself. The record of each day will be read on the succeeding day at the hour for business. The teacher will perhaps have a committee to take care of the fire, and another to see that the room is constantly in good order. He will have distributors for each division of seats, to distribute books, and compositions, and pens, and to collect votes. And thus, in a short time, his school will become *regularly organized as a society or legislative assembly*. The boys will learn submission to the majority in such unimportant things as may be committed to them; they will learn system and regularity, and every thing else, indeed, that belongs to the science of political self-government.

There are dangers, however. What useful practice has not its dangers? One of these is, that the teacher will allow these arrangements to take up too much time. He must guard against this. I have found from experience that fifteen minutes each day, with a school of 135, is enough. This ought never to be exceeded.

Another danger is, that the boys will be so engaged in the duties of their *offices* as to neglect their *studies*. This would be, and ought to be, fatal to the whole plan. This danger may be avoided in the following manner. State publicly that you will not appoint any to office who are not good scholars, always punctual, and always prepared; and when any boy who holds an office is going behindhand in his studies, say to him kindly, "You have not time to get your lessons, and I am afraid it is owing to the fact that you spend so much time in helping me. Now if you wish to resign your office, so as to have more time for your lessons, you can. In fact, I think you ought to do it. You may try it for a day or two, and I will notice how you recite, and then we can decide."

Such a communication will generally be found to have a powerful effect. If it does not remedy the evil, the resignation must be insisted on. A few decided cases of this kind will effectually remove the evil I am considering.

Another difficulty which is likely to attend the plan of allowing the pupils of a school to take some part in this way in the administration of it is that it may tend to make them insubordinate, so that they will, in many instances, submit with less good humor to such decisions as you may consider necessary. I do not mean that this will be the case with all, but that there will be a few who will be ungenerous enough, if you allow them to decide sometimes what shall be done, to endeavor to make trouble, or at least to show symptoms of impatience and vexation because you do not allow them always to decide.

Sometimes this feeling may show itself by the discontented looks, or gestures, or even words with which some unwelcome regulation or order on the part of the teacher will be received. Such a spirit should be immediately and decidedly checked whenever it appears. It will not be difficult to check, and even entirely to remove it. On one occasion when, after learning the wish of the scholars on some subject which had been brought before them, I decided contrary to it, there arose a murmur of discontent all over the room. This was the more distinct, because I have always accustomed my pupils to answer questions asked, and to express their wishes and feelings on any subject I may present to them with great freedom.

I asked all those who had expressed their dissatisfaction to rise.

About one third of the scholars arose.

"Perhaps you understood that when I put the question to vote I meant to abide by your decision, and that, consequently, I ought not to have reversed it, as I did afterward?"

"Yes, sir," "Yes, sir," they replied.

"Do you suppose it would be safe to leave the decision of important questions to the scholars in this school?"

"Yes, sir;" "No, sir." The majority were, however, in the affirmative.

Thus far, only those who were standing had answered. I told them that, as they were divided in opinion, they might sit, and I would put the question to the whole school.

"You know," I continued, addressing the whole, "what sort of persons the girls who compose this school are. You know about how many are governed habitually by steady principle, and how many by impulse and feeling. You know, too, what proportion have judgment and foresight necessary to consider and decide independently such questions as continually arise in the management of a school. Now suppose I should resign the school into your own hands as to its management, and only come in to give instruction to the classes, leaving all general control of its arrangements with you, would it go on safely or not?"

As might have been foreseen, there was, when the question was fairly proposed, scarcely a solitary vote in favor of government by scholars. They seemed to see clearly the absurdity of such a scheme.

"Besides," I continued, "the trustees of this school have committed it to my charge; they hold me responsible; the public hold *me* responsible, not you. Now if I should surrender it into your hands, and you, from any cause, should manage the trust unfaithfully or unskillfully, I should necessarily be held accountable. I could never shift the responsibility upon you. Now it plainly is not just or right that one party should hold the power, and another be held accountable for its exercise. It is clear, therefore, in every view of the subject, that I should retain the management of this school in my own hands. Are you not satisfied that it is?"

The scholars universally answered "Yes, sir." They seemed satisfied, and doubtless were.

It was then stated to them that the object in asking them to vote was, in some cases, to obtain an expression of their opinion or their wishes in order to help *me* decide, and only in those cases where it was expressly stated did I mean to give the final decision to them.

Still, however, if cases are often referred to them, the feeling will gradually creep in that the school is managed on republican principles, as they call it, and they will, unless this point is specially guarded, gradually lose that spirit of entire and cordial subordination so necessary for the success of any school. It should often be distinctly explained to them that a republican government is one where the power essentially resides in the community, and is exercised by a ruler only so far as the community delegates it to him, whereas in the school the government is based on the principle that the power, primarily and essentially, resides in the teacher, the scholars exercising only such as *he* may delegate to *them*.

With these limitations and restrictions, and with this express understanding in regard to what is, in all cases, the ultimate authority, I think there will be no danger in throwing a very large share of the business which will, from time to time, come up in the school, upon the scholars themselves for decision. In my own experience this plan has been adopted with the happiest results. In the Mount Vernon School a small red morocco wrapper lies constantly on a little shelf, accessible to all. By its side is a little pile of papers, about one inch by six, on which any one may write her motion, or her *proposition*, as the scholars call it, whatever it may be, and when written it is inclosed in the wrapper, to be brought to me at the appointed time for attending to the general business of the school. Through this wrapper all questions are asked, all complaints entered, all proposals made. Is there discontent in the school? It shows itself by "*propositions*" in the wrapper. Is any body aggrieved or injured? I learn it through the wrapper. In fact, it is a little safety-valve, which lets off what, if confined, might threaten explosion—an index—a thermometer, which reveals to me, from day to day, more of the state of public opinion in the little community than any thing beside.

These propositions are generally read aloud. Some cases are referred to the scholars for decision; some I decide myself; others are laid aside without notice of any kind; others still, merely suggest remarks on the subjects to which they allude.

The principles, then, which this chapter has been intended to establish, are simply these: in making your general arrangements, look carefully over your ground, consider all the objects which you have to accomplish, and the proper degree of time and attention which each deserves. Then act upon system. Let the mass of particulars which would otherwise crowd upon you in promiscuous confusion be arranged and classified. Let each be assigned to its proper time and place, so that your time may be your own, under your own command, and not, as is too often the case, at the mercy of the thousand accidental circumstances which may occur.

In a word, be, in the government of your school, yourself supreme, and let your supremacy be that of *authority;* but delegate power, as freely as possible, to those under your care. Show them that you are desirous of reposing trust in them just so far as they show themselves capable of exercising it. Thus interest them in your plans, and make them feel that they participate in the honor or the disgrace of success or failure.

I have gone much into detail in this chapter, proposing definite measures by which the principles I have recommended may be carried into effect. I wish, however, that it may be distinctly understood that all I contend for is the *principles* themselves, no matter what the particular measures are by which they are secured. Every good school must be systematic, but all need not be on precisely the same system. As this work is intended almost exclusively for beginners, much detail has been admitted, and many of the specific measures here proposed may perhaps be safely adopted where no others are established. There may also, perhaps, be cases where teachers, whose schools are already in successful operation, may ingraft upon their own plans some things which are here proposed. If they should attempt it, it must be done cautiously and gradually. There is no other way by which they can be safely introduced, or even introduced at all. This is a point of so much importance, that I must devote a paragraph to it before closing the chapter.

Let a teacher propose to his pupils, formally, from his desk, the plan of writing propositions, for example, as explained above, and procure his wrapper, and put it in its place, and what would be the result? Why, not a single paper, probably, could he get, from one end of the week to the other. But let him, on the other hand, when a boy comes to him to ask some question, the answer to which many in the school would equally wish to hear, say to the inquirer,

"Will you be so good as to write that question, and put it on my desk, and then, at the regular time, I will answer it to all the school."

When he reads it, let him state that it was written at his request, and give the other boys permission to leave their proposals or questions on his desk in the same way. In a few days he will have another, and thus the plan may be gently and gradually introduced.

So with officers. They should be appointed among the scholars only *as fast as they are actually needed*, and the plan should thus be cautiously carried only so far as it proves good on trial. Be always cautious about innovations and changes. Make no rash experiments on a large scale, but always test your principle in the small way, and then, if it proves good, gradually extend its operation as circumstances seem to require.

By thus cautiously and slowly introducing plans, founded on the systematic principles here brought to view, a very considerable degree of quiet, and order, and regularity may be introduced into the largest and most miscellaneous schools. And this order and quiet are absolutely necessary to enable the teacher to find that interest and enjoyment in his work which were exhibited in the last chapter; the pleasure of *directing and controlling mind*, and doing it, not by useless and anxious complaints, or stern threats and painful punishments, but by regarding the scene of labor in its true light, as a community of intellectual and moral beings, and governing it by moral and intellectual power. It is, in fact, the pleasure of exercising *power*. I do not mean arbitrary, personal authority, but the power to produce, by successful but quiet contrivance, extensive and happy results; the pleasure of calmly considering every difficulty, and, without irritation or anger, devising the proper moral means to remedy the moral evil; and then the interest and pleasure of witnessing its effects.

CHAPTER III.

INSTRUCTION.

E come now to consider the subject of Instruction.

There are three kinds of human knowledge which stand strikingly distinct from all the rest. They lie at the foundation. They constitute the roots of the tree. In other words, they are the *means* by which all other knowledge is attained. I need not say that I mean Reading, Writing, and Calculation.

Teachers do not perhaps always consider how entirely and essentially distinct these three branches of learning are from all the rest. They are arts; the acquisition of them is not to be considered as knowledge, so much as the means by which knowledge may be obtained. A child who is studying Geography, or History, or Natural Science, is learning *facts*—gaining information; on the other hand, the one who is learning to write, or to read, or to calculate, may be adding little or nothing to his stock of knowledge. He is acquiring *skill*, which, at some future time, he may make the means of increasing his knowledge to any extent.

This distinction ought to be kept constantly in view, and the teacher should feel that these three fundamental branches stand by themselves, and stand first in importance. I do not mean to undervalue the others, but only to insist upon the superior value and importance of these. Teaching a pupil to read before he enters upon the active business of life is like giving a new settler an axe as he goes to seek his new home in the forest. Teaching him a lesson in history is, on the other hand, only cutting down a tree or two for him. A knowledge of natural history is like a few bushels of grain gratuitously placed in his barn; but the art of ready reckoning is the plow which will remain by him for years, and help him to draw out from the soil a new treasure every year of his life.

The great object, then, of the common schools in our country is to teach the whole population to read, to write, and to calculate. In fact, so essential is it that the accomplishment of these objects should be secured, that it is even a question whether common schools should not be confined to them. I say it is a *question*, for it is sometimes made so, though public opinion has decided that some portion of attention, at least, should be paid to the acquisition of additional knowledge. But, after all, the amount of *knowledge* which is actually acquired at schools is very small. It must be very small. The true policy is to aim at making all the pupils good readers, writers, and calculators, and to consider the other studies of the school important chiefly as practice in turning these arts to useful account. In other words, the scholars should be taught these arts thoroughly first of all, and in the other studies the main design should be to show them how to use, and interest them in using, the arts they have thus acquired.

A great many teachers feel a much stronger interest in the one or two scholars they may have in Surveying or in Latin than they do in the large classes in the elementary branches which fill the school. But a moment's reflection will show that such a preference is founded on a very mistaken view. Leading forward one or two minds from step to step in an advanced study is certainly far inferior in real dignity and importance to opening all the stores of written knowledge to fifty or a hundred. The man who neglects the interests of his school in these great branches to devote his time to two or three, or half a dozen older scholars, is unjust both to his employers and to himself.

It is the duty, therefore, of every teacher who commences a common district school for a single season to make, when he commences, an estimate of the state of his pupils in reference to these three branches. How do they all write? How do they all read? How do they calculate? It would be well if he would make a careful examination of the school in this respect. Let them all write a specimen. Let all read, and let him make a memorandum of the manner, noticing how many read fluently, how many with difficulty, how many know only their letters, and how many are to be taught these. Let him ascertain, also, what progress they have made in arithmetic—how many can readily perform the elementary processes, and what number need instruction in these. After thus surveying the ground, let him form his plan, and lay out his whole strength in carrying forward as rapidly as possible the *whole school* in these studies. By this means he is acting most directly and powerfully on the intelligence of the whole future community in that place. He is opening to fifty or a hundred minds stores of knowledge which they will go on exploring for years to come. What a descent now from such a work as this to the mere hearing of the recitation of two or three boys in Trigonometry!

I repeat it, that a thorough and enlightened survey of the whole school should be taken, and plans formed for elevating the whole mass in those great branches of knowledge which are to be of immediate practical use to them in future life.

If the school is one more advanced in respect to the age and studies of the pupils, the teacher should, in the same manner, before he forms his plans, consider well what are the great objects which he has to accomplish. He should ascertain what is the existing state of his school both as to knowledge and character; how long, generally, his pupils are to remain under his care; what are to be their future stations and conditions in life, and what objects he can reasonably hope to effect for them while they remain under his influence. By means of this forethought and consideration he will be enabled to work understandingly.

It is desirable, too, that what I have recommended in reference to the whole school should be done in respect to the case of each individual. When a new pupil comes under your charge, ascertain (by other means, however, than formal examination) to what stage his education has advanced, and deliberately consider what objects you can reasonably expect to effect for him while he remains under your care. You can not, indeed, always form your plans to suit so exactly your general views in regard to the school and to individuals as you could wish. But these general views will, in a thousand cases, modify your plans, or affect in a greater or less degree all your arrangements. They will keep you to a steady purpose, and your work will go on far more systematically and regularly than it would do if, as in fact many teachers do, you were to come headlong into your school, take things just as you find them, and carry them forward at random without end or aim.

This survey of your field being made, you are prepared to commence definite operations, and the great difficulty in carrying your plans into effect is how to act more efficiently on *the greatest numbers at a time*. The whole business of public instruction, if it goes on at all, must go on by the teacher's skill in multiplying his power, by acting on *numbers at once*. In most books on education we are taught, almost exclusively, how to operate on the *individual*. It is the error into which theoretic writers almost always fall. We meet in every periodical, and in every treatise, and, in fact, in almost every conversation on the subject, with remarks which sound very well by the fireside, but they are totally inefficient and useless in school, from their being apparently based upon the supposition that the teacher has but *one* pupil to attend to at a time. The great question in the management of schools is not how you can take *one* scholar, and lead him forward most rapidly in a prescribed course, but how you can classify and arrange *numbers*, comprising every possible variety both as to knowledge and capacity, so as to carry them all forward effectually together.

The extent to which a teacher may multiply his power by acting on numbers at a time is very great. In order to estimate it, we must consider carefully what it is when carried to the greatest extent to which it is capable of being carried under the most favorable circumstances. Now it is possible for a teacher to speak so as to be easily heard by three hundred persons, and three hundred pupils can be easily so seated as to see his illustrations or diagrams. Now suppose that three hundred pupils, all ignorant of the method of reducing fractions to a common denominator, and yet all old enough to learn, are collected in one room. Suppose they are all attentive and desirous of learning, it is very plain that the process may be explained to the whole at once, so that half an hour spent in that exercise would enable a very large proportion of them to understand the subject. So, if a teacher is explaining to a class in Grammar the difference between a noun and verb, the explanation would do as well for several hundred as for the dozen who constitute the class, if arrangements could only be made to have the hundreds hear it; but there are, perhaps, only a hundred pupils in the school, and of these a large part understand already the point to be explained, and another large part are too young to attend to it. I wish the object of these remarks not to be misunderstood. I do not recommend the attempt to teach on so extensive a scale; I admit that it is impracticable; I only mean to show in what the impracticability consists, namely, in the difficulty of making such arrangements as to derive the full benefit from the instructions rendered. The instructions of the teacher are, *in the nature of things*, available to the extent I have represented, but in actual practice the full benefit can not be derived. Now, so far as we thus fall short of this full benefit, so far there is, of course, waste; and it is difficult or impossible to make such arrangements as will avoid the waste, in this manner, of a large portion of every effort which the teacher makes.

A very small class instructed by an able teacher is like a factory of a hundred spindles, with a water-wheel of power sufficient for a thousand. In such a case, even if the owner, from want of capital or any other cause, can not add the other nine hundred, he ought to know how much of his power is in fact unemployed, and make arrangements to bring it into useful exercise as soon as he can. The teacher, in the same manner, should understand what is the full beneficial effect which it is possible, *in theory*, to derive from his instructions. He should understand, too, that just so far as he falls short of this full effect there is waste. It may be unavoidable; part of it unquestionably is, like the friction of machinery, unavoidable. Still, it is waste; and it ought to be so understood, that, by the gradual perfection of the machinery, it may be more and more fully prevented.

Always bear in mind, then, when you are devoting your time to two or three individuals in a class, that your are losing a large part of your labor. Your instructions are conducive to good effect only to the one tenth or one twentieth of the extent to which, under more favorable circumstances, they might be made available. And though you can not always avoid this loss, you ought to be aware of it, and so to shape your measures as to diminish it as much as possible.

We come now to consider the particular measures to be adopted in giving instruction.

The objects which are to be secured in the management of the classes are twofold:

1. Recitation.
2. Instruction.

These two objects are, it is plain, entirely distinct. Under the latter is included all the explanation, and assistance, and additional information which the teacher may give his pupils, and under the former, such an *examination* of individuals as is necessary to secure their careful attention to their lessons. It is unsafe to neglect either of these points. If the class meetings are mere *recitations*, they soon become dull and mechanical; the pupils generally take little interest in their studies, and imbibe no literary spirit. Their intellectual progress will, accordingly, suddenly cease the moment they leave school, and so cease to be called upon to recite lessons. On the other hand, if *instruction* is all that is aimed at, and *recitation* (by which I mean, as above explained, such an examination of individuals as is necessary to ascertain that they have faithfully performed the tasks assigned) is neglected, the exercise soon becomes not much more than a lecture, to which those, and those only, will attend who please.

The business, therefore, of a thorough examination of the class must not be omitted. I do not mean that each individual scholar must every day be examined, but simply that the teacher must, in some way or other, satisfy himself by reasonable evidence that the whole class are really prepared. A great deal of ingenuity may be exercised in contriving means for effecting this object in the shortest possible time. I know of no part of the field of a teacher's labors which may be more facilitated by a little ingenuity than this.

One teacher, for instance, has a spelling lesson to hear. He begins at the head of the line, and putting one word to each boy, goes regularly down, each successive pupil calculating the chances whether a word which he can accidentally spell will or will not come to him. If he spells it, the teacher can not tell whether he is prepared or not. That word is only one among fifty constituting the lesson. If he misses it, the teacher can not decide that he was unprepared. It might have been a single accidental error.

Another teacher, hearing the same lesson, requests the boys to bring their slates, and, as he dictates the words one after another, requires all to write them. After they are all written, he calls upon the pupils to spell them aloud as they have written them, simultaneously, pausing a moment after each, to give those who are wrong an opportunity to indicate it by some mark opposite the word misspelled. They all count the number of errors and report them. He passes down the class, glancing his eye at the work of each one to see that all is right, noticing particularly those slates which, from the character of the boys, need a more careful inspection. A teacher who had never tried this experiment would be surprised at the rapidity with which such work will be performed by a class after a little practice.

Now how different are these two methods in their actual results! In the latter case the whole class are thoroughly examined. In the former not a single member of it is. Let me not be understood to recommend exactly this method of teaching spelling as the best one to be adopted in all cases. I only bring it forward as an illustration of the idea that a little machinery, a little ingenuity in contriving ways of acting on the *whole* rather than on individuals, will very much promote the teacher's designs.

In order to facilitate such plans, it is highly desirable that the classes should be trained to military precision and exactness in these manipulations. What I mean by this may perhaps be best illustrated by describing a case: it will show, in another branch, how much will be gained by acting upon numbers at once instead of upon each individual in succession.

Imagine, then, that a teacher requested all the pupils of his school who could write to take out their slates at the hour for a general exercise. As soon as the first bustle of opening and shutting the desks was over, he looked around the room, and saw some ruling lines across their slates, others wiping them all over on both sides with sponges, others scribbling, or writing, or making figures.

"All those," says he, speaking, however, with a pleasant tone and with a pleasant look, "who have taken out any thing besides slates, may rise."

Several, in various parts of the room, stood up.

"All those who have written any thing since they took out their slates may rise too, and those who have wiped their slates."

When all were up, he said to them, though not with a frown or a scowl, as if they had committed a great offense,

"Suppose a company of soldiers should be ordered to *form a line*, and instead of simply obeying that order they should all set at work, each in his own way, doing something else. One man at one end of the line begins to load and fire his gun; another takes out his knapsack and begins to eat his luncheon; a third amuses himself by going as fast as possible through the exercise; and another still, begins to march about hither and thither, facing to the right and left, and performing all the evolutions he can think of. What should you say to such a company as that?"

The boys laughed.

"It is better," said the teacher, "when numbers are acting under the direction of one, that they should all act *exactly together*. In this way we advance much faster than we otherwise should. Be careful, therefore, to do exactly what I command, and nothing more.

"*Provide a place on your slates large enough to write a single line*," added the teacher, in a distinct voice. I print his orders in Italics, and his remarks and explanations in Roman letters.

"*Prepare to write.*

"I mean by this," he continued, "that you place your slates before you with your pencils at the place where you are to begin, so that all may commence precisely at the same instant."

The teacher who tries such an experiment as this will find at such a juncture an expression of fixed and pleasant attention upon every countenance in school. All will be intent, all will be interested. Boys love order, and system, and acting in concert, and they will obey with great alacrity such commands as these if they are good-humoredly, though decidedly expressed.

The teacher observed in one part of the room a hand raised, indicating that the boy wished to speak to him. He gave him liberty by pronouncing his name.

"I have no pencil," said the boy.

A dozen hands all around him were immediately seen fumbling in pockets and desks, and in a few minutes several pencils were reached out for his acceptance.

The boy looked at the pencils and then at the teacher; he did not exactly know whether he was to take one or not.

"All those boys," said the teacher, pleasantly, "who have taken out pencils, may rise.

"Have these boys done right or wrong?"

"Right;" "Wrong;" "Right," answered their companions, variously.

"Their motive was to help their class-mate out of his difficulties; that is a good feeling, certainly."

"Yes, sir, right;" "Right."

"But I thought you promised me a moment ago," replied the teacher, "not to do any thing unless I commanded it. Did I ask for pencils?"

A pause.

"I do not blame these boys at all in this case; still, it is better to adhere rigidly to the principle of *exact obedience* when numbers are acting together. I thank them, therefore, for being so ready to assist a companion, but they must put their pencils away, as they were taken out without orders."

Now such a dialogue as this, if the teacher speaks in a good-humored, though decided manner, would be universally well received in any school. Whenever strictness of discipline is unpopular, it is rendered so simply by the ill-humored and ill-judged means by which it is attempted to be introduced. But all children will love strict discipline if it is pleasantly, though firmly maintained. It is a great, though very prevalent mistake, to imagine that boys and girls like a lax and inefficient government, and dislike the pressure of steady control. What they dislike is sour looks and irritating language, and they therefore very naturally dislike every thing introduced or sustained by means of them. If, however, exactness and precision in all the operations of a class and of the school are introduced and enforced in the proper manner, that is, by a firm, but mild and good-humored authority, scholars will universally be pleased with them. They like to see the uniform appearance, the straight line, the simultaneous movement. They like to feel the operation of system, and to realize, while they are at the school-room, that they form a community, governed by fixed and steady laws, firmly but kindly administered. On the other hand, laxity of discipline, and the disorder which will result from it, will only lead the pupils to contemn their teacher and to hate their school.

By introducing and maintaining such a discipline as I have described, great facilities will be secured for examining the classes. For example, to take a case different from the one before described, let us suppose that a class have been performing a number of examples in Addition. They come together to the recitation, and, under one mode of managing classes, the teacher is immediately beset by a number of the pupils with excuses. One had no slate; another was absent when the lesson was assigned; a third performed the work, but it got rubbed out, and a fourth did not know what was to be done. The teacher stops to hear all these, and to talk about them, fretting himself, and fretting the delinquents by his impatient remarks. The rest of the class are waiting, and, having nothing good to do, the temptation is almost irresistible to do something bad. One boy is drawing pictures on his slate to make his neighbors laugh, another is whispering, and two more are at play. The disorder continues while the teacher goes round examining slate after slate, his whole attention being engrossed by each individual, as the pupils come to him successively, while the rest are left to themselves, interrupted only by an occasional harsh, or even angry, but utterly useless rebuke from him.

But, under another mode of managing classes and schools, a very different result would be produced.

A boy approaches the teacher to render an excuse; the teacher replies, addressing himself, however, to the whole class, "I shall give all an opportunity to offer their excuses presently. No one must come till he is called."

The class then regularly take their places in the recitation seats, the prepared and unprepared together. The following commands are given and obeyed promptly. They are spoken pleasantly, but still in the tone of command.

"The class may rise.

"All those that are not fully prepared with this lesson may sit."

A number sit; and others, doubtful whether they are prepared or not, or thinking that there is something peculiar in their cases, which they wish to state, raise their hands, or make any other signal which is customary to indicate a wish to speak. Such a signal ought always to be agreed upon, and understood in school.

The teacher shakes his head, saying, "I will hear you presently. If there is, on any account whatever, any doubt whether you are prepared, you must sit.

"Those that are standing may read their answers to No. 1. Unit figure?"

Boys. "Five."

Teacher. "Tens?"

B. "Six."

T. "Hundreds?"

B. "Seven."

While these numbers are thus reading, the teacher looks at the boys, and can easily see whether any are not reading their own answers, but only following the rest. If they have been trained to speak exactly together, his ear will also at once detect any erroneous answer which any one may give. He takes down the figures given by the majority on his own slate, and reads them aloud.

"This is the answer obtained by the majority; it is undoubtedly right. Those who have different answers may sit."

These directions, if understood and obeyed, would divide the class evidently into two portions. Those standing have their work done, and done correctly, and those sitting have some excuse or error to be examined. A new lesson may now be assigned, and the first portion may be dismissed, which in a well-regulated school will be two thirds of the class. Their slates may be slightly examined as they pass by the teacher on their way to their seats to see that all is fair; but it will be safe to take it for granted that a result in which a majority agree will be right. Truth is consistent with itself, but error, in such a case, never is. This the teacher can at any time show by comparing the answers that are wrong; they will always be found, not only to differ from the correct result, but to contradict each other.

The teacher may now, if he pleases, after the majority of the class have gone, hear the reasons of those who were unprepared, and look for the errors of those whose work was incorrect; but it is better to spend as little time as possible in such a way. If a scholar is not prepared, it is not of much consequence whether it is because he forgot his book or mistook the lesson; or if it is ascertained that his answer is incorrect, it is ordinarily a mere waste of time to search for the particular error.

"I have looked over my work, sir," says the boy, perhaps, "and I can not find where it is wrong." He means by it that he does not believe that it is wrong.

"It is no matter if you can not," would be the proper reply, "since it certainly is wrong; you have made a mistake in adding somewhere, but it is not worth while for me to spend two or three minutes apiece with all of you to ascertain where. Try to be careful next time."

Indeed the teacher should understand and remember what many teachers are very prone to forget, namely, that the mere fact of finding an arithmetical error in a pupil's work on the slate, and pointing it out to him, has very little effect in correcting the false habit in his mind from which it arose.

The cases of those who are unprepared at a recitation ought by no means to be passed by unnoticed, although it would be unwise to spend much time in examining each in detail.

"It is not of much consequence," the teacher might say, "whether you have good excuses or bad, so long as you are not prepared. In future life you will certainly be unsuccessful if you fail, no matter for what reason, to discharge the duties which devolve upon you. A carpenter, for instance, would certainly lose his custom if he should not perform his work faithfully and in season. Excuses, no matter how reasonable, will do him little good. It is just so in respect to punctuality in time as well as in respect to performance of duty. What we want is that every boy should be in his place at the proper moment; not that he should be late, and have good excuses for it. When you come to be men, tardiness will always be punished. Excuses will not help the matter at all. Suppose, hereafter, when you are about to take a journey, you reach the pier five minutes after the steamer has gone, what good will excuses do you? There you are, left hopelessly behind, no matter if your excuses are the best in the world. So in this school. I want good punctuality and good recitations, not good excuses. I hope every one will be prepared to-morrow."

It is not probable, however, that every one would be prepared the next day in such a case, but by acting steadily on these principles the number of delinquencies would be so much diminished that the very few which should be left could easily be examined in detail, and the remedies applied.

Simultaneous recitation, by which I mean the practice of addressing a question to all the class to be answered by all together, is a practice which has been for some years rapidly extending in our schools, and, if adopted with proper limits and restrictions, is attended with great advantage. The teacher must guard against some dangers, however, which will be likely to attend it.

1. Some will answer very eagerly, instantly after the question is completed. They wish to show their superior readiness. Let the teacher mention this, expose kindly the motive which leads to it, and tell them it is as irregular to answer before the rest as after them.

2. Some will defer their answers until they can catch those of their comrades for a guide. Let the teacher mention this fault, expose the motive which leads to it, and tell them that if they do not answer independently and at once, they had better not answer at all.

3. Some will not answer at all. The teacher can see by looking around the room who do not, for they can not counterfeit the proper motion of the lips with promptness and decision unless they know what the answer is to be. He ought occasionally to say to such a one, "I perceive you do not answer," and ask him questions individually.

4. In some cases there is danger of confusion in the answers, from the fact that the question may be of such a nature that the answer is long, and may by different individuals be differently expressed. This evil must be guarded against by so shaping the question as to admit of a reply in a single word. In reading large numbers, for example, each figure may be called for by itself, or they may be given one after another, the pupils keeping exact time. When it is desirable to ask a question to which the answer is necessarily long it may be addressed to an individual, or the whole class may write their replies, which may then be read in succession.

In a great many cases where simultaneous answering is practiced, after a short time the evils above specified are allowed to grow, until at last some half a dozen bright members of a class answer for all, the rest dragging after them, echoing their replies, or ceasing to take any interest in an exercise which brings no personal and individual responsibility upon them. To prevent this, the teacher should exercise double vigilance at such a time. He should often address questions to individuals alone, especially to those most likely to be inattentive and careless, and guard against the ingress of every abuse which might, without close vigilance, appear.

With these cautions, the method here alluded to will be found to be of very great advantage in many studies; for example, all the arithmetical tables may be recited in this way; words may be spelled, answers to sums given, columns of figures added, or numbers multiplied, and many questions in history, geography, and other miscellaneous studies answered, especially the general questions asked for the purpose of a review.

But, besides being useful as a mode of examination, this plan of answering questions simultaneously is a very important means of fixing in the mind any facts which the teacher may communicate to his pupils. If, for instance, he says some day to a class that Vasco de Gama was the discoverer of the passage round the Cape of Good Hope, and leaves it here, in a few days not one in twenty will recollect the name. But let him call upon them all to spell it simultaneously, and then to pronounce it distinctly three or four times in concert, and the word will be very strongly impressed upon their minds. The reflecting teacher will find a thousand cases in the instruction of his classes, and in his general exercises in the school, in which this principle will be of great utility. It is universal in its application. What we *say* we fix, by the very act of saying it, in the mind. Hence, reading aloud, though a slower, is a far more thorough method of acquiring knowledge than reading silently, and it is better, in almost all cases, whether in the family, or in Sabbath or common schools, when general instructions are given, to have the leading points fixed in the mind by questions answered simultaneously.

But we are wandering a little from our subject, which is, in this part of our chapter, the methods of *examining* a class, not of giving or fixing instructions.

Another mode of examining classes, which it is important to describe, consists in requiring *written answers* to the questions asked. The form and manner in which this plan may be adopted is various. The class may bring their slates to the recitation, and the teacher may propose questions successively, the answers to which all the class may write, numbering them carefully. After a dozen answers are written, the teacher may call at random for them, or he may repeat a question, and ask each pupil to read the answer he had written, or he may examine the slates. Perhaps this method may be very successfully employed in reviews by dictating to the class a list of questions relating to the ground they have gone over for a week, and then instructing them to prepare answers written out at length, and to bring them in at the next exercise. This method may be made more formal still by requiring a class to write a full and regular abstract of all they have learned during a specified time. The practice of thus reducing to writing what has been learned will be attended with many advantages so obvious that they need not be described.

It will be perceived that three methods of examining classes have now been named, and these will afford the teacher the means of introducing a very great variety in his mode of conducting his recitations, while he still carries his class forward steadily in their prescribed course. Each is attended with its peculiar advantages. The *single replies*, coming from individuals specially addressed, are more rigid, and more to be relied upon, but they consume a great deal of time, and, while one is questioned, it requires much skill to keep up interest in the rest. The *simultaneous answers* of a class awaken more general interest, but it is difficult, without special care, to secure by this means a special examination of all. The *written replies* are more thorough, but they require more time and attention, and while they habituate the pupil to express himself in writing, they would, if exclusively adopted, fail to accustom him to an equally important practice, that of the oral communication of his thoughts. A constant variety, of which these three methods should be the elements, is unquestionably the best mode. We not only, by this means, secure in a great degree the advantages which each is fitted to produce, but we gain also the additional advantage and interest of variety.

By these, and perhaps by other means, it is the duty of the teacher to satisfy himself that his pupils are really attentive to their duties. It is not perhaps necessary that every individual should be every day minutely examined; this is, in many cases, impossible; but the system of examination should be so framed and so administered as to be daily felt by all, and to bring upon every one a daily responsibility.

We come now to consider the second general head which was to be discussed in this chapter.

The study of books alone is insufficient to give knowledge to the young. In the first stage, learning to read a book is of no use whatever without the voice of the living teacher. The child can not take a step alone. As the pupil, however, advances in his course, his dependence upon his teacher for guidance and help continually diminishes, until at last the scholar sits in his solitary study, with no companion but his books, and desiring, for a solution of every difficulty, nothing but a larger library. In schools, however, the pupils have made so little progress in this course, that they all need more or less of the oral assistance of a teacher. Difficulties must be explained; questions must be answered; the path must be smoothed, and the way pointed out by a guide who has traveled it before, or it will be impossible for the pupil to go on. This is the part of our subject which we now approach.

The great principle which is to guide the teacher in this part of his duty is this: *Assist your pupils in such a way as to lead them, as soon as possible, to do without assistance.* This is fundamental. In a short time they will be away from your reach; they will have no teacher to consult; and unless you teach them how to understand books themselves, they must necessarily stop suddenly in their course the moment you cease to help them forward. I shall proceed, therefore, to consider the subject in the following plan:

1. Means of exciting interest in study.
2. The kind and degree of assistance to be rendered.
3. Miscellaneous suggestions.

1. Interesting the pupils in their studies. There are various principles of human nature which may be of great avail in accomplishing this object. Making intellectual effort and acquiring knowledge are always pleasant to the human mind, unless some peculiar circumstances render them otherwise. The teacher has, therefore, only to remove obstructions and sources of pain, and the employment of his pupils will be of itself a pleasure.

"I am going to give you a new exercise to-day," said a teacher to a class of boys in Latin. "I am going to have you parse your whole lesson in writing. It will be difficult, but I think you may be able to accomplish it."

The class looked surprised. They did not know what *parsing in writing* could be.

"You may first, when you take your seats, and are ready to prepare the lesson, write upon your slates a list of the ten first nouns that you find in the lesson, arranging them in a column. Do you understand so far?"

"Yes, sir."

"Then rule lines for another column, just beyond this. In parsing nouns, what is the first particular to be named?"

"What the noun is from."

"Yes; that is, its nominative. Now you may write, at the head of the first column, the word *Nouns*, and at the head of the second, *Nom.*, for nominative. Then rule a line for the third column. What shall this contain?" "The declension." "Yes; and the fourth?" "Gender." "The fifth?" "Number."

In the same manner the other columns were designated. The sixth was to contain case; the seventh, the word with which the noun was connected in construction; and the eighth, a reference to the rule.

"Now I wish you," continued the teacher, "to fill up such a table as this with *ten* nouns. Do you understand how I mean?"

"Yes, sir;" "No, sir," they answered, variously.

"All who do understand may take their seats, as I wish to give as little explanation as possible. The more you can depend upon yourselves, the better."

Those who saw clearly what was to be done left the class, and the teacher continued his explanation to those who were left behind. He made the plan perfectly clear to them by taking a particular noun and running it through the table, showing what should be written opposite to the word in all the columns, and then dismissed them.

The class separated, as every class would, in such a case, with a strong feeling of interest in the work before them. It was not so difficult as to perplex them, and yet it required attention and care. They were interested and pleased—pleased with the effort which it required them to make, and they anticipated, with interest and pleasure, the time of coming again to the class to report and compare their work.

When the time for the class came, the teacher addressed them somewhat as follows:

"Before looking at your slates, I am going to predict what the faults are. I have not seen any of your work, but shall judge altogether from my general knowledge of school-boys, and the difficulties I know they meet with. Do you think I shall succeed?"

The scholars made no reply, and an unskillful teacher would imagine that time spent in such remarks would be wholly wasted. By no means. The influence of them was to awaken universal interest in the approaching examination of the slates. Every scholar would be intent, watching, with eager interest, to see whether the imagined faults would be found upon his work. The class was, by that single pleasant remark, put into the best possible state for receiving the criticisms of the teacher.

"The first fault which I suppose will be found is that some are unfinished."

The scholars looked surprised. They did not expect to have that called a fault.

"How many plead guilty to it?"

A few raised their hands, and the teacher continued:

"I suppose that some will be found partly effaced. The slates were not laid away carefully, or they were not clean, so that the writing is not distinct. How many find this the case with their work?

"I suppose that, in some cases, the lines will not be perpendicular, but will slant, probably toward the left, like writing.

"I suppose, also, that, in some cases, the writing will be careless, so that I can not easily read it. How many plead guilty to this?"

After mentioning such other faults as occurred to him, relating chiefly to the form of the table, and the mere mechanical execution of he work, he said,

"I think I shall not look at your slates to-day. You can all see, I have no doubt, how you can considerably improve them in mechanical execution in your next lesson; and I suppose you would a little prefer that I should not see your first imperfect efforts. In fact, I should rather not see them. At the next recitation they probably will be much better."

One important means by which the teacher may make his scholars careful of their reputation is to show them, thus, that he is careful of it himself.

Now in such a case as this, for it is, except in the principles which it is intended to illustrate, imaginary, a very strong interest would be awakened in the class in the work assigned them. Intellectual effort in new and constantly varied modes is in itself a pleasure, and this pleasure the teacher may deepen and increase very easily by a little dexterous management, designed to awaken curiosity and concentrate attention. It ought, however, to be constantly borne in mind that this variety should be confined to the modes of pursuing an object—the object itself being permanent, and constant, and steadily pursued. For instance, if a little class are to be taught simple addition, after the process is once explained, which may be done, perhaps, in two or three lessons, they will need many days of patient practice to render it familiar, to impress it firmly in their recollection, and to enable them to work with rapidity. Now this object must be steadily pursued. It would be very unwise for the teacher to say to himself, My class are tired of addition; I must carry them on to subtraction, or give them some other study. It would be equally unwise to keep them many days performing example after example in monotonous succession, each lesson a mere repetition of the last. He must steadily pursue his object of familiarizing them fully with this elementary process, but he may give variety and spirit to the work by changing occasionally the modes. One week he may dictate examples to them, and let them come together to compare their results, one of the class being appointed to keep a list of all who are correct each day. At another time each one may write an example, which he may read aloud to all the others, to be performed and brought in at the next time. Again, he may let them work on paper with pen and ink, that he may see how few mistakes they make, as mistakes in ink can not be easily removed. He may excite interest by devising ingenious examples, such as finding out how much all the numbers from one to fifty will make when added together, or the amount of the ages of the whole class, or any such investigation, the result of which they might feel an interest in learning. Thus the object is steadily pursued, though the means of pursuing it are constantly changing. We have the advantage of regular progress in the acquisition of knowledge truly valuable, while this progress is made with all the spirit and interest which variety can give.

The necessity of making such efforts as this, however, to keep up the interest of the class in their work, and to make it pleasant to them, will depend altogether upon circumstances; or, rather, it will vary much with circumstances. A class of pupils somewhat advanced in their studies, and understanding and feeling the value of knowledge, will need very little of such effort as this; while young and giddy children, who have been accustomed to dislike books and school, and every thing connected with them, will need more. It ought, however, in all cases, to be made a means, not an end—the means to lead on a pupil to an *interest in progress in knowledge itself*, which is, after all, the great motive which ought to be brought as soon and as extensively as possible to operate in the school-room.

Another way to awaken interest in the studies of the school is to bring out, as frequently and as distinctly as possible, the connection between these studies and the practical business of life. The events which are occurring around you, and which interest the community in which you are placed, may, by a little ingenuity, be connected in a thousand ways with the studies of the school. If the practice, which has been already repeatedly recommended, of appropriating a quarter of an hour each day to a general exercise, should be adopted, it will afford great facilities for doing this.

There is no branch of study attended to in school which may, by judicious efforts, be made more effectual in accomplishing this object, leading the pupils to see the practical utility and the value of knowledge, than composition. If such subjects as are suitable themes for *moral essays* are assigned, the scholars will indeed dislike the work of writing, and derive little benefit from it. The mass of pupils in our schools are not to be writers of moral essays or orations, and they do not need to form that style of empty, florid, verbose declamation which the practice of writing composition in our schools, as it is too frequently managed, tends to form. Assign practical subjects—subjects relating to the business of the school, or the events taking place around you. Is there a question before the community on the subject of the loca-

tion of a new school-house? Assign it to your pupils as a question for discussion, and direct them not to write empty declamation, but to obtain from their parents the real arguments in the case, and to present them distinctly and clearly, and in simple language, to their companions. Was a building burned by lightning in the neighborhood? Let those who saw the scene describe it, their productions to be read by the teacher aloud, and let them see that clear descriptions please, and that good legible writing can be read fluently, and that correct spelling, and punctuation, and grammar make the article go smoothly and pleasantly, and enable it to produce its full effect. Is the erection of a public building going forward in the neighborhood of your school? You can make it a very fruitful source of subjects and questions to give interest and impulse to the studies of the school-room. Your classes in geometry may measure, your arithmeticians may calculate and make estimates, your writers may describe its progress from week to week, and anticipate the scenes which it will in future years exhibit.

By such means the practical bearings and relations of the studies of the school-room may be constantly kept in view; but I ought to guard the teacher, while on this subject, most distinctly against the danger of making the school-room a scene of literary amusement instead of study. These means of awakening interest and relieving the tedium of the uninterrupted and monotonous study of text-books must not encroach on the regular duties of the school. They must be brought forward with judgment and moderation, and made subordinate and subservient to these regular duties. Their design is to give spirit and interest, and a feeling of practical utility to what the pupils are doing; and if resorted to with these restrictions and within these limits, they will produce powerful, but safe results.

Another way to excite interest, and that of the right kind, in school, is not to *remove* difficulties, but to teach the pupils how to *surmount* them. A text-book so contrived as to make study mere play, and to dispense with thought and effort, is the worst text-book that can be made, and the surest to be, in the end, a dull one. The great source of literary enjoyment, which is the successful exercise of intellectual power, is, by such a mode of presenting a subject, cut off. Secure, therefore, severe study. Let the pupil see that you are aiming to secure it, and that the pleasure which you expect that they will receive is that of firmly and patiently encountering and overcoming difficulty; of penetrating, by steady and persevering effort, into regions from which the idle and the inefficient are debarred, and that it is your province to lead them forward, not to carry them. They will soon understand this, and like it.

Never underrate the difficulties which your pupils will have to encounter, or try to persuade them that what you assign is *easy*. Doing easy things is generally dull work, and it is especially discouraging and disheartening for a pupil to spend his strength in doing what is really difficult for him when his instructor, by calling his work easy, gives him no credit for what may have been severe and protracted labor. If a thing is really hard for the pupil, his teacher ought to know it and admit it. The child then feels that he has some sympathy.

It is astonishing how great an influence may be exerted over a child by his simply knowing that his efforts are observed and appreciated. You pass a boy in the street wheeling a heavy load in a barrow; now simply stop to look at him, with a countenance which says, "That is a heavy load; I should not think that boy could wheel it;" and how quick will your look give fresh strength and vigor to his efforts. On the other hand, when, in such a case, the boy is faltering under his load, try the effect of telling him, "Why, that is not heavy; you can wheel it easily enough; trundle it along." The poor boy will drop his load, disheartened and discouraged, and sit down upon it in despair. It is so in respect to the action of the young in all cases. They are animated and incited by being told *in the right way* that they have something difficult to do. A boy is performing some service for you. He is watering your horse, perhaps, at a well by the road-side as you are traveling. Say to him, "Hold up the pail high, so that the horse can drink; it is not heavy." He

will be discouraged, and will be ready to set the pail down. Say to him, on the other hand, "I had better dismount myself. I don't think you can hold the pail up. It is very heavy;" and his eye will brighten up at once. "Oh no, sir," he will reply, "I can hold it very easily." Hence, even if the work you are assigning to a class *is* easy, do not tell them so unless you wish to destroy all their spirit and interest in doing it; and if you wish to excite their spirit and interest, make your work difficult, and let them see that you know it is so; not so difficult as to tax their powers too heavily, but enough so to require a vigorous and persevering effort. Let them distinctly understand, too, that you know it is difficult, that you mean to make it so, but that they have your sympathy and encouragement in the efforts which it calls them to make.

You may satisfy yourself that human nature is, in this respect, what I have described by some such experiment as the following. Select two classes not very familiar with elementary arithmetic, and offer to each of them the following example in addition:

1	2	3	4	5	6	7	8	9
2	3	4	5	6	7	8	9	1
3	4	5	6	7	8	9	1	2

etc., etc.

The numbers may be continued, according to the obvious law regulating the above, until each one of the nine digits has commenced the line. Or, if you choose Multiplication, let the example be this:

Multiply 123456789
by 123456789

Now, when you bring the example to one of the classes, address the pupils as follows:

"I have contrived for you a very difficult sum. It is the most difficult one that can be made with the number of figures contained in it, and I do not think that any of you can do it, but you may try. I shall not be surprised if every answer should contain mistakes."

To the other class say as follows:

"I have prepared an example for you, which I wish you to be very careful to perform correctly. It is a little longer than those you have had heretofore, but it is to be performed upon the same principles, and you can all do it correctly, if you really try."

Now under such circumstances the first class will go to their seats with ardor and alacrity, determined to show you that they can do work, even if it is difficult; and if they succeed, they come to the class the next day with pride and pleasure. They have accomplished something which you admit it was not easy to accomplish. On the other hand, the second class will go to their seats with murmuring looks and words, and with a hearty dislike of the task you have assigned them. They know that they have something to do, which, however easy it may be to the teacher, is really difficult for them; and they have to be perplexed and wearied with the work, without having, at last, even the little satisfaction of knowing that the teacher appreciates the difficulties with which they had to contend.

2. We now come to consider the subject of rendering assistance to the pupil, which is one of the most important and delicate parts of a teacher's work. The great difference which exists among teachers in regard to the skill they possess in this part of their duty, is so striking that it is very often noticed by others; and perhaps skill here is of more avail in deciding the question of success or failure than any thing besides. The first great principle is, however, simple and effectual.

(1.) *Divide and subdivide a difficult process, until your steps are so short that the pupil can easily take them.*

Most teachers forget the difference between the pupil's capacity and their own, and they pass rapidly forward, through a difficult train of thought, in their own ordinary gait, their unfortunate followers vainly trying to keep up with them. The case is precisely analogous to that of the father, who walks with the step of a man, while his little son is by his side, wearying and exhausting himself with fruitless efforts to reach his feet as far, and to move them as rapidly as a full-grown man.

But to show what I mean by subdividing a difficult process so as to make each step simple, I will take a case which may serve as an example. I will suppose that the teacher of a common school undertakes to show his boys, who, we will suppose, are acquainted with nothing but elementary arithmetic, how longitude is determined by means of the eclipses of Jupiter's satellites; not a very simple question, but still one which, like all others, may be, merely by the power of the subdivision alluded to, easily explained. I will suppose that the subject has come up at a general exercise; perhaps the question was asked in writing by one of the older boys. I will present the explanation chiefly in the form of question and answer, that it may be seen that the steps are so short that the boys may take them themselves.

"Which way," asks the teacher, "are the Rocky Mountains from us?"

"West," answer two or three of the boys.

In such cases as this, it is very desirable that the answers should be general, so that throughout the school there should be a spirited interest in the questions and replies. This will never be the case if a small number of the boys only take part in the answers, and many teachers complain that when they try this experiment they can seldom induce many of the pupils to take a part.

The reason ordinarily is that they say that *any* of the boys may answer instead of that *all* of them may. The boys do not get the idea that it is wished that a universal reply should come from all parts of the room, in which every one's voice should be heard. If the answers were feeble in the instance we are supposing, the teacher would perhaps say,

"I only heard one or two answers; do not more of you know where the Rocky Mountains are? Will you all think and answer together? Which way are they from us?"

"West," answer a large number of boys.

"You do not answer fully enough yet; I do not think more than forty answered, and there are about sixty here. I should like to have *every one in the room* answer, and all precisely together."

He then repeats the question, and obtains a full response. A similar effort will always succeed.

"Now does the sun, in going round the earth, pass over the Rocky Mountains, or over us, first?"

To this question the teacher hears a confused answer. Some do not reply; some say, "Over the Rocky Mountains;" others, "Over us;" and others still, "The sun does not move at all."

"It is true that the sun, strictly speaking, does not move; the earth turns round, presenting the various countries in succession to the sun, but the effect is precisely the same as it would be if the sun moved, and, accordingly, I use that language. Now how long does it take the sun to pass round the earth?"

"Twenty-four hours."

"Does he go toward the west or toward the east from us?"

"Toward the west."

But it is not necessary to give the replies; the questions alone will be sufficient. The reader will observe that they inevitably lead the pupil, by short and simple steps, to a clear understanding of the point to be explained.

"Will the sun go toward or from the Rocky Mountains after leaving us?"

"How long did you say it takes the sun to go round the globe and come to us again?"

"How long to go half round?" "Quarter round?"

"How long will it take him to go to the Rocky Mountains?"

No answer.

"You can not tell. It would depend upon the distance. Suppose, then, the Rocky Mountains were half round the globe, how long would it take the sun to go to them?" "Suppose they were quarter round?"

"The whole distance is divided into portions called degrees—360 in all. How many will the sun pass in going half round?" "In going quarter round?"

"Ninety degrees, then, make one quarter of the circumference of the globe. This, you have already said, will take six hours. In one hour, then, how many degrees will the sun pass over?"

Perhaps no answer. If so, the teacher will subdivide the question on the principle we are explaining, so as to make the steps such that the pupils *can* take them.

"How many degrees will the sun pass over in three hours?"

"Forty-five."

"How large a part of that, then, will he pass in one hour?"

"One third of it."

"And what is one third of forty-five?"

The boys would readily answer fifteen, and the teacher would then dwell for a moment on the general truth thus deduced, that the sun, in passing round the earth, passes over fifteen degrees every hour.

"Suppose, then, it takes the sun one hour to go from us to the River Mississippi, how many degrees west of us would the river be?"

Having thus familiarized the pupils to the fact that the motion of the sun is a proper measure of the difference of longitude between two places, the teacher must dismiss the subject for a day, and when the next opportunity of bringing it forward occurs, he would, perhaps, take up the subject of the sun's motion as a measure of *time.*

"Is the sun ever exactly over our heads?"

"Is he ever exactly south of us?"

"When he is exactly south of us, or, in other words, exactly opposite to us in his course round the earth, he is said to be in our meridian; for the word meridian means a line drawn exactly north or south from any place."

There is no limit to the simplicity which may be imparted, even to the most difficult subjects, by subdividing the steps. This point, for instance, the meaning of meridian, may be the subject, if it were necessary, of many questions, which would render it simple to the youngest child. The teacher may point to the various articles in the room, or buildings, or other objects without, and ask if they are or are not in his meridian. But to proceed:

"When the sun is exactly opposite to us, in the south, at the highest point to which he rises, what o'clock is it?"

"When the sun is exactly opposite to us, can he be opposite to the Rocky Mountains?"

"Does he get opposite to the Rocky Mountains before or after he is opposite to us?"

"When he is opposite to the Rocky Mountains, what o'clock is it there?"

"Is it twelve o'clock here, then, before or after it is twelve o'clock there?"

"Suppose the River Mississippi is fifteen degrees from us, how long is it twelve o'clock here before it is twelve o'clock there?"

"When it is twelve o'clock here, then, what time will it be there?"

Some will probably answer "one," and some "eleven." If so, the step is too long, and may be subdivided thus:

"When it is noon here, is the sun going toward the Mississippi, or has he passed it?"

"Then has noon gone by at that river, or has it not yet come?"

"Then will it be one hour before or one hour after noon?"

"Then will it be eleven or one?"

Such minuteness and simplicity would, in ordinary cases, not be necessary. I go into it here merely to show how, by simply subdividing the steps, a subject ordinarily perplexing may be made plain. The reader will observe that in the above there are no explanations by the teacher—there are not even leading questions; that is, there are no questions the form of which suggests the answers desired. The pupil goes on from step to step simply because he has but one short step to take at a time.

"Can it be noon, then," continues the teacher, "here and at a place fifteen degrees west of us at the same time?"

"Can it be noon here and at a place ten miles west of us at the same time?"

It is unnecessary to continue the illustration, for it will be very evident to every reader that, by going forward in this way, the whole subject may be laid out before the pupils so that they shall perfectly understand it. They can, by a series of questions like the above, be led to see, by their own reasoning, that time, as denoted by the clock, must differ in every two places not upon the same meridian, and that the difference must be exactly proportional to the difference of longitude. So that a watch which is right in one place can not, strictly speaking, be right in any other place east or west of the first; and that, if the time of day at two places can be compared, either by taking a chronometer from one to another, or by observing some celestial phenomenon, like the eclipses of Jupiter's satellites, and ascertaining precisely the time of their occurrence, according to the reckoning at both, the distance east or west by degrees may be determined. The reader will observe, too, that the method by which this explanation is made is strictly in accordance with the principle I am illustrating, which is by simply *dividing the process into short steps.* There is no ingenious reasoning on the part of the teacher, no happy illustrations, no apparatus, no diagrams. It is a pure process of mathematical reasoning, made clear and easy by *simple analysis.*

In applying this method, however, the teacher should be very careful not to subdivide too much. It is best that the pupils should walk as fast as they can. The object of the teacher should be to smooth the path not much more than barely enough to enable the pupil to go on. He should not endeavor to make it very easy.

(2.) Truths must not only be taught to the pupils, but they must be *fixed*, and *made familiar*. This is a point which seems to be very generally overlooked.

"Can you say the Multiplication Table?" said a teacher to a boy who was standing before him in his class.

"Yes, sir."

"Well, I should like to have you say the line beginning nine times one."

The boy repeated it slowly, but correctly.

"Now I should like to have you try again, and I will, at the same time, say another line, to see if I can put you out."

The boy looked surprised. The idea of his teacher's trying to perplex and embarrass him was entirely new.

"You must not be afraid," said the teacher. "You will undoubtedly not succeed in getting through, but you will not be to blame for the failure. I only try it as a sort of intellectual experiment."

The boy accordingly began again, but was soon completely confused by the teacher's accompaniment. He stopped in the middle of his line, saying,

"I could say it, only you put me out."

"Well, now try to say the Alphabet, and let me see if I can put you out there."

As might have been expected, the teacher failed. The boy went regularly onward to the end.

"You see, now," said the teacher to the class who had witnessed the experiment, "that this boy knows his Alphabet in a different sense from that in which he knows his Multiplication Table. In the latter, his knowledge is only imperfectly his own; he can make use of it only under favorable circumstances. In the former it is entirely his own; circumstances have no control over him."

A child has a lesson in Latin Grammar to recite. She hesitates and stammers, miscalls the cases, and then corrects herself, and, if she gets through at last, she considers herself as having recited well, and very many teachers would consider it well too. If she hesitates a little longer than usual in trying to summon to her recollection a particular word, she says, perhaps, "Don't tell me," and if she happens at last to guess right, she takes her book with a countenance beaming with satisfaction.

"Suppose you had the care of an infant school," might the instructor say to such a scholar, "and were endeavoring to teach a little child to count, and she should recite her lesson to you in this way, 'One, two, four—no, three—one, two, three — — stop, don't tell me—five—no, four—four—five— — — — I shall think in a minute—six—is that right? five, six,' &c. Should you call that reciting well?"

Nothing is more common than for pupils to say, when they fail of reciting their lesson, that they could say it at their seats, but that they can not now say it before the class. When such a thing is said for the first time it should not be severely reproved, because nine children in ten honestly think that if the lesson were learned so that it could be recited any where, their duty is discharged. But it should be kindly, though distinctly explained to them, that in the business of life they must have their knowledge so much at command that they can use it at all times and in all circumstances, or it will do them little good.

One of the most common cases of difficulty in pursuing mathematical studies, or studies of any kind where the succeeding lessons depend upon those which precede, is the fact that the pupil, though he may understand what precedes, is not *familiar* with it. This is very strikingly the case with Geometry. The class study the definitions, and the teacher supposes they fully understand them; in fact, they do *understand* them, but the name and the thing are so feebly connected in their minds that a direct effort and a short pause are necessary to recall the idea when they hear or see the word. When they come on, therefore, to the demonstrations, which in themselves would be difficult enough, they have double duty to perform. The words used do not readily suggest the idea, and the connection of the ideas requires careful study.

Under this double burden many a young geometrician sinks discouraged.

A class should go on slowly, and dwell on details so long as to fix firmly and make perfectly familiar whatever they undertake to learn. In this manner the knowledge they acquire will become their own. It will be incorporated, as it were, into their very minds, and they can not afterward be deprived of it.

The exercises which have for their object this rendering familiar what has been learned may be so varied as to interest the pupil very much, instead of being tiresome, as it might at first be supposed.

Suppose, for instance, a teacher has explained to a large class in grammar the difference between an adjective and an adverb; if he leave it here, in a fortnight one half of the pupils would have forgotten the distinction, but by dwelling upon it a few lessons he may fix it forever. The first lesson might be to require the pupils to write twenty short sentences containing only adjectives. The second to write twenty containing only adverbs. The third to write sentences in two forms, one containing the adjective, and the other expressing the same idea by means of the adverb, arranging them in two columns, thus:

He writes well.	His writing is good.

Again, they may make out a list of adjectives, with the adverbs derived from each in another column. Then they may classify adverbs on the principle of their meaning, or according to their termination. The exercise may be infinitely varied, and yet the object of the whole may be to make *perfectly familiar*, and to fix forever in the mind the distinction explained.

These two points seem to me to be fundamental, so far as assisting pupils through the difficulties which lie in their way is concerned. Diminish the difficulties as far as is necessary by shortening and simplifying the steps, and make thorough work as you go on. These principles, carried steadily into practice, will be effectual in leading any mind through any difficulties which may occur. And though they can not, perhaps, be fully applied to every mind in a large school, yet they can be so far acted upon in reference to the whole mass as to accomplish the object for a very large majority.

3. *General cautions.* A few miscellaneous suggestions, which we shall include under this head, will conclude this chapter.

(1.) Never do any thing *for* a scholar, but teach him to do it for himself. How many cases occur in the schools of our country where the boy brings his slate to the teacher, saying he can not do a certain sum. The teacher takes the slate and pencil, performs the work in silence, brings the result, and returns the slate to the hands of his pupil, who walks off to his seat, and goes to work on the next example, perfectly satisfied with the manner in which he is passing on. A man who has not done this a hundred times himself will hardly believe it possible that such a practice can prevail, it is so evidently a mere waste of time both for master and scholar.

(2.) Never get out of patience with dullness. Perhaps I ought to say, never get out of patience with any thing. That would, perhaps, be the wisest rule. But, above all things, remember that dullness and stupidity—and you will certainly find them in every school—are the very last things to get out of patience with. If the Creator has so formed the mind of a boy that he must go through life slowly and with difficulty, impeded by obstructions which others do not feel, and depressed by discouragements which others never know, his lot is surely hard enough without having you to add to it the trials and suffering which sarcasm and reproach from you can heap upon him. Look over your school-room, therefore, and wherever you find one whom you perceive the Creator to have endued with less intellectual power than others, fix your eye upon him with an expression of kindness and sympathy. Such a boy will have suffering enough from the selfish tyranny of his companions; he ought to find in you a protector and friend. One of the greatest enjoyments which a teacher's life affords is the interest of seeking out such a one, bowed down with burdens of depression and discouragement, unaccustomed to sympathy and kindness, and expecting nothing for the future but a weary continuation of the cheerless toils which have imbittered the past; and the pleasure of taking off the burden, of surprising the timid, disheartened sufferer by kind words and cheering looks, and of seeing in his countenance the expression of ease and even of happiness gradually returning.

(3.) The teacher should be interested in *all* his scholars, and aim equally to secure the progress of all. Let there be no neglected ones in the school-room. We should always remember that, however unpleasant in countenance and manners that bashful boy in the corner may be, or however repulsive in appearance, or unhappy in disposition, that girl, seeming to be interested in nobody, and nobody appearing interested in her, they still have, each of them, a mother, who loves her own child, and takes a deep and constant interest in its history. Those mothers have a right, too, that their children should receive their full share of attention in a school which has been established for the common and equal benefit of all.

(4.) Do not hope or attempt to make all your pupils alike. Providence has determined that human minds should differ from each other for the very purpose of giving variety and interest to this busy scene of life. Now if it were possible for a teacher so to plan his operations as to send his pupils forth upon the community formed on the same model, as if they were made by machinery, he would do so much toward spoiling one of the wisest of the plans which the Almighty has formed for making this world a happy scene. Let it be the teacher's aim to co-operate with, not vainly to attempt to thwart, the designs of Providence. We should bring out those powers with which the Creator has endued the minds placed under our control. We must open our garden to such influences as shall bring forward all the plants, each in a way corresponding to its own nature. It is impossible if it were wise, and it would be foolish if it were possible, to stimulate, by artificial means, the rose, in hope of its reaching the size and magnitude of the apple-tree, or to try to cultivate the fig and the orange where wheat only will grow. No; it should be the teacher's main design to shelter his pupils from every deleterious influence, and to bring every thing to bear upon the community of minds before him which will encourage in each one the development of its own native powers. For the rest, he must remember that his province is to cultivate, not to create.

Error on this point is very common. Many teachers, even among those who have taken high rank through the success with which they have labored in the field, have wasted much time in attempting to do what never can be done, to form the character of those brought under their influence after a certain uniform model, which they have conceived as the standard of excellence. Their pupils must write just such a hand, they must compose in just such a style, they must be similar in sentiment and feeling, and their manners must be formed according to a fixed and uniform model; and when, in such a case, a pupil comes under their charge whom Providence has designed to be entirely different from the beau ideal adopted as the standard, more time, and pains, and anxious solicitude is wasted in vain attempts to produce the desired conformity than half the school require beside.

(5.) Do not allow the faults or obliquities of character, or the intellectual or moral wants of any individual of your pupils to engross a disproportionate share of your time. I have already said that those who are peculiarly in need of sympathy or help should receive the special attention they seem to require ; what I mean to say now is, do not carry this to an extreme. When a parent sends you a pupil who, in consequence of neglect or mismanagement at home, has become wild and ungovernable, and full of all sorts of wickedness, he has no right to expect that you shall turn your attention away from the wide field which, in your whole school-room, lies before you, to spend your time, and exhaust your spirits and strength in endeavoring to repair the injuries which his own neglect has occasioned. When you open a school, you do not engage, either openly or tacitly, to make every pupil who may be sent to you a learned or a virtuous man. You do engage to give them all faithful instruction, and to bestow upon each such a degree of attention as is consistent with the claims of the rest. But it is both unwise and unjust to neglect the many trees in your nursery which, by ordinary attention, may be made to grow straight and tall, and to bear good fruit, that you may waste your labor upon a crooked stick, from which all your toil can secure very little beauty or fruitfulness.

Let no one now understand me to say that such cases are to be neglected. I admit the propriety, and, in fact, have urged the duty, of paying to them a little more than their due share of attention. What I now condemn is the practice, of which all teachers are in danger, of devoting such a disproportionate and unreasonable degree of attention to them as to encroach upon their duties to others. The school, the whole school, is your field, the elevation *of the mass* in knowledge and virtue, and no individual instance, either of dullness or precocity, should draw you away from its steady pursuit.

(6.) The teacher should guard against unnecessarily imbibing those faulty mental habits to which his station and employment expose him. Accustomed to command, and to hold intercourse with minds which are immature and feeble compared with our own, we gradually acquire habits that the rough collisions and the friction of active life prevent from gathering around other men. Narrow-minded prejudices and prepossessions are imbibed through the facility with which, in our own little community, we adopt and maintain opinions. A too strong confidence in our own views on every subject almost inevitably comes from never hearing our opinions contradicted or called in question, and we express those opinions in a tone of authority, and even sometimes of arrogance, which we acquire in the school-room, for there, when we speak, nobody can reply.

These peculiarities show themselves first, and, in fact, most commonly, in the school-room; and the opinions thus formed very often relate to the studies and management of the school. One has a peculiar mode of teaching spelling, which is successful almost entirely through the magic influence of his interest in it, and he thinks no other mode of teaching this branch is even tolerable. Another must have all his pupils write on the angular system, or the anti-angular system, and he enters with all the zeal into a controversy on the subject, as if the destiny of the whole rising generation depended upon its decision. Tell him that all that is of any consequence in any handwriting is that it should be legible, rapid, and uniform, and that, for the rest, it would be better that every human being should write a different hand, and he looks upon you with astonishment, wondering that you can not see the vital importance of the question whether the vertex of an *o* should be pointed or round. So in every thing. He has *his way* in every minute particular—a way from which he can not deviate, and to which he wishes every one else to conform.

This set, formal mannerism is entirely inconsistent with that commanding intellectual influence which the teacher should exert in the administration of his school. He should work with what an artist calls boldness and freedom of touch.

Activity and enterprise of mind should characterize all his measures if he wishes to make bold, original, and efficient men.

(7.) Assume no false appearances in your school either as to knowledge or character. Perhaps it may justly be said to be the common practice of teachers in this country to affect a dignity of deportment in the presence of their pupils which in other cases is laid aside, and to pretend to superiority in knowledge and an infallibility of judgment which no sensible man would claim before other sensible men, but which an absurd fashion seems to require of the teacher. It can, however, scarcely be said to be a fashion, for the temptation is almost exclusively confined to the young and the ignorant, who think they must make up by appearance what they want in reality. Very few of the older, and more experienced, and successful instructors in our country fall into it at all; but some young beginner, whose knowledge is very limited, and who, in manner and habits, has only just ceased to be a boy, walks into his school-room with a countenance of forced gravity, and with a dignified and solemn step, which is ludicrous even to himself. I describe accurately, for I describe from recollection. This unnatural, and forced, and ludicrous dignity cleaves to him like a disease through the whole period of his duty. In the presence of his scholars he is always under restraint, assuming a stiff and formal dignity which is as ridiculous as it is unnatural. He is also obliged to resort to arts which are certainly not very honorable to conceal his ignorance.

A scholar, for example, brings him a sum in arithmetic which he does not know how to perform. This may be the case with a most excellent teacher, and one well qualified for his business. In order to be successful as a teacher, it is not necessary to understand every thing. Instead, however, of saying frankly, "I do not understand that example; I will examine it," he looks at it embarrassed and perplexed, not knowing how he shall escape the exposure of his ignorance. His first thought is to give some general directions to the pupil, and send him to his seat to make a new experiment, hoping that in some way or other, he scarcely knows how, he will get through; and, at any rate, if he should not, the teacher thinks that he himself at least gains time by the manœuvre, and he is glad to postpone his trouble, though he knows it must soon return.

All efforts to conceal ignorance, and all affectation of knowledge not possessed, are as unwise as they are dishonest. If a scholar asks a question which you can not answer, or brings you a difficulty which you can not solve, say frankly, "I do not know." It is the only way to avoid continual anxiety and irritation, and the surest means of securing real respect. Let the scholars understand that the superiority of the teacher does not consist in his infallibility, or in his universal acquisitions, but in a well-balanced mind, where the boundary between knowledge and ignorance is distinctly marked; in a strong desire to go forward in mental improvement, and in fixed principles of action and systematic habits. You may even take up in school a study entirely new to you, and have it understood at the outset that you know no more of it than the class commencing, but that you can be their guide on account of the superior maturity and discipline of your powers, and the comparative ease with which you can meet and overcome difficulties. This is the understanding which ought always to exist between master and scholars. The fact that the teacher does not know every thing can not long be concealed if he tries to conceal it, and in this, as in every other case, HONESTY IS THE BEST POLICY.

CHAPTER IV.

MORAL DISCIPLINE.

UNDER the title which I have placed at the head of this chapter I intend to discuss the methods by which the teacher is to secure a moral ascendency over his pupils, so that he may lead them to do what is right, and bring them back to duty when they do what is wrong. I shall use, in what I have to say, a very plain and familiar style; and as very much depends not only on the general principles by which the teacher is actuated, but also on the tone and manner in which, in cases of discipline, he addresses his pupils, I shall describe particular cases, real and imaginary, because by this method I can better illustrate the course to be pursued. I shall also present and illustrate the various principles which I consider important, and in the order in which they occur to my mind.

1. The first duty, then, of the teacher when he enters his school is to beware of the danger of making an unfavorable impression at first upon his pupils. Many years ago, when I was a child, the teacher of the school where my early studies were performed closed his connection with the establishment, and after a short vacation another was expected. On the appointed day the boys began to collect, some from curi-

osity, at an early hour, and many speculations were started as to the character of the new instructor. We were standing near a table with our hats on—and our position, and the exact appearance of the group, is indelibly fixed on my memory—when a small and youthful-looking man entered the room, and walked up toward us. Supposing him to be some stranger, or, rather, not making any supposition at all, we stood looking at him as he approached, and were thunderstruck at hearing him accost us with a stern voice and sterner brow, "Take off your hats. Take off your hats and go to your seats." The conviction immediately rushed upon our minds that this must be our new teacher. The first emotion was that of surprise, and the second was that of the ludicrous, though I believe we contrived to smother the laugh until we got out into the open air.

So long since was this little occurrence that I have entirely forgotten the name of the teacher, and have not the slightest recollection of any other act in his administration of the school. But this recollection of his first greeting of his pupils, and the expression of his countenance at the moment, will go with me to the end of life. So strong are first impressions.

Be careful, then, when you first see your pupils, that you meet them with a smile. I do not mean a pretended cordiality, which has no existence in the heart, but think of the relation which you are to sustain to them, and think of the very interesting circumstances under which, for some months at least, your destinies are to be united to theirs, until you can not help feeling a strong interest in them. Shut your eyes for a day or two to their faults, if possible, and take an interest in all their pleasures and pursuits, that the first attitude in which you exhibit yourself before them may be one which shall allure, not repel.

2. In endeavoring to correct the faults of your pupils, do not, as many teachers do, seize only upon *those particular cases*

of transgression which may happen to come under your notice. These individual instances are very few, probably, compared with the whole number of faults against which you ought to exert an influence. And though you perhaps ought not to neglect those which may accidentally come under your notice, yet the observing and punishing such cases is a very small part of your duty.

You accidentally hear, I will suppose, as you are walking home from school, two of your boys in earnest conversation, and one of them uses profane language. Now the course to be pursued in such a case is, most evidently, not to call the boy to you the next day and punish him, and there let the matter rest. This would, perhaps, be better than nothing. But the chief impression which it would make upon the individual and upon the other scholars would be, "I must take care how I *let the master hear me* use such language again." A wise teacher, who takes enlarged and extended views of his duty in regard to the moral progress of his pupils, would act very differently. He would look at the whole subject. "Does this fault," he would say to himself, "prevail among my pupils? If so, how extensively? It is comparatively of little consequence to punish the particular transgression. The great point is to devise some plan to reach the whole evil, and to correct it if possible."

In one case where such a circumstance occurred, the teacher managed it most successfully in the following manner.

He said nothing to the boy, and, in fact, the boy did not know that he was overheard. He allowed a day or two to elapse, so that the conversation might be forgotten, and then took an opportunity one day, after school, when all things had gone on pleasantly, and the school was about to be closed, to bring forward the whole subject. He told the boys that he had something to say to them after they had laid by their books and were ready to go home. The desks were soon closed, and every face in the room was turned toward the master with a look of fixed attention. It was almost evening. The sun had gone down. The boys' labors were over. Their duties for the day were over; their minds were at rest, and every thing was favorable for making a deep and permanent impression.

"A few days ago," says the teacher, when all was still, "I accidentally overheard some conversation between two of the boys of this school, and one of them swore."

There was a pause.

"Perhaps you expect that I am now going to call the boy out and punish him. Is that what I ought to do?"

There was no answer.

"I think a boy who uses bad language of any kind does what he knows is wrong. He breaks God's commands. He does what he knows would be displeasing to his parents, and he sets a bad example. He does wrong, therefore, and justly deserves punishment."

There were, of course, many boys who felt that they were in danger. Every one who had used profane language was aware that he might be the one who had been overheard, and, of course, all were deeply interested in what the teacher was saying.

"He might, I say," continued the teacher, "justly be punished; but I am not going to punish him; for if I should, I am afraid that it would only make him a little more careful hereafter not to commit this sin when I could possibly be within hearing, instead of persuading him, as I wish to, to avoid such a sin in future altogether. I am satisfied that that boy would be far happier, even in this world, if he would make it a principle always to do his duty, and never, in any case, to do wrong. And then, when I think how soon he and all of us will be in another world, where we shall all be judged for what we do here, I feel strongly desirous of persuading him to abandon entirely this practice. I am afraid that punishing him now would not do that.

"Besides," continues the teacher, "I think it very probable that there are many other boys in this school who are sometimes guilty of this fault, and I have thought that it would be a great deal better and happier for us all if, instead of punishing this particular boy whom I have accidentally overheard, and who probably is not more to blame than many other boys in school, I should bring up the whole subject, and endeavor to persuade all the boys to reform."

I am aware that there are, unfortunately, in our country a great many teachers from whose lips such an appeal as this would be wholly in vain. The man who is accustomed to scold, and storm, and punish with unsparing severity every transgression, under the influence of irritation and anger, must not expect that he can win over his pupils to confidence in him and to the principles of duty by a word. But such an appeal will not be lost when it comes from a man whose daily and habitual management corresponds with it. But to return to the story:

The teacher made some farther remarks, explaining the nature of the sin, not in the language of execration and affected abhorrence, but calmly, temperately, and without any disposition to make the worst of the occurrence which had taken place. In concluding what he said, he addressed the boys as follows:

"Now, boys, the question is, do you wish to abandon this habit or not? If you do, all is well. I shall immediately forget all the past, and will do all I can to help you resist and overcome temptation in future. But all I can do is only to help you; and the first thing to be done, if you wish to engage in this work of reform, is to acknowledge your fault; and I should like to know how many are willing to do this."

"I wish all those who are willing to tell me whether they use profane language would rise."

Every individual but one rose.

"I am very glad to see so large a number," said the

teacher; "and I hope you will find that the work of confessing and forsaking your faults is, on the whole, pleasant, not painful business. Now those who can truly and honestly say that they never do use profane language of any kind may take their seats."

Three only of the whole number, which consisted of not far from twenty, sat down. It was in a sea-port town, where the temptation to yield to this vice is even greater than would be, in the interior of our country, supposed possible.

"Those who are now standing," pursued the teacher, "admit that they do, sometimes at least, commit this sin. I suppose all, however, are determined to reform; for I do not know what else should induce you to rise and acknowledge it here, unless it is a desire hereafter to break yourselves of the habit. But do you suppose that it will be enough for you merely to resolve here that you will reform?"

"No, sir," said the boys.

"Why not? If you now sincerely determine never more to use a profane word, will you not easily avoid it?"

The boys were silent. Some said faintly, "No, sir."

"It will not be easy for you to avoid the sin hereafter," continued the teacher, "even if you do now sincerely and resolutely determine to do so. You have formed the habit of sin, and the habit will not be easily overcome. But I have detained you long enough now. I will try to devise some method by which you may carry your plan into effect, and to-morrow I will tell you what it is."

So the boys were dismissed for the day; the pleasant countenance and cheerful tone of the teacher conveying to them the impression that they were engaging in the common effort to accomplish a most desirable purpose, in which they were to receive the teacher's help, not that he was pursuing them, with threatening and punishment, into the forbidden practice into which they had wickedly strayed. Great caution is, however, in such a case, necessary to guard against the danger that the teacher, in attempting to avoid the tones of irritation and anger, should so speak of the sin as to blunt his pupils' sense of its guilt, and lull their consciences into a slumber.

At the appointed time on the following day the subject was again brought before the school, and some plans proposed by which the resolutions now formed might be more certainly kept. These plans were readily and cheerfully adopted by the boys, and in a short time the vice of profaneness was, in a great degree, banished from the school.

I hope the reader will keep in mind the object of the above illustration, which is to show that it is the true policy of the teacher not to waste his time and strength in contending against *such accidental instances* of transgression as may chance to fall under his notice, but to take an enlarged and extended view of the whole ground, endeavoring to remove *whole classes of faults*—to elevate and improve *multitudes together*.

By these means, his labors will not only be more effectual, but far more pleasant. You can not come into collision with an individual scholar, to punish him for a mischievous spirit, or even to rebuke him for some single act by which he has given you trouble, without an uncomfortable and uneasy feeling, which makes, in ordinary cases, the discipline of a school the most unpleasant part of a teacher's duty. But you can plan a campaign against a whole class of faults, and put into operation a system of measures to correct them, and watch from day to day the operation of that system with all the spirit and interest of a game. It is, in fact, a game where your ingenuity and moral power are brought into the field, in opposition to the evil tendencies of the hearts which are under your influence. You will notice the success or the failure of the means you may put into operation with all the interest with which the experimental philosopher observes the curious processes he guides, though your interest may be much purer and higher, for he works upon matter, but you are experimenting upon mind.

Remember, then, as for the first time you take your new station at the head of your school, that it is not your duty simply to watch with an eagle eye for those accidental instances of transgression which may chance to fall under your notice. You are to look over the whole ground. You are to make yourself acquainted, as soon as possible, with the classes of character and classes of faults which may prevail in your dominions, and to form deliberate and well-digested plans for improving the one and correcting the other.

And this is to be the course pursued not only with great delinquencies, such as those to which I have already alluded, but to every little transgression against the rules of order and propriety. You can correct them far more easily and pleasantly in the mass than in detail.

To illustrate this principle by another case. A teacher, who takes the course I am condemning, approaches the seat of one of his pupils, and asks to see one of his books. As the boy opens his desk, the teacher observes that it is in complete disorder. Books, maps, papers, play-things, are there in promiscuous confusion, and, from the impulse of the moment, the displeased teacher pours out upon the poor boy a torrent of reproach.

"What a looking desk! Why, John, I am really ashamed of you! Look!" continues he, holding up the lid, so that the boys in the neighborhood can look in; "see what a mass of disorder and confusion. If ever I see your desk in such a state again, I shall most certainly punish you."

The boys around laugh, very equivocally, however, for, with the feeling of amusement, there is mingled the fear that the angry master may take it into his head to inspect their domains. The boy accidentally exposed looks sullen, and begins to throw his books into some sort of arrangement, just enough to shield himself from the charge of absolutely disobeying the injunction that he has received, and there the matter ends.

Another teacher takes no apparent notice of the confusion which he thus accidentally witnesses. "I must take up," thinks he to himself, "the subject of order before the whole school. I have not yet spoken of it." He thanks the boy for the book he borrowed, and goes away. He makes a memorandum of the subject, and the boy does not know that the condition of his desk was noticed; perhaps he does not even know that there was any thing amiss.

A day or two after, at a time regularly appropriated to such subjects, he addresses the boys as follows:

"In our efforts to improve the school as much as possible, there is one subject which we must not forget. I mean the order of the desks."

The boys all begin to open their desk lids.

"You may stop a moment," says the teacher. "I shall give you all an opportunity to examine your desks presently.

"I do not know what the condition of your desks is. I have not examined them, and have not, in fact, seen the inside of more than one or two. As I have not brought up this subject before, I presume that there are a great many which can be arranged better than they are. Will you all now look into your desks, and see whether you consider them in good order? Stop a moment, however. Let me tell you what good order is. All those things which are alike should be arranged together. Books should be in one place, papers in another, and thus every thing should be classified. Again, every thing should be so placed that it can be taken out without disturbing other things. There is another principle, also, which I will mention: the various articles should have *constant* places, that is, they should not be changed from day to day. By this means you soon remember where every thing belongs, and you can put away your things much more easily every night than if you had every night to arrange them in a new way. Now will you look into your desks, and tell me whether they are, on these three principles, well arranged?"

The boys of most schools, where this subject had not been regularly attended to, would nearly all answer in the negative.

"I will allow you, then, some time to-day, fifteen minutes to arrange your desks, and I hope you will try to keep them in good order hereafter. A few days hence I shall examine them. If any of you wish for assistance or advice from me in putting them in order, I shall be happy to render it."

By such a plan, which will occupy but little more time than the irritating and useless scolding which I supposed in the other case, how much more will be accomplished. Such an address would of itself, probably, be the means of putting in order, and keeping in order, at least one half of the desks in the room, and following up the plan in the same manner and in the same spirit with which it was begun would secure the rest.

I repeat it, therefore, make it a principle in all cases to aim as much as possible at the correction of those faults which are likely to be general by *general measures.* You avoid by this means a vast amount of irritation and impatience, both on your own part and on the part of your scholars, and you produce twenty times the useful effect.

3. The next principle which occurs to me as deserving the teacher's attention in the outset of his course is this:

Interest your scholars in doing something themselves to elevate the moral character of the school, so as to secure a *decided majority who will, of their own accord, co-operate with you.*

Let your pupils understand, not by any formal speech which you make to that effect, but by the manner in which, from time to time, you incidentally allude to the subject, that you consider the school, when you commence it, as *at par*, so to speak—that is, on a level with other schools, and that your various plans for improving and amending it are not to be considered in the light of finding fault, and punishing transgressions, and controlling evil propensities, so as just to keep things in a tolerable state, but as efforts to improve and carry forward the institution to a still higher state of excellence. Such is the tone and manner of some teachers that they never appear to be more than merely satisfied. When the scholars do right, nothing is said about it. The teacher seems to consider that a matter of course. It does not appear to interest or please him at all. Nothing arouses him but when they do wrong, and that only excites him to anger and frowns. Now in such a case there can, of course, be no stimulus to effort on the part of the pupils but the cold and heartless stimulus of fear.

Now it is wrong for the teacher to expect that things will go right in his school as a matter of course. All that he can expect *as a matter of course* is, that things should go on as well as they do ordinarily in schools—the ordinary amount of idleness, the ordinary amount of misconduct. This is the most that he can expect to come as a matter of course. He should feel this, and then all he can gain which will be better than this will be a source of positive pleasure; a pleasure which his pupils have procured for him, and which, consequently, they should share. They should understand that the teacher is engaged in various plans for improving the school, in which they should be invited to engage, not from the selfish desire of thereby saving him trouble, but because it will really be happy employment for them to engage in such an enterprise, and because, by such efforts, their own moral powers will be exerted and strengthened in the best possible way.

In another chapter I have explained to what extent, and in what manner, the assistance of the pupils may be usefully and successfully employed in carrying forward the general arrangements of the school. The same *principles* will apply here, though perhaps a little more careful and delicate management is necessary in interesting them in subjects which relate to moral discipline.

One important method of accomplishing this end is to present these plans before the minds of the scholars as experiments—moral experiments, whose commencement, progress, and results they may take a great interest in witnessing. Let us take, for example, the case alluded to under the last head—the plan of effecting a reform in regard to keeping desks in order. Suppose the teacher were to say, when the time had arrived at which he had promised to give them an opportunity to put the desks in order,

"I think it would be a good plan to keep some account of our efforts for improving the school in this respect. We might make a record of what we do to-day, noting the day of the month and the number of desks which may be found to be disorderly. Then, at the end of any time you may propose, we will have the desks examined again, and see how many are disorderly then. We can thus see how much improvement has been made in that time. Should you like to adopt the plan?"

If the boys should appear not much interested in the proposal, the teacher might, at his own discretion, waive it. In all probability, however, they would like it, and would indicate their interest by their countenances, or perhaps by a response. If so, the teacher might proceed.

"You may all examine your desks, then, and decide whether they are in order or not. I do not know, however, but that we ought to appoint a committee to examine them; for perhaps all the boys would not be honest, and report their desks as they really are."

"Yes, sir;" "yes, sir," say the boys.

"Do you mean that you will be honest, or that you would like to have a committee appointed?"

There was a confused murmur. Some answer one, and some the other.

"I think," proceeds the teacher, "the boys will be honest, and report their desks just as they are. At any rate, the number of dishonest boys in this school can not be so large as materially to affect the result. I think we had better take your own statements. As soon as the desks are all examined, those who have found theirs in a condition which does not satisfy them are requested to rise and be counted."

The teacher then looks around the room, and selecting some intelligent boy who has influence among his companions, and whose influence he is particularly desirous of enlisting on the side of good order, says, "Shall I nominate some one to keep an account of the number?"

"Yes, sir," say the boys.

"Well, I nominate William Jones. How many are in favor of requesting William Jones to perform this duty?"

"It is a vote. William, I will thank you to write upon a piece of paper that on the 8th of December the subject of order in the desks was brought up, and that the boys resolved on making an effort to improve the school in this respect. Then say that the boys reported all their desks which they thought were disorderly, and that the number was thirty-five; and that after a week or two, the desks are to be examined again, and the disorderly ones counted, that we may see how much we have improved. After you have written it you may bring it to me, and I will tell you whether it is right."

"How many desks do you think will be found to be disorderly when we come to make the examination?"

The boys hesitate.

The teacher names successively several numbers, and asks whether they think the real number will be greater or less. He notices their votes upon them, and at last fixes upon one which seems to be about the general sense of the school. Then the teacher himself mentions the number which he supposes will be found to be disorderly. His estimate will ordinarily be larger than that of the scholars, because he knows better how easily resolutions are broken. This number, too, is recorded, and then the whole subject is dismissed.

Now, of course, no reader of these remarks will understand

me to be recommending, by this imaginary dialogue, a particular course to be taken in regard to this subject, far less the particular language to be used. All I mean is to show by a familiar illustration how the teacher is to endeavor to enlist the interest and to excite the curiosity of his pupils in his plans for the improvement of his school, by presenting them as moral experiments, which they are to assist him in trying—experiments whose progress they are to watch, and whose results they are to predict. If the precise steps which I have described should actually be taken, although it would occupy but a few minutes, and would cause no thought and no perplexing care, yet it would undoubtedly be the means of awakening a very general interest in the subject of order throughout the school. All would be interested in the work of arrangement.

All would watch, too, with interest the progress and the result of the experiment; and if, a few days afterward, the teacher should accidentally, in recess, see a disorderly desk, a good-humored remark made with a smile to the by-standers, "I suspect my prediction will turn out the correct one," would have far more effect than the most severe reproaches, or the tingling of a rap over the knuckles with a ratan.

I know from experience that scholars of every kind can be led by such measures as these, or rather by such a spirit as this, to take an active interest, and to exert a most powerful influence in regard to the whole condition of the institution. I have seen the experiment successful in boys' schools and in girls' schools, among very little children, and among the seniors and juniors at college.

In one of the colleges of New England a new and beautiful edifice was erected. The lecture-rooms were fitted up in handsome style, and the officers, when the time for the occupation of the building approached, were anticipating with regret what seemed to be the unavoidable defacing, and cutting, and marking of the seats and walls. It was, however,

thought that if the subject was properly presented to the students, they would take an interest in preserving the property from injury. They were accordingly addressed somewhat as follows:

"It seems, young gentlemen, to be generally the custom in colleges for the students to ornament the walls and benches of their recitation-rooms with various inscriptions and caricatures, so that after the premises have been for a short time in the possession of a class, every thing within reach, which will take an impression from a penknife or a trace from a pencil, is covered with names, and dates, and heads, and inscriptions of every kind. The faculty do not know what you wish in this respect in regard to the new accommodations which the trustees have now provided for you, and which you are soon to enter. They have had them fitted up for you handsomely, and if you wish to have them kept in good order, we will assist you. If the students think proper to express by a vote, or in any other way, their wish to keep them in good order, we will engage to have such incidental injuries as may from time to time occur immediately repaired. Such injuries will, of course, be done; for, whatever may be the wish and general opinion of the whole, it is not to be expected that every individual in so large a community will be careful. If, however, as a body, you wish to have the building preserved in its present state, and will, as a body, take the necessary precautions, we will do our part."

The students responded to this appeal most heartily. They passed a vote expressing a desire to preserve the premises in order, and for many years, and, for aught I know, to the present hour, the whole is kept as a room occupied by gentlemen should be kept. At some other colleges, and those, too, sustaining the very highest rank among the institutions of the country, the doors of the public buildings are sometimes *studded with nails as thick as they can possibly be driven, and then covered with a thick coat of sand dried into the paint, as a protection from the knives of the students!!*

The particular methods by which the teacher is to interest his pupils in his various plans for their improvement can not be fully described here. In fact, it does not depend so much on the methods he adopts as upon the view which he himself takes of these plans, and the *tone and manner in which he speaks of them to his pupils.*

A teacher, for example, perhaps on the first day of his labors in a new school, calls a class to read. They pretend to form a line, but it crooks in every direction. One boy is leaning back against a desk; another comes forward as far as possible, to get near the fire; the rest lounge in every position and in every attitude. John is holding up his book high before his face to conceal an apple from which he is endeavoring to secure an enormous bite. James is, by the same sagacious device, concealing a whisper which he is addressing to his next neighbor, and Moses is seeking amusement by crowding and elbowing the little boy who is unluckily standing next him.

"What a spectacle!" says the master to himself, as he looks at this sad display. "What shall I do?" The first impulse is to break forth upon them at once with all the artillery of reproof, and threatening, and punishment. I have seen, in such a case, a scolding and frowning master walk up and down before such a class with a stern and angry air, commanding this one to stand back, and that one to come forward, ordering one boy to put down his book, and scolding at a second for having lost his place, and knocking the knees of another with his ruler because he was out of the line. The boys scowl at their teacher, and, with ill-natured reluctance, they obey just enough to escape punishment.

Another teacher looks calmly at the scene, and says to himself, "What shall I do to remove effectually these evils? If I can but interest the boys in reform, it will be far more easy to effect it than if I attempt to accomplish it by the mere exercise of my authority."

In the mean time things go on during the reading in their own way. The teacher simply *observes*. He is in no haste to commence his operations. He looks for the faults; watches, without seeming to watch, the movements which he is attempting to control. He studies the materials with which he is to work, and lets their true character develop itself. He tries to find something to approve in the exercise as it proceeds, and endeavors to interest the class by narrating some fact connected with the reading, or making some explanation which interests the boys. At the end of the exercise he addresses them, perhaps, as follows:

"I have observed, boys, in some military companies, that the officers are very strict, requiring implicit and precise obedience. The men are required to form a precise line." (Here there is a sort of involuntary movement all along the line, by which it is very sensibly straightened.) "They make all the men stand erect" (at this word heads go up, and straggling feet draw in all along the class), "in the true military posture. They allow nothing to be done in the ranks but to attend to the exercise" (John hastily crowds his apple into his pocket), "and thus they regulate every thing in exact and steady discipline, so that all things go on in a most systematic and scientific manner. This discipline is so admirable in some countries, especially in Europe, where much greater attention is paid to military tactics than in our country, that I have heard it said by travelers that some of the soldiers who mount guard at public places look as much like statues as they do like living men.

"Other commanders act differently. They let the men do pretty much as they please. So you will see such a company lounging into a line when the drum beats, as if they took little interest in what was going on. While the captain is giving his commands, one is eating his luncheon, another is talking with his next neighbor. Part are out of the line; part lounge on one foot; they hold their guns in every position; and, on the whole, present a very disorderly and unsoldier-like appearance.

"I have observed, too, that boys very generally prefer to *see* the strict companies, but perhaps they would prefer to *belong* to the lax ones."

"No, sir;" "No, sir," say the boys.

"Suppose you all had your choice either to belong to a company like the first one I described, where the captain was strict in all his requirements, or to one like the latter, where you could do pretty much as you pleased, which should you prefer?"

Unless I am entirely mistaken in my idea of the inclinations of boys, it would be very difficult to get a single honest expression of preference for the latter. They would say with one voice,

"The first."

"I suppose it would be so. You would be put to some inconvenience by the strict commands of the captain, but then you would be more than paid by the beauty of regularity and order which you would all witness. There is nothing so pleasant as regularity, and nobody likes regularity more than boys do. To show this, I should like to have you now form a line as exact as you can."

After some unnecessary shoving and pushing, increased by the disorderly conduct of a few bad boys, a line is formed. Most of the class are pleased with the experiment, and the teacher takes no notice of the few exceptions. The time to attend to *them* will come by-and-by.

"Hands down." The boys obey.

"Shoulders back."

"There; there is a very perfect line."

"Do you stand easily in that position?"

"Yes, sir."

"I believe your position is the military one now, pretty nearly; and military men study the postures of the human body for the sake of finding the one most easy; for they wish to preserve as much as possible of the soldiers' strength for the time of battle. I should like to try the experiment of your standing thus at the next lesson. It is a very great improvement upon your common mode. Are you willing to do it?"

"Yes, sir," say the boys.

"You will get tired, I have no doubt; for the military position, though most convenient and easy in the end, is not to be learned and fixed in practice without effort. In fact, I do not expect you will succeed the first day very well. You will probably become restless and uneasy before the end of the lesson, especially the smaller boys. I must excuse it, I suppose, if you do, as it will be the first time."

By such methods as these the teacher will certainly secure a majority in favor of all his plans. But perhaps some experienced teacher, who knows from his own repeated difficulties with bad boys what sort of spirits the teacher of district schools has sometimes to deal with, may ask, as he reads this,

"Do you expect that such a method as this will succeed in keeping your school in order? Why there are boys in almost every school whom you would no more coax into obedience and order in this way than you would persuade the northeast wind to change its course by reasoning."

I know there are. And my readers are requested to bear in mind that my object is not to show how the whole government of the school may be secured, but how one important advantage may be gained, which will assist in accomplishing the object. All I should expect or hope for, by such measures as these, is *to interest and gain over to our side the majority.* What is to be done with those who can not be reached by such kinds of influence I shall endeavor presently to show. The object now is simply to gain the *majority*—to awaken a general interest, which you can make effectual in promoting your plans, and thus to narrow the field of discipline by getting those right who can be got right by such measures.

Thus securing a majority to be on your side in the general administration of the school is absolutely indispensable to success. A teacher may, indeed, by the force of mere authority, so control his pupils as to preserve order in the school-room, and secure a tolerable progress in study, but the progress will be slow, and the cultivation of moral principle must be, in such a case, entirely neglected. The principles of duty can not be inculcated by fear; and though pain and terror must in many instances be called in to coerce an individual offender, whom milder measures will not reach, yet these agents, and others like them, can never be successfully employed as the ordinary motives to action. They can not produce any thing but mere external and heartless obedience in the presence of the teacher, with an inclination to throw off all restraint when the pressure of stern authority is removed.

We should all remember that our pupils are but for a very short time under our direct control. Even when they are in school the most untiring vigilance will not enable us to watch, except for a very small portion of the time, any one individual. Many hours of the day, too, they are entirely removed from our inspection, and a few months will take them away from us altogether. Subjecting them, then, to mere external restraint is a very inadequate remedy for the moral evil to which they are exposed. What we aim at is to bring forward and strengthen an internal principle which will act when both parent and teacher are away, and control where external circumstances are all unfavorable.

I have thus far, under this head, been endeavoring to show the importance of securing, by gentle measures, a majority of the scholars to co-operate with the teacher in his plans. The particular methods of doing this demand a little attention.

(1.) The teacher should study human nature as it exhibits itself in the school-room by taking an interest in the sports and enjoyments of the pupils, and connecting, as much as possible, what is interesting and agreeable with the pursuits of the school, so as to lead the scholars to like the place. An attachment to the institution, and to the duties of it, will give the teacher a very strong hold upon the community of mind which exists there.

(2.) Every thing which is unpleasant in the discipline of the school should be attended to, as far as possible, privately. Sometimes it is necessary to bring a case forward in public for reproof or punishment, but this is seldom required. In some schools it is the custom to postpone cases of discipline till the close of the day, and then, just before the boys are dismissed at night, all the difficulties are settled. Thus, day after day, the impression which is last made upon their minds is received from a season of suffering, and terror, and tears.

Now such a practice may be attended with many advant-

ages, but it seems to be, on the whole, unwise. Awing the pupils, by showing them the painful consequences of doing wrong, should be very seldom resorted to. It is far better to allure them by showing them the pleasures of doing right. Doing right is pleasant to every body, and no persons are so easily convinced of this, or, rather, so easily led to see it, as children. Now the true policy is to let them experience the pleasure of doing their duty, and they will easily be allured to it.

In many cases, where a fault has been publicly committed, it seems, at first view, to be necessary that it should be publicly punished; but the end will, in most cases, be answered if it is *noticed* publicly, so that the pupils may know that it received attention, and then the ultimate disposal of the case may be made a private affair between the teacher and the individual concerned. If, however, every case of disobedience, or idleness, or disorder, is brought out publicly before the school, so that all witness the teacher's displeasure and feel the effects of it (for to witness it is to feel its most unpleasant effects), the school becomes, in a short time, hardened to such scenes. Unpleasant associations become connected with the management of the school, and the scholars are prepared to do wrong with less reluctance, since the consequence is only a repetition of what they are obliged to see every day.

Besides, if a boy does something wrong, and you severely reprove him in the presence of his class, you punish the class almost as much as you do him. In fact, in many cases you punish them more; for I believe it is almost invariably more unpleasant for a good boy to stand by and listen to rebukes, than for a bad boy to take them. Keep these things, therefore, as much as possible out of sight. Never bring forward cases of discipline except on mature deliberation, and for a distinct and well-defined purpose.

(3.) Never bring forward a case of discipline of this kind

unless you are sure that public opinion will go in your favor. If a case comes up in which the sympathy of the scholars is excited for the criminal in such a way as to be against yourself, the punishment will always do more harm than good. Now this, unless there is great caution, will often happen. In fact, it is probable that a very large proportion of the punishments which are ordinarily inflicted in schools only prepare the way for more offenses.

It is, however, possible to bring forward individual cases in such a way as to produce a very strong moral effect of the right kind. This is to be done by seizing upon those peculiar emergencies which will arise in the course of the administration of a school, and which each teacher must watch for and discover himself. They can not be pointed out. I may, however, give a clearer idea of what is meant by such emergencies by an example. It is a case which actually occurred as here narrated.

In a school where nearly all the pupils were faithful and docile, there were one or two boys who were determined to find amusement in those mischievous tricks so common in schools and colleges. There was one boy, in particular, who was the life and soul of all these plans. Devoid of principle, idle as a scholar, morose and sullen in his manners, he was, in every respect, a true specimen of the whole class of mischief-makers, wherever they are to be found. His mischief consisted, as usual, in such exploits as stopping up the keyhole of the door, upsetting the teacher's inkstand, or fixing something to his desk to make a noise and interrupt the school.

It so happened that there was a standing feud between the boys of his neighborhood and those of another situated a mile or two from it. By his malicious activity he had stimulated this quarrel to a high pitch, and was very obnoxious to the boys of the other party. One day, when taking a walk, the teacher observed a number of boys with excited looks, and armed with sticks and stones, standing around a shoemaker's shop, to which his poor pupil had gone for refuge from them. They had got him completely within their power, and were going to wait until he should be wearied with his confinement and come out, when they were going to inflict upon him the punishment they thought he deserved.

The teacher interfered, and by the united influence of authority, management, and persuasion, succeeded in effecting a rescue. The boy would probably have preferred to owe his safety to any one else than to the teacher whom he had so often tried to tease, but he was glad to escape in any way. The teacher said nothing about the subject, and the boy soon supposed it was entirely forgotten.

But it was not forgotten. The teacher knew perfectly well that the boy would before long be at his old tricks again, and was reserving this story as the means of turning the whole current of public opinion against such tricks, should they again occur.

One day he came to school in the afternoon, and found the room filled with smoke; the doors and windows were all closed, though, as soon as he came in, some of the boys opened them. He knew by this circumstance that it was roguery, not accident, which caused the smoke. He appeared not to notice it, however, said he was sorry it smoked, and asked the mischievous boy—for he was sure to be always near in such a case—to assist him in putting up the wood of the fire more compactly. The boy supposed that the smoke was understood to be accidental, and perhaps secretly laughed at the dullness of his master.

In the course of the afternoon, the teacher ascertained by private inquiries that his suspicions were correct as to the author of the mischief. At the close of school, when the studies were ended, and the books laid away, he said to the scholars that he wanted to tell them a story.

He then, with a pleasant tone and manner, gave a very

minute, and, to the boys, a very interesting narrative of his adventure two or three weeks before, when he rescued this boy from his danger. He called him, however, simply *a boy*, without mentioning his name, or even hinting that he was a member of the school. No narrative could excite a stronger interest among an audience of school-boys than such a one as this, and no act of kindness from a teacher would make as vivid an impression as interfering to rescue a trembling captive from such a situation as the one this boy had been in.

The scholars listened with profound interest and attention, and though the teacher said little about his share in the affair, and spoke of what he did as if it were a matter of course that he should thus befriend a boy in distress, an impression very favorable to himself must have been made. After he had finished his narrative, he said,

"Now should you like to know who this boy was?"

"Yes, sir," "Yes, sir," said they, eagerly.

"It was a boy that you all know."

The boys looked around upon one another. Who could it be?

"He is a member of this school."

There was an expression of fixed, and eager, and increasing interest on every face in the room.

"He is here now," said the teacher, winding up the interest and curiosity of the scholars, by these words, to the highest pitch.

"But I can not tell you his name; for what return do you think he made to me? To be sure it was no very great favor that I did him; I should have been unworthy the name of teacher if I had not done it for him, or for any boy in my school. But, at any rate, it showed my good wishes for him; it showed that I was his friend; and what return do you think he made me for it? Why, to-day he spent his time between schools in filling the room with smoke, that he might torment his companions here, and give me trouble, and

anxiety, and suffering when I should come. If I should tell you his name, the whole school would turn against him for his ingratitude."

The business ended here, and it put a stop, a final stop, to all malicious tricks in the school. Now it is not very often that so fine an opportunity occurs to kill, by a single blow, the disposition to do willful, wanton injury, as this circumstance afforded; but the principle illustrated by it, bringing forward individual cases of transgression in a public manner, only for the sake of the general effect, and so arranging what is said and done as to produce the desired effect upon the public mind in the highest degree, may very frequently be acted upon. Cases are continually occurring, and if the teacher will keep it constantly in mind, that when a particular case comes before the whole school, the object is an influence upon the whole, and not the punishment or reform of the guilty individual, he will insensibly so shape his measures as to produce the desired result.

(4.) There should be a great difference made between the *measures which you take* to prevent wrong, and the *feelings of displeasure which you express* against the wrong when it is done. The former should be strict, authoritative, unbending; the latter should be mild and gentle. Your measures, if uniform and systematic, will never give offense, however powerfully you may restrain and control those subject to them. It is the morose look, the harsh expression, the tone of irritation and fretfulness, which is so unpopular in school. The sins of childhood are by nine tenths of mankind enormously overrated, and perhaps none overrate them more extravagantly than teachers. We confound the trouble they give us with their real moral turpitude, and measure the one by the other. Now if a fault prevails in school, one teacher will scold and fret himself about it day after day, until his scholars are tired both of school and of him; and yet he will *do* nothing effectual to remove it. Another will take efficient and decided measures, and yet say very little on the subject, and the whole evil will be removed without suspending for a moment the good-humor and pleasant feeling which should prevail in school.

The expression of your displeasure on account of any thing that is wrong will seldom or never do any good. The scholars consider it scolding; it is scolding; and though it may, in many cases, contain many sound arguments and eloquent expostulations, it operates simply as a punishment. It is unpleasant to hear it. General instruction must indeed be given, but not general reproof.

(5.) Feel that in the management of the school *you* are under obligation as well as the scholars, and let this feeling appear in all that you do. Your scholars wish you to dismiss school earlier than usual on some particular occasion, or to allow them an extra holiday. Show by the manner in which you consider and speak of the question that your main inquiry is what is *your duty*. Speak often of your responsibility to your employers—not formally, but incidentally and naturally, as you will speak if you feel this responsibility.

It will assist very much, too, in securing cheerful, good-humored obedience to the regulations of the school, if you extend their authority over yourself. Not that the teacher is to have no liberty from which the scholars are debarred; this would be impossible. But the teacher should submit, himself, to every thing which he requires of his scholars, unless it is in cases where a different course is necessary.

Suppose, for instance, a study-card, like the one described in a preceding chapter, is made so as to mark the time of recess and of study. The teacher, near the close of recess, is sitting with a group of his pupils around him, telling them some story. They are all interested, and they see he is interested. He looks at his watch, and shows by his manner that he is desirous of finishing what he is saying, but that he knows that the striking of the bell will cut short his story.

Perhaps he says not a word about it, but his pupils see that he is submitting to the control which is placed over them; and when the card goes up, and he stops instantly in the middle of his sentence and rises with the rest, each one to go to his own place, to engage at once in their several duties, he teaches them a most important lesson, and in the most effectual way. Such a lesson of fidelity and obedience, and such an example of it, will have more influence than half an hour's scolding about whispering without leave, or a dozen public punishments. At least so I found it, for I have tried both.

Show then continually that you see and enjoy the beauty of system and strict discipline, and that you submit to law yourself as well as require submission of others.

(6.) Lead your pupils to see that they must share with you the credit or the disgrace which success or failure in the management of the school may bring. Lead them to feel this, not by telling them so, for there are very few things which can be impressed upon children by direct efforts to impress them, but by so speaking of the subject, from time to time, as to lead them to see that you understand it so.

Repeat, with judicious caution, what is said of the school, both for and against it, and thus endeavor to interest the scholars in its public reputation. This feeling of interest in the institution may very easily be awakened. It sometimes springs up spontaneously, and, where it is not guided aright by the teacher, sometimes produces very bad effects upon the minds of the pupils in rival institutions. When two schools are situated near each other, evil consequences will result from this feeling, unless the teacher manages it so as to deduce good consequences. I recollect that in my boyish days there was a standing quarrel between the boys of a town school and an academy which were in the same village. We were all ready at any time, when out of school, to fight for the honor of our respective institutions, each for his own, but very few were ready to be diligent and faithful when in it, though it would seem that that might have been rather a more effectual means of establishing the point. If the scholars are led to understand that the school is to a great extent their institution, that they must assist to sustain its character, and that they share the honor of its excellence, if any honor is acquired, a feeling will prevail in the school which may be turned to a most useful account.

(7.) In giving instruction on moral duty, the subject should generally be taken up in reference to imaginary cases, or cases which are unknown to most of the scholars. If this is done, the pupils feel that the object of bringing up the subject is to do good; whereas, if questions of moral duty are only introduced from time to time, when some prevailing or accidental fault in school calls for reproof, the feeling will be that the teacher is only endeavoring to remove from his own path a source of inconvenience and trouble. The most successful mode of giving general moral instruction that I have known, and which has been adopted in many schools with occasional variations of form, is the following:

When the time has arrived, a subject is assigned, and small papers are distributed to the whole school, that all may write something concerning it. These are then read and commented on by the teacher, and become the occasion of any remarks which he may wish to make. The interest of the pupils is strongly excited to hear the papers read, and the instruction which the teacher may give produces a deeper effect when ingrafted thus upon something which originates in the minds of the pupils.

To take a particular case. A teacher addresses his scholars thus: "The subject for the moral exercise to-day is *Prejudice*. Each one may take one of the papers which have been distributed, and you may write upon them any thing you please relating to the subject. As many as have thought of any thing to write may raise their hands."

One or two only of the older scholars gave the signal.

"I will mention the kinds of communications you can make, and perhaps what I say will suggest something to you. As fast as you think of any thing, you may raise your hands, and as soon as I see a sufficient number up, I will give directions to begin.

"You can describe any case in which you have been prejudiced yourselves either against persons or things."

Here a number of the hands went up.

"You can mention any facts relating to antipathies of any kind, or any cases where you know other persons to be prejudiced. You can ask any questions in regard to the subject —questions about the nature of prejudice, or the causes of it, or the remedy for it."

As he said this, many hands were successively raised, and at last directions were given for all to begin to write. Five minutes were allowed, and at the end of that time the papers were collected and read. The following specimens, transcribed verbatim from the originals, with the remarks made as nearly as could be remembered immediately after the exercise, will give an idea of the ordinary operation of this plan.

"I am very much prejudiced against spiders and every insect in the known world with scarcely an exception. There is a horrid sensation created by their ugly forms that makes me wish them all to Jericho. The butterfly's wings are pretty, but he is dreadful ugly. There is no affectation in this, for my pride will not permit me to show this prejudice to any great degree when I can help it. I do not fear the little wretches, but I do hate them. ANTI-SPIDER-SPARER."

"This is not expressed very well; the phrases '*to Jericho*' and '*dreadful ugly*' are vulgar, and not in good taste. Such a dislike, too, is more commonly called an antipathy than a prejudice, though perhaps it comes under the general head of prejudices."

"How may we overcome prejudice? I think that when we are prejudiced against a person, it is the hardest thing in the world to overcome it."

"A prejudice is usually founded on some unpleasant association connected with the subject of it. The best way to overcome the prejudice, therefore, is to connect some pleasant association with it.

"For example (to take the case of the antipathy to the spider, alluded to in the last article), the reason why that young lady dislikes spiders is undoubtedly because she has some unpleasant idea associated with the thought of that animal, perhaps, for example, the idea of their crawling upon her, which is certainly not a very pleasant one for any body. Now the way to correct such a prejudice is to try to connect some pleasant thoughts with the sight of the animal.

"I once found a spider in an empty apartment hanging in its web on the wall, with a large ball of eggs which it had suspended by its side. My companion and myself cautiously brought up a tumbler under the web, and pressed it suddenly against the wall, so as to inclose both spider and eggs within it. We then contrived to run in a pair of shears, so as to cut off the web, and let both the animal and its treasure fall down into the tumbler. We put a book over the top, and walked off with our prize to a table to see what the spider would do.

"At first it tried to climb up the side of the tumbler, but its feet slipped on account of the smoothness of the glass. We then inclined the glass so as to favor its climbing, and to enable it to reach the book at the top. As soon as it touched the book, it was safe. It could cling to the book easily, and we placed the tumbler again upright to watch its motions.

"It attached a thread to the book, and let itself down by it to the bottom of the tumbler, and walked round and round the ball of eggs, apparently in great trouble. Presently it ascended by its thread, and then came down again. It attached a new thread to the ball, and then went up, drawing the ball with it. It hung the ball at a proper distance from the book, and bound it firmly in its place by threads running from it in every direction to the parts of the book which were near, and then the animal took its place quietly by its side.

"Now I do not say that if any body had a strong antipathy to a spider, seeing one perform such a work as this would entirely remove it, but it would certainly soften it. It would *tend* to remove it. It would connect an interesting and pleasant association with the object. So if she should watch a spider in the fields making his web. You have all seen those beautiful regular webs in the morning dew ("Yes, sir;"

"Yes, sir"), composed of concentric circles, and radii diverging in every direction. ("Yes, sir.") Well, watch a spider when making one of these, or observe his artful ingenuity and vigilance when he is lying in wait for a fly. By thus connecting pleasant ideas with the sight of the animal, you will destroy the unpleasant association which constitutes the prejudice. In the same manner, if I wished to create an antipathy to a spider in a child, it would be very easily done. I would tie her hands behind her, and put three or four upon her to crawl over her face.

"Thus you must destroy prejudices in all cases by connecting pleasant thoughts and associations with the objects of them."

"I am very often prejudiced against new scholars without knowing why."

"We sometimes hear a person talk in this way: 'I do not like such or such a person at all.'

"'Why?'

"'Oh, I don't know; I do not like her at all. I can't bear her.'

"'But why not? What is your objection to her?'

"'Oh, I don't know; I have not any particular reason, but I never did like her.'

"Now, whenever you hear any person talk so, you may be sure that her opinion on any subject is worth nothing at all. She forms opinions in one case without grounds, and it depends merely upon accident whether she does or not in other cases."

"Why is it that so many of our countrymen *are*, or seem to be, prejudiced against the unfortunate children of Africa? Almost every *large white* boy who meets a *small black* boy insults him in some way or other."

"It is so hard to *overcome* prejudices, that we ought to be careful how we *form* them."

"When I see a new scholar enter this school, and she does not happen to suit me exactly in her ways and manners, I very often get prejudiced against her; though sometimes I find her a valuable friend after I get acquainted with her."

"There is an inquiry I should like very much to make, though I suppose it would not be quite right to make it. I should like to ask all those who have some particular friend in school, and who can recollect the impression which the individual made upon them when they first saw her, to rise, and then I should like to inquire in how many cases the first impression was favorable, and in how many unfavorable."

"Yes, sir;" "Yes, sir."

"Do you mean you would like to have the inquiry made?"

"Yes, sir."

"All, then, who have intimate friends, and can recollect the impression which they first made upon them, may rise."

[About thirty rose; more than two thirds of whom voted that the first impression made by the persons who had since become their particular friends was unfavorable.]

"This shows how much dependence you can justly place on first impressions."

"It was the next Monday morning after I had attained the wise age of four years that I was called up into my mother's room, and told that I was the next day going to school.

"I called forth all my reasoning powers, and with all the ability of a child of four years, I reasoned with my mother, but to no purpose. I told her that I *hated* the school-mistress then, though I had never seen her. The very first day I tottered under the weight of the mighty fool's-cap. I only attended her school two quarters; with prejudice I went, and with prejudice I came away.

"The old school-house is now torn down, and a large brick house takes the place of it. But I never pass by without remembering my teacher. I am prejudiced to [against] the very spot."

"Is it not right to allow prejudice to have influence over our minds as far as this? If any thing comes to our knowledge with which wrong *seems* to be connected, and one in whom we have always felt confidence is engaged in it, is it not right to allow our prejudice in favor of this individual to have so much influence over us as to cause us to believe that all is really right, though every circumstance which has come to our knowledge is against such a conclusion? I felt this influence, not many weeks since, in a very great degree."

"The disposition to judge favorably of a fraud in such a case would not be prejudice; or, at least, if it were so, it would not be a sufficient ground to justify us in withholding blame. Well-grounded confidence in such a person, if there was reason for it, ought to have such an effect, but not prejudice."

The above may be considered as a fair specimen of the ordinary operation of such an exercise. It is taken as an illustration, not by selection, from the large number of similar exercises which I have witnessed, but simply because it was an exercise occurring at the time when a description was to be written. Besides the articles quoted above, there were thirty or forty others which were read and commented on. The above will, however, be sufficient to give the reader a clear idea of the exercise, and to show what is the nature of the moral effect it is calculated to produce.

The subjects which may be advantageously brought forward in such a way are, of course, very numerous. They are such as the following:

1. Duties to Parents.—Anecdotes of good or bad conduct at home. Questions. Cases where it is most difficult to obey. Dialogues between parents and children. Excuses which are often made for disobedience.

2. Selfishness.—Cases of selfishness any of the pupils have observed. Dialogues they have heard exhibiting it. Questions about its nature. Indications of selfishness.

3. Faults of the School.—Any bad practices the scholars may have observed in regard to general deportment, recitations, habits of study, or the scholars' treatment of one another. Each scholar may write what is his own greatest trouble in school, and whether he thinks any thing can be done to remove it. Any thing they think can be improved in the management of the school by the teacher. Unfavorable things they have heard said about it out of school, though without names.

4. Excellences of the School.—Good practices which ought to be persevered in. Any little incidents the scholars may have noticed illustrating good character. Cases which have occurred in which scholars have done right in temptation, or when others around were doing wrong. Favorable reports in regard to the school in the community around.

5. The Sabbath.—Any thing the scholars may have known to be done on the Sabbath which they doubt whether right or wrong. Questions in regard to the subject. Various opinions they have heard expressed. Difficulties they have in regard to proper ways of spending the Sabbath.

(8.) We have one other method to describe by which a favorable moral influence may be exerted in school. The method can, however, go into full effect only where there are

several pupils who have made considerable advances in mental cultivation.

It is to provide a way by which teachers and pupils may write anonymously for the school. This may be done by having a place of deposit for such articles as may be written, where any person may leave what he wishes to have read, nominating by a memorandum upon the article itself the reader. If a proper feeling on the subject of good discipline and the formation of good character prevails in school, many articles, which will have a great deal of effect upon the pupils, will find their way through such an avenue once opened. The teacher can himself often bring forward in this way his suggestions with more effect than he otherwise could do. Such a plan is, in fact, like the plan of a newspaper for an ordinary community, where sentiments and opinions stand on their own basis, and influence the community just in proportion to their intrinsic merits, unassisted by the authority of the writer's name, and unimpeded by any prejudice which may exist against him.

The following articles, which were really offered for such a purpose in the Mount Vernon school, will serve as specimens to illustrate the actual operation of the plan. One or two of them were written by teachers. I do not know the authors of the others. I do not offer them as remarkable compositions: every teacher will see that they are not so. The design of inserting them is merely to show that the ordinary literary ability to be found in every school may be turned to useful account by simply opening a channel for it, and to furnish such teachers as may be inclined to try the experiment the means of making the plan clearly understood by their pupils.

MARKS OF A BAD SCHOLAR.

"At the time when she should be ready to take her seat at school, she commences preparation for leaving home. To the extreme annoyance of those about her, all is now hurry, and bustle, and ill-humor. Thorough search is to be made for every book or paper for which she has occasion; some are found in one place, some in another, and others are forgotten altogether. Being finally equipped, she casts her eye at the clock, hopes to be in tolerable good season (notwithstanding that the hour for opening the school has already arrived), and sets out in the most violent hurry.

"After so much haste, she is unfitted for attending properly to the duties of the school until a considerable time after her arrival. If present at the devotional exercises, she finds it difficult to command her attention even when desirous of so doing, and her deportment at this hour is, accordingly, marked with an unbecoming listlessness and abstraction.

"When called to recitations, she recollects that some task was assigned, which, till that moment, she had forgotten; of others she had mistaken the extent, most commonly thinking them to be shorter than her companions suppose. In her answers to questions with which she should be familiar, she always manifests more or less of hesitation, and what she ventures to express is very commonly in the form of a question. In these, as in all exercises, there is an inattention to general instructions. Unless what is said be addressed particularly to herself, her eyes are directed toward another part of the room; it may be, her thoughts are employed about something not at all connected with the school. If reproved by her teacher for negligence in any respects, she is generally provided with an abundance of excuses, and however mild the reproof, she receives it as a piece of extreme severity.

"Throughout her whole deportment there is an air of indolence and a want of interest in those exercises which should engage her attention. In her seat, she most commonly sits in some lazy posture—either with her elbows upon her desk, her head leaning upon her hands, or with her seat tipped forward or backward. When she has occasion to leave her seat, it is in a sauntering, lingering gait—perhaps some trick is contrived on the way for exciting the mirth of her companions.

"About every thing in which it is possible to be so, she is untidy. Her books are carelessly used, and placed in her desk without order. If she has a piece of waste paper to dispose of, she finds it much more convenient to tear it into small pieces and scatter it about her desk, than to put it in a proper place. Her hands and clothes are usually covered with ink. Her written exercises are blotted and full of mistakes."

THE CONSEQUENCES OF BEING BEHINDHAND.

"The following incident, which I witnessed on a late journey, illustrates an important principle, and I will relate it.

"When our steam-boat started from the wharf, all our passengers had not come. After we had proceeded a few yards, there appeared among the crowd on the wharf a man with his trunk under his arm, out of breath, and with a most disappointed and disconsolate air. The captain determined to stop for him; but stopping an immense steam-boat, moving swiftly through the water, is not to be done in a moment; so we took a grand sweep, wheeling majestically around an English ship which was at anchor in the harbor. As we came toward the wharf again, we saw the man in a small boat coming off from it. As the steam-boat swept round, they barely succeeded in catching a rope from the stern, and then immediately the steam-engine began its work again, and we pressed forward, the little boat following us so swiftly that the water around her was all in a foam.

"They pulled upon the rope attached to the little boat until they drew it alongside. They then let down a rope, with a hook in the end of it, from an iron crane which projected over the side of the steam-boat, and hooked it into a staple in the front of the small boat. '*Hoist away!*' said the captain. The sailors hoisted, and the front part of the little boat began to rise, the stern plowing and foaming through the water, and the man still in it, with his trunk under his arm. They 'hoisted away' until I began to think that the poor man would actually tumble out behind. He clung to the seat, and looked as though he was saying to himself, 'I will take care how I am tardy the next time.' However, after a while, they hoisted up the stern of the boat, and he got safely on board.

"*Moral.*—Though coming to school a few minutes earlier or later may not in itself be a matter of much consequence, yet the habit of being five minutes too late, if once formed, will, in actual life, be a source of great inconvenience, and sometimes of lasting injury."

NEW SCHOLARS.

"There is at ——— a young ladies' school, taught by Mr. ———.

* * * * * * *

"But, with all these excellences, there is one fault, which I considered a great one, and which does not comport with the general character of the school for kindness and good feeling. It is the little effort made by the scholars to become acquainted with the new ones who enter. Whoever goes there must push herself forward, or she will never feel at home. The young ladies seem to forget that the new-comer must feel rather unpleasantly in the midst of a hundred persons to whom she is wholly a stranger, and with no one to speak to. Two or three will stand together, and instead of deciding upon some plan by which the individual may be made to feel at ease, something like the following conversation takes place:

"*Miss X.* How do you like the looks of Miss A., who entered school to-day?

"*Miss Y.* I don't think she is very pretty, but she looks as if she might be a good scholar.

"*Miss X.* She does not strike me very pleasantly. Did you ever see such a face? And her complexion is so dark, I should think she had always lived in the open air; and what a queer voice she has!

"*Miss Y.* I wonder if she has a taste for Arithmetic?

"*Miss X.* She does not look as if she had much taste for any thing. See how strangely she arranges her hair!

"*Miss S.* Whether she has much taste or not, some one of us ought to go and get acquainted with her. See how unpleasantly she feels!

"*Miss X.* I don't want to get acquainted with her until I know whether I shall like her or not.

"Thus nothing is done to relieve her. When she does become acquainted, all her first strange appearance is forgotten; but this is sometimes not the case for several weeks. It depends entirely on the character of the individual herself. If she is forward, and willing to make the necessary effort, she can find many friends; but if she is diffident, she has much to suffer. This arises principally from thoughtlessness. The young ladies do not seem to realize that there is any thing for them to do. They feel enough at home themselves, and the remembrance of the time when they entered school does not seem to arise in their minds."

A SATIRICAL SPIRIT.

"I witnessed, a short time since, a meeting between two friends, who had had but little intercourse before for a long while. I thought a part of their conversation might be useful, and I shall therefore relate it, as nearly as I can recollect, leaving each individual to draw her own inferences.

"For some time I sat silent, but not uninterested, while the days of 'Auld Lang Syne' came up to the remembrance of the two friends. After speaking of several individuals who were among their former acquaintances, one asked, 'Do you remember Miss W.?' 'Yes,' replied the former, 'I remember her as the fear, terror, and abhorrence of all who knew her.' *I* knew the lady by report, and asked why she was so regarded. The reply was, 'Because she was so severe, so satirical in her remarks upon others. She spared neither friend nor foe.'

"The friends resumed their conversation. 'Did you know,' said the one who had first spoken of Miss W., 'that she sometimes had seasons of bitter repentance for indulging in this unhappy propensity of hers? She would, at such times, resolve to be more on her guard, but, after all her good resolutions, she would yield to the slightest temptations. When she was expressing, and apparently really *feeling* sorrow for having wounded the feelings of others, those who knew her would not venture to express any sympathy, for, very likely, the next moment *that* would be turned into ridicule. No confidence could be placed in her.'

"A few more facts will be stated respecting the same individual, which I believe are strictly true. Miss W. possessed a fine and well-cultivated mind, great penetration, and a tact at discriminating character rarely equaled. She could, if she chose, impart a charm to her conversation that would interest and even fascinate those who listened to it; still, she was not beloved. Weaknesses and foibles met with unmerciful severity, and well-meaning intentions and kind actions did not always escape without the keen sarcasm which it is so difficult for the best regulated mind to bear unmoved. The mild and gentle seemed to shrink from her; and thus she, who might have been the bright and beloved ornament of the circle in which she moved, was regarded with distrust, fear, and even hatred. This dangerous habit of making satirical remarks was evinced in childhood; it was cherished; it 'grew with her growth, and strengthened with her strength,' until she became what I have described. LAURA."

Though such a satirical spirit is justly condemned, a little good-humored raillery may sometimes be allowed as a mode of attacking faults in school which can not be reached by graver methods. The teacher must not be surprised if some things connected with his own administration come in sometimes for a share.

VARIETY.

"I was walking out a few days since, and not being particularly in haste, I concluded to visit a certain school for an hour or two. In a few minutes after I had seated myself on the sofa, the '*Study Card*' was dropped, and the general noise and confusion indicated that recess had arrived. A line of military characters, bearing the title of the 'Freedom's Band,' was soon called out, headed by one of their own number. The tune chosen to guide them was Kendall's March.

"'Please to form a regular line,' said the lady commander. 'Remember that there is to be no speaking in the ranks. Do not begin to step until I strike the bell. Miss B., I requested you not to step until I gave the signal.'

"Presently the command was given, and the whole line *stepped* for a few minutes to all intents and purposes. Again the bell sounded. 'Some of you have lost the step,' said the general. 'Look at me, and begin again. Left! right! left! right!' The line was once more in order, and I observed a new army on the opposite side of the room, performing the same manœuvres, always to the tune of 'Kendall's March.' After a time the recess closed, and order was again restored. In about half an hour I approached a class which was reciting behind the railing. 'Miss A.,' said a teacher, 'how many kinds of magnitude are there?' *Miss A.* (Answer inaudible.) *Several voices.* 'We can't hear.' *Teacher.* 'Will you try to speak a little louder, Miss A.?'

"Some of the class at length seemed *to guess* the meaning of the young lady, but *I* was unable to do even that until the answer was repeated by the teacher. Finding that I should derive little instruction from the recitation, I returned to the sofa.

"In a short time the *propositions* were read. 'Proposed, that the committee be impeached for not providing suitable pens.' 'Lost, a pencil, with a piece of India-rubber attached to it by a blue ribbon,' &c., &c.

"Recess was again announced, and the lines commenced their evolutions to the tune of 'Kendall's March.' Thought I, 'Oh that there were a new tune under the sun!'

"Before the close of school some compositions were read. One was entitled 'The Magic Ring,' and commenced, 'As I was sitting alone last evening, I heard a gentle tap on the door, and immediately a beautiful fairy appeared before me. She placed a ring on my finger, and left me.' The next began, 'It is my week to write composition, but I do not know what to say. However, I must write something, so it shall be a dialogue.' Another was entitled the 'Magical Shoe,' and contained a marvelous narration of adventures made in a pair of shoes more valuable than the far-famed 'seven-league boots.' A fourth began, 'Are you acquainted with that new scholar?' 'No; but I don't believe I shall like her.' And soon the 'Magical Thimble,' the 'Magical Eye-glass,' &c., were read in succession, until I could not but exclaim, 'How pleasing is variety!' School was at length closed, and the young ladies again attacked the piano. 'Oh,' repeated I to myself, '*how pleasing is variety!*' as I left the room to the tune of Kendall's March."

By means like these, and others similar to them, it will not be difficult for any teacher to obtain so far an ascendency over the minds of his pupils as to secure an overwhelming majority in favor of good order and co-operation with him in his plans for elevating the character of the school. But let it be distinctly understood that this, and this only, has been the object of this chapter thus far. The first point

brought up was the desirableness of making at first a favorable impression; the second, the necessity of taking general views of the condition of the school, and aiming to improve it in the mass, and not merely to rebuke or punish accidental faults; and the third, the importance and the means of gaining a general influence and ascendency over the minds of the pupils. But, though an overwhelming majority can be reached by such methods as these, all can not. We must have the majority secured, however, in order to enable us to reach and to reduce the others. But to this work we must come at last.

4. I am, therefore, now to consider, under a fourth general head, what course is to be taken with *individual* offenders whom the general influences of the school-room will not control.

The teacher must always expect that there will be such cases. They are always to be found in the best and most skillfully-managed schools. The following suggestions will perhaps assist the teacher in dealing with them.

(1.) The first point to be attended to is to ascertain who they are. Not by appearing suspiciously to watch any individuals, for this would be almost sufficient to make them bad, if they were not so before. Observe, however; notice, from day to day, the conduct of individuals, not for the purpose of reproving or punishing their faults, but to enable you to understand their characters. This work will often require great adroitness and very close scrutiny, and you will find, as the results of it, a considerable variety of character, which the general influences above described will not be sufficient to control. The number of individuals will not be great, but the diversity of character comprised in it will be such as to call into exercise all your powers of vigilance and discrimination. On one seat you will find a coarse, rough-looking boy, who openly disobeys your commands and opposes your wishes while in school, and makes himself a continual source of trouble and annoyance during play-hours by bullying and

hectoring every gentle and timid schoolmate. On another sits a more sly rogue, whose demure and submissive look is assumed to conceal a mischief-making disposition. Here is one whose giddy spirit is always leading him into difficulty, but who is of so open and frank a disposition that you will most easily lead him back to duty; but there is another who, when reproved, will fly into a passion; and then a third, who will stand sullen and silent before you when he has done wrong, and is not to be touched by kindness nor awed by authority.

Now all these characters must be studied. It is true that the caution given in a preceding part of this chapter, against devoting undue and disproportionate attention to such persons, must not be forgotten. Still, these individuals will require, and it is right that they should receive, a far greater degree of attention, so far as the moral administration of the school is concerned, than their mere numbers would appear to justify. This is the field in which the teacher is to study human nature, for here it shows itself without disguise. It is through this class, too, that a very powerful moral influence is to be exerted upon the rest of the school. The manner in which such individuals are managed, the tone the teacher assumes toward them, the gentleness with which he speaks of their faults, and the unbending decision with which he restrains them from wrong, will have a most powerful effect upon the rest of the school. That he may occupy this field, therefore, to the best advantage, it is necessary that he should first thoroughly explore it.

By understanding the dispositions and characters of such a class of pupils as I have described, I do not mean merely watching them with vigilance in school, so that none of their transgressions shall go unobserved and unpunished. I intend a far deeper and more thorough examination of character. Every boy has something or other which is good in his disposition and character which he is aware of, and on which he prides himself; find out what it is, for it may often be made the foundation on which you may build the superstructure of reform. Every one has his peculiar sources of enjoyment and objects of pursuit, which are before his mind from day to day. Find out what they are, that by taking an interest in what interests him, and perhaps sometimes assisting him in his plans, you can bind him to you. Every boy is, from the circumstances in which he is placed at home, exposed to temptations which have perhaps had far greater influence in the formation of his character than any deliberate and intentional depravity of his own; ascertain what these temptations are, that you may know where to pity him and where to blame. The knowledge which such an examination of character will give you, will not be confined to making you acquainted with the individual. It will be the most valuable knowledge which a man can possess, both to assist him in the general administration of the school and in his intercourse among mankind in the business of life. Men are but boys, only with somewhat loftier objects of pursuit. Their principles, motives, and ruling passions are essentially the same. Extended commercial speculations are, so far as the human heart is concerned, substantially what trading in jack-knives and toys is at school, and building a snow fort, to its own architects, the same as erecting a monument of marble.

(2.) After exploring the ground, the first thing to be done as a preparation for reforming individual character in school is to secure the personal attachment of the individuals to be reformed. This must not be attempted by professions and affected smiles, and still less by that sort of obsequiousness, common in such cases, which produces no effect but to make the bad boy suppose that his teacher is afraid of him; which, by the way, is, in fact, in such cases, usually true. Approach the pupil in a bold and manly, but frank and pleasant manner. Approach him as his superior, but still as his friend; desirous to make him happy, not merely to obtain his good-will. And the best way to secure these appearances is just to secure the reality. Actually be the boy's friend. Really desire to make him happy—happy, too, in his own way, not in yours. Feel that you are his superior, and that you must and will enforce obedience; but with this, feel that probably obedience will be rendered without any contest. If these are really the feelings which reign within you, the boy will see it, and they will exert a strong influence over him; but you can not counterfeit appearances.

A most effectual way to secure the good-will of a scholar is to ask him to assist you. The Creator has so formed the human heart that doing good must be a source of pleasure, and he who tastes this pleasure once will almost always wish to taste it again. To do good to any individual creates or increases the desire to do it.

There is a boy in your school who is famous for his skill in making whistles from the green branches of the poplar. He is a bad boy, and likes to turn his ingenuity to purposes of mischief. You observe him some day in school, when he thinks your attention is engaged in another way, blowing softly upon one which he has concealed in his desk for the purpose of amusing his neighbors without attracting the attention of the teacher. Now there are two remedies. Will you try the physical one? Then call him out into the floor,

inflict painful punishment, and send him smarting to his seat, with his heart full of anger and revenge, to plot some new and less dangerous scheme of annoyance. Will you try the moral one? Then wait till the recess, and while he is out at his play, send a message out by another boy, saying that you have heard he is very skillful in making whistles, and asking him to make one for you to carry home to a little child at your boarding-house. What would, in ordinary cases, be the effect? It would certainly be a very simple application, but its effect would be to open an entirely new train of thought and feeling for the boy. "What!" he would say to himself, while at work on his task, "give the master *pleasure* by making whistles! Who would have conceived of it? I never thought of any thing but giving him trouble and pain. I wonder who told him I could make whistles?" He would find, too, that the new enjoyment was far higher and purer than the old, and would have little disposition to return to the latter.

I do not mean by this illustration that such a measure as this would be the only notice that ought to be taken of such an act of willful disturbance in school. Probably it would not. What measures in direct reference to the fault committed would be necessary would depend upon the circumstances of the case. It is not necessary to our purpose that they should be described here.

The teacher can awaken in the hearts of his pupils a personal attachment for him by asking in various ways their assistance in school, and then appearing honestly gratified with the assistance rendered. Boys and girls are delighted to have what powers and attainments they possess brought out into action, especially where they can lead to useful results. They love to be of some consequence in the world, and will be especially gratified to be able to assist their teacher. Even if the studies of a turbulent boy are occasionally interrupted for half an hour, that he might help you arrange papers, or rule books, or distribute exercises, it will be time well spent. Get him to co-operate with you in any thing, and he will feel how much more pleasant it is to co-operate than to thwart and oppose; and, by judicious measures of this kind, almost any boy may be brought over to your side.

Another means of securing the personal attachment of boys is to notice them, to take an interest in their pursuits, and the qualities and powers which they value in one another. It is astonishing what an influence is exerted by such little circumstances as stopping at a play-ground a moment to notice with interest, though perhaps without saying a word, speed of running, or exactness of aim, the force with which a ball is struck, or the dexterity with which it is caught or thrown. The teacher must, indeed, in all his intercourse with his pupils, never forget his station, nor allow them to lay aside the respect, without which authority can not be maintained. But he may be, notwithstanding this, on the most intimate and familiar footing with them all. He may take a strong and open interest in all their enjoyments, and thus awaken on their part a personal attachment to himself, which will exert over them a constant and powerful control.

(3.) The efforts described under the last head for gaining a personal influence over those who, from their disposition and character, are most in danger of doing wrong, will not be sufficient entirely to prevent transgression. Cases of deliberate, intentional wrong will occur, and the question will rise, What is the duty of the teacher in such an emergency? When such cases occur, the course to be taken is, first of all, to come to a distinct understanding on the subject with the guilty individual. Think of the case calmly, until you have obtained just and clear ideas of it. Endeavor to understand precisely in what the guilt of it consists. Notice every palliating circumstance, and take as favorable a view of the thing as you can, while, at the same time, you fix most firm-

ly in your mind the determination to put a stop to it. Then go to the individual, and lay the subject before him, for the purpose of understanding distinctly from his own lips what he intends to do. I can, however, as usual, explain more fully what I mean by describing a particular case, substantially true.

The teacher of a school observed himself, and learned from several quarters, that a certain boy was in the habit of causing disturbance during time of prayer, at the opening and close of school, by whispering, playing, making gestures to the other boys, and throwing things about from seat to seat. The teacher's first step was to speak of the subject generally before the whole school, not alluding, however, to any particular instance which had come under his notice. These general remarks produced, as he expected, but little effect.

He waited for some days, and the difficulty still continued. Had the irregularity been very great, it would have been necessary to have taken more immediate measures, but he thought the case admitted of a little delay. In the mean time, he took pains to cultivate the acquaintance of the boy, to discover, and to show that he noticed, what was good in his character and conduct, occasionally to ask some assistance from him, and thus to gain some personal ascendency over him.

One day, when every thing had gone smoothly and prosperously, the teacher told the boy, at the close of the school, that he wished to talk with him a little, and asked him to walk home with him. It was not uncommon for the teacher to associate thus with his pupils out of school, and this request, accordingly, attracted no special attention. On the walk the teacher thus accosted the criminal:

"Do you like frank, open dealing, James?"

James hesitated a moment, and then answered, faintly,

"Yes, sir."

"Most boys do, and I do, and I supposed that you would prefer being treated in that way. Do you?"

"Yes, sir."

"Well, I am going to tell you of one of your faults. I have asked you to walk with me, because I supposed it would be more agreeable for you to have me see you privately than to bring it up in school."

James said it would be more agreeable.

"Well, the fault is being disorderly at prayer-time. Now, if you like frank and open dealing, and are willing to deal so with me, I should like to talk with you a little about it, but if you are not willing, I will dismiss the subject. I do not wish to talk with you now about it unless you yourself desire it; but if we talk at all, we must both be open, and honest, and sincere. Now, should you rather have me talk with you or not?"

"Yes, sir, I should rather have you talk with me now than in school."

The teacher then described his conduct in a mild manner, using the style of simple narration, admitting no harsh epithets, no terms of reproach. The boy was surprised, for he supposed that he had not been noticed. He thought, perhaps, that he should have been punished if he had been observed. The teacher said, in conclusion,

"Now, James, I do not suppose you have done this from any designed irreverence toward God, or deliberate intention of giving me trouble and pain. You have several times lately assisted me in various ways, and I know, from the cheerful manner with which you comply with my wishes, that your prevailing desire is to give me pleasure, not pain. You have fallen into this practice through thoughtlessness, but that does not alter the character of the sin. To do so is a great sin against God, and a great offense against good order in school. You see, yourself, that my duty to the school will require me to adopt the most decided measures to prevent the continuance and the spread of such a practice. I should be imperiously bound to do it, even if the individual was the very best friend I had in school, and if the measures necessary should bring upon him great disgrace and suffering. Do you not think it would be so?"

"Yes, sir," said James, seriously, "I suppose it would."

"I wish to remove the evil, however, in the pleasantest way. Do you remember my speaking on this subject in school the other day?"

"Yes, sir."

"Well, my object in what I said then was almost entirely to persuade you to reform without having to speak to you directly. I thought it would be pleasanter to you to be reminded of your duty in that way. But I do not think it did you much good. Did it?"

"I don't think I have played *so much* since then."

"Nor I. You have improved a little, but you have not decidedly and thoroughly reformed. So I was obliged to take the next step which would be least unpleasant to you, that is, talking with you alone. Now you told me when we began that you would deal honestly and sincerely with me, if I would with you. I have been honest and open. I have told you all about it so far as I am concerned. Now I wish you to be honest, and tell me what you are going to do. If you think, from this conversation, that you have done wrong, and if you are fully determined to do so no more, and to break off at once, and forever, from this practice, I should like to have you tell me, and then the whole thing will be settled. On the other hand, if you feel about it pretty much as you have done, I should like to have you tell me that too, honestly and frankly, that we may have a distinct understanding, and that I may be considering what to do next. I shall not be offended with you for giving me either of these answers, but be sure that you are honest; you promised to be so."

The boy looked up in his master's face, and said, with great earnestness,

"Mr. T., I *will* do better. I *will not* trouble you any more."

I have detailed this case thus particularly because it exhibits clearly what I mean by going directly and frankly to the individual, and coming at once to a full understanding. In nine cases out of ten this course will be effectual. For four years, with a very large school, I found this sufficient in every case of discipline which occurred, except in three or four instances, where something more was required. To make it successful, however, the work must be done properly. Several things are necessary. It must be deliberate; generally better after a little delay. It must be indulgent, so far as the view which the teacher takes of the guilt of the pupil is concerned; every palliating consideration must be felt. It must be firm and decided in regard to the necessity of a change, and the determination of the teacher to effect it. It must also be open and frank; no insinuations, no hints, no surmises, but plain, honest, open dealing.

In many cases the communication may be made most delicately and most successfully in writing. The more delicately you touch the feelings of your pupils, the more tender these feelings will become. Many a teacher hardens and stupefies the moral sense of his pupils by the harsh and rough exposures to which he drags out the private feelings of the heart. A man may easily produce such a state of feeling in his schoolroom, that to address even the gentlest reproof to any individual, in the hearing of the next, would be a most severe punishment; and, on the other hand, he may so destroy that sensitiveness that his vociferated reproaches will be as unheeded as the idle wind.

If, now, the teacher has taken the course recommended in this chapter—if he has, by his general influence in the school, done all in his power to bring the majority of his pupils to the side of order and discipline—if he has then studied, attentively and impartially, the characters of those who can not thus be led—if he has endeavored to make them his friends, and to acquire, by every means, a personal influence over

them—if, finally, when they do wrong, he goes plainly, but in a gentle and delicate manner, to them, and lays before them the whole case—if he has done all this, he has gone as far as moral influence will carry him. My opinion is, that this course, faithfully and judiciously pursued, will, in almost all instances, succeed; but it will not in all; and where it fails, there must be other, and more vigorous and decided measures. What these measures of restraint or punishment shall be must depend upon the circumstances of the case; but in resorting to them, the teacher must be decided and unbending.

The course above recommended is not trying lax and inefficient measures for a long time in hopes of their being ultimately successful, and then, when they are found not to be so, changing the policy. There should be, through the whole, the tone and manner of *authority*, not of *persuasion*. The teacher must be a *monarch*, and, while he is gentle and forbearing, always looking on the favorable side of conduct so far as guilt is concerned; he must have an eagle eye and an efficient hand, so far as relates to arresting the evil and stopping the consequences. He may slowly and cautiously, and even tenderly, approach a delinquent. He may be several days in gathering around him the circumstances of which he is ultimately to avail himself in bringing him to submission; but, while he proceeds thus slowly and tenderly, he must come with the air of authority and power. The fact that the teacher bases all his plans on the idea of his ultimate authority in every case may be perfectly evident to all the pupils, while he proceeds with moderation and gentleness in all his specific measures. Let it be seen, then, that the constitution of your school is a monarchy, absolute and unlimited; but let it also be seen that the one who holds the power is himself under the control of moral principle in all that he does, and that he endeavors to make the same moral principle which guides him go as far as it is possible to make it go in the government of his subjects.

CHAPTER V.

RELIGIOUS INFLUENCE.

IN consequence of the unexampled religious freedom possessed in this country, for which it is happily distinguished above all other countries on the face of the earth, there necessarily results a vast variety of religious sentiment and action. We can not enjoy the blessings without the inconveniences of freedom. Where every man is allowed to believe as he pleases, some will, undoubtedly, believe wrong, and others will be divided, by embracing views of a subject which are different, though perhaps equally consistent with truth. Hence we have among us every shade and every variety of religious opinion, and, in many cases, contention and strife, resulting from hopeless efforts to produce uniformity.

A stranger who should come among us would suppose, from the tone of our religious journals, and from the general aspect of society on the subject of religion, that the whole community was divided into a thousand contending sects, who hold nothing in common, and whose sole objects are the annoyance and destruction of each other. But if we leave out of view some hundreds, or, if you please, some thousands of theological controversialists who manage the public discussions, and say and do all that really comes before the public on this subject, it will be found that there is vastly more religious truth admitted by common consent among the people of New England than is generally supposed. This common ground I shall endeavor briefly to describe; for it is very plain that the teacher must, in ordinary cases, confine himself to it. By common consent, however, I do not mean the consent of every body; I mean that of the great majority of serious, thinking men.

But let us examine first, for a moment, what right any member of the community has to express and to disseminate his opinions with a view to the inquiry whether the teacher is really bound to confine himself to what he can do on this subject with the common consent of his employers.

The various monarchical nations of Europe have been for many years, as is well known, strongly agitated with questions of politics. It is with difficulty that public tranquillity is preserved. Every man takes sides. Now, in this state of things, a wealthy gentleman residing in one of these countries is opposed to the revolutionary projects so constantly growing up there, and being, both from principle and feeling, strongly attached to monarchical government, wishes to bring up his children with the same feelings which he himself cherishes. He has a right to do so. No matter if his opinions are wrong. He ought, it will be generally supposed in this country, to be republican. I suppose him to adopt opinions which will generally, by my readers, be considered wrong, that I may bring more distinctly to view the right he has to educate his children as *he thinks* it proper that they should be educated. He may be wrong to *form* such opinions; but the opinions once formed, he has a right, with which no human power can justly interfere, to educate his children in conformity with those opinions. It is alike the law of God and nature that the father should control, as he alone is responsible, the education of his child.

Now, under these circumstances, he employs an American mechanic, who is residing in Paris, to come to his house and teach his children the use of the lathe. After some time he comes into their little work-shop, and is astonished to find the lathe standing still, and the boys gathered round the Republican turner, who is relating to them stories of the tyranny of kings, the happiness of republicans, and the glory of war. The parent remonstrates. The mechanic defends himself.

"I am a Republican," he says, "upon principle, and wherever I go I must exert all the influence in my power to promote free principles, and to expose the usurpations and the tyranny of kings."

To this the monarchist might very properly reply,

"In your efforts to promote your principles, you are limited, or you ought to be limited, to modes that are proper and honorable. I employ you for a distinct and specific purpose, which has nothing to do with questions of government, and you ought not to allow your love of republican principles to lead you to take advantage of the position in which I place you, and interfere with my plans for the political education of my children."

Now for the parallel case. A member of a Congregational society is employed to teach a school in a district occupied exclusively by Friends—a case not uncommon. He is employed there, not as a religious teacher, but for another specific and well-defined object. It is for the purpose of teaching the children of that district *reading*, *writing*, and *calculation*, and for such other purposes analogous to this as the law providing for the establishment of district schools contemplated. Now, when he is placed in such a situation, with such a trust confided to him, and such duties to discharge, it is not right for him to make use of the influence which this official station gives him over the minds of the children committed to his care for the accomplishment of *any other purposes whatever* which the parents would disapprove. It would not be considered right by men of the world to attempt to accomplish any other purposes in such a case; and are the pure and holy principles of piety to be extended by methods more exceptionable than those by which political and party contests are managed?

There is a very great and obvious distinction between the general influence which the teacher exerts as a member of the community and that which he can employ in his schoolroom as teacher. He has unquestionably a right to exert *upon the community, by such means as he shares in common with every other citizen*, as much influence as he can command for the dissemination of his own political, or religious, or scientific opinions. But the strong ascendency which, in consequence of his official station, he has obtained over the minds of his pupils, is sacred. He has no right to use it for any purpose *foreign to the specific objects* for which he is employed, unless *by the consent, expressed or implied*, of those by whom he is intrusted with his charge. The parents who send their children to him to be taught to read, to write, and to calculate, may have erroneous views of their duty as parents in other respects. He *may know* that their views are erroneous. They may be taking a course which the teacher *knows* is wrong. But he has not, on this account, a right to step in between the parent and child, to guide the latter according to his own opinions, and to violate the wishes and thwart the plans of the former.

God has constituted the relation between the parent and the child, and according to any view which a rational man can take of this relation, the parent is alone responsible for the guidance he gives to that mind, so entirely in his power. He is responsible to God; and where our opinions in regard to the manner in which any of the duties arising from the relation are to be performed, differ from his, we have no right to interfere, without his consent, to rectify what we thus imagine to be wrong. I know of but one exception which any man whatever would be inclined to make to this principle, and that is where the parent would, if left to himself, take such a course as would ultimately make his children *unsafe members of society*. The *community* have a right to interfere in such a case, as they in fact do by requiring every man to provide for the instruction of his children, and in some other ways which need not now be specified. Beyond this, however, no interference contrary to the parent's consent is justifiable. Where parents will do wrong, notwithstanding any persuasions which we can address to them, we must not violate the principles of an arrangement which God has himself made, but must submit patiently to the awful consequences which will in some cases occur, reflecting that the responsibility for these consequences is on the head of those who neglect their duty, and that the being who makes them liable will settle the account.

Whatever, then, the teacher attempts to do beyond the *specific* and *defined* duties which are included among the objects for which he is employed, must be done *by permission*—by the voluntary consent, whether tacit or openly expressed, of those by whom he is employed. This, of course, confines him to what is generally common ground among his particular employers. In a republican country, where all his patrons are republican, he may, without impropriety, explain and commend to his pupils, as occasion may occur, the principles of free governments, and the blessings which may be expected to flow from them. But it would not be justifiable for him to do this under a monarchy, or in a community divided in regard to this subject, because this question does not come within the objects for the promotion of which his patrons have associated and employed him, and consequently he has no right, while continuing their teacher, to go into it without their consent. In the same manner, an Episcopal teacher, in a private school formed and supported by Episcopalians, may use and commend forms of prayer, and explain the various usages of that church, exhibiting their excellence, and their adaptation to the purposes for which they are intended. He may properly do this, because, in the case supposed, the patrons of the school are *united* on this subject, and their *tacit consent* may be supposed to be given. But place the same teacher over a school of Friends, whose parents dislike forms and ceremonies of every kind in religion, and his duty would be changed altogether. So, if a Roman Catholic is intrusted with the instruction of a common district school in a community composed of many Protestant denominations, it would be plainly his duty to avoid all influence, direct or indirect, over the minds of his pupils, except in those religious sentiments and opinions which are common to himself and all his employers. I repeat the principle. *He is employed for a specific purpose, and he has no right to wander from that purpose, except as far as he can go with the common consent of his employers.*

Now the common ground on religious subjects in this country is very broad. There are, indeed, many principles which are, in my view, essential parts of Christianity, which are subjects of active discussion among us. But, setting these aside, there are other principles equally essential, in regard to which the whole community are agreed; or, at least, if there is a dissenting minority, it is so small that it is hardly to be considered. Let us look at some of these principles.

1. Our community is agreed that *there is a God.* There is probably not a school in our country where the parents of the scholars would not wish to have the teacher, in his conversation with his pupils, take this for granted, and allude reverently to that great Being, with the design of leading them to realize his existence and to feel his authority.

2. Our community are agreed that *we are responsible to God for all our conduct.* Though some persons absurdly pretend to believe that the Being who formed this world, if, indeed, they think there is any such Being, has left it and its inhabitants to themselves, not inspecting their conduct, and never intending to call them to account, they are too few among us to need consideration. A difference of opinion on this subject might embarrass the teacher in France, and in other countries in Europe, but not here. However negligent men may be in *obeying* God's commands, they do almost universally in our country admit in theory the authority from which they come, and believing this, the parent, even if he is aware that he himself does not obey these commands, chooses to have his children taught to respect them. The teacher will thus be acting with the consent of his employers, in almost any part of our country, in endeavoring to influence his pupils to perform moral duties, not merely from worldly motives, nor from mere abstract principles of right and wrong, but *from regard to the authority of God.*

3. The community are agreed, too, in the belief of *the immortality of the soul.* They believe, almost without exception, that there is a future state of being to which this is introductory and preparatory, and almost every father and mother in our country wish to have their children keep this in mind, and to be influenced by it in all their conduct.

4. The community are agreed that *we have a revelation from Heaven.* I believe there are very few instances where the parents would not be glad to have the Bible read from time to time, its geographical and historical meanings illustrated, and its moral lessons brought to bear upon the hearts and lives of their children. Of course, if the teacher is so unwise as to make such a privilege, if it were allowed him, the occasion of exerting an influence upon one side or the other of some question which divides the community around him, he must expect to excite jealousy and distrust, and to be ex-

cluded from a privilege which he might otherwise have been permitted freely to enjoy. There may, alas! be some cases where the use of the Scriptures is altogether forbidden in school; but probably in almost every such case it would be found that it is from fear of its perversion to sect or party purposes, and not from any unwillingness to have the Bible used in the way I have described.

5. The community are agreed, in theory, that *personal attachment to the Supreme Being is the duty of every human soul;* and every parent, with exceptions so few that they are not worth naming, wishes that his children should cherish that affection, and yield their hearts to its influence. He is willing, therefore, that the teacher, of course without interfering with the regular duties for the performance of which he holds his office, should, from time to time, so speak of this duty, of God's goodness to men, of his daily protection and his promised favors, as to awaken, if possible, this attachment in the hearts of his children. Of course, it is very easy for the teacher, if he is so disposed, to abuse this privilege also. He can, under pretense of awakening and cherishing the spirit of piety in the hearts of his pupils, present the subject in such aspects and relations as to arouse the sectarian or denominational feelings of some of his employers; but I believe, if this was honestly and fully avoided, there are few, if any parents in our country who would not be gratified to have the great principle of love to God manifest itself in the instructions of the school-room, and showing itself, by its genuine indications, in the hearts and conduct of their children.

6. The community are agreed not only in believing that piety consists primarily in love to God, but that *the life of piety is to be commenced by penitence for past sins, and forgiveness, in some way or other, through a Savior.* I am aware that one class of theological writers, in the heat of controversy, charge the other with believing that Jesus Christ was nothing more nor less than a teacher of religion, and there are

unquestionably individuals who take this view. But these individuals are few. There are very few in our community who do not in some sense look upon Jesus Christ as our *Savior*—our Redeemer; who do not feel themselves *in some way* indebted to him for the offer of pardon. There may be here and there a theological student, or a contributor to the columns of a polemical magazine, who ranks Jesus Christ with Moses and with Paul. But the great mass of the fathers and mothers, of every name and denomination through all the ranks of society, look up to the Savior of sinners with something at least of the feeling that he is the object of extraordinary affection and reverence. I am aware, however, that I am approaching the limit which, in many parts of our country, ought to bound the religious influence of the teacher in a public school, and on this subject, as on every other, he ought to do nothing directly or indirectly which would be displeasing to those who have intrusted children to his care.

So much ground, it seems, the teacher may occupy, by common consent, in this country, and it certainly is a great deal. It may be doubted whether, after all our disputes, there is a country in the world whose inhabitants have so much in common in regard to religious belief. There is, perhaps, no country in the world where the teacher may be allowed to do so much toward leading his pupils to fear God and to obey his commands, with the cordial consent of parents, as he can here.*

* In speaking of this common ground, and in commenting upon it, I wish not to be understood that I consider these truths as comprising all that is essential in Christianity. Very far from it. A full expression of the Christian faith would go far in advance of all here presented. We must not confound, however, what is essential to prepare the way for the forgiveness of sin with what is essential that a child should understand in order to secure his penitence and forgiveness. The former is a great deal, the latter very little.

The ground which I have been laying out is common all over our country; in particular places there will be even much more that is common. Of course the teacher, in such cases, will be at much greater liberty. If a Roman Catholic community establish a school, and appoint a Roman Catholic teacher, he may properly, in his intercourse with his scholars, allude, with commendation, to the opinions and practices of that church. If a college is established by the Methodist denomination, the teacher of that institution may, of course, explain and enforce there the views of that society. Each teacher is confined only to *those views which are common to the founders and supporters of the particular institution to which he is attached.*

I trust the principle which I have been attempting to enforce is fully before the reader's mind, namely, that moral and religious instruction in a school being in a great degree extra-official in its nature, must be carried no farther than the teacher can go with the common consent, either expressed or implied, of those who have founded, and who support his school. Of course, if those founders forbid it altogether, they have a right to do so, and the teacher must submit. The only question that can justly arise is whether he will remain in such a situation, or go and seek employment where a door of usefulness, here closed against him, will be opened. While he remains, he must honestly and fully submit to the wishes of those in whose hands Providence has placed the ultimate responsibility of training up the children of his school. It is only for a partial and specific purpose that they are placed under his care.

The religious reader may inquire why I am so anxious to restrain, rather than to urge on, the exercise of religious influence in schools. "There is far too little," some one will say, "instead of too much, and teachers need to be encouraged and led on in this duty, not to be restrained from it." There is, indeed, far too little religious influence exerted in common schools. What I have said has been intended to prepare the way for an increase of it. My view of it is this: If teachers do universally confine themselves to the limits which I have been attempting to define, they may accomplish within these limits a vast amount of good. By attempting, however, to exceed them, the confidence of parents is destroyed or weakened, and the door is closed. In this way, injury to a very great extent has been done in many parts of our country. Parents are led to associate with the very idea of religion, indirect and perhaps secret efforts to influence their children in a way which they themselves would disapprove. They transfer to the cause of piety itself the dislike which was first awakened by exceptionable means to promote it; and other teachers, seeing these evil effects, are deterred from attempting what they might easily have accomplished. Before, therefore, attempting to enforce the duty and to explain the methods of exerting religious influence in school, I thought proper distinctly to state with what restrictions and within what limits the work is to be done.

There are many teachers who profess to cherish the spirit and to entertain the hopes of piety, who yet make no effort whatever to extend its influence to the hearts of their pupils. Others appeal sometimes to religious truth merely to assist them in the government of the school. They perhaps bring it before the minds of disobedient pupils in a vain effort to make an impression upon the conscience of one who has done wrong, and who can not by other means be brought to submission. But the pupil in such cases understands, or at least he believes, that the teacher applies to religious truth only to eke out his own authority, and of course it produces no effect. Another teacher thinks he must, to discharge his duty, give a certain amount, weekly, of what he considers religious instruction. He accordingly appropriates a regular portion of time to a formal lecture or exhortation, which he delivers without regard to the mental habits of thought and feeling which prevail among his charge. He forgets that the heart must be led, not driven to piety, and that unless his efforts are adapted to the nature of the minds he is acting upon, and suited to influence them, he must as certainly fail of success as when there is a want of adaptedness between the means and the end in any other undertaking whatever.

The arrangement which seems to me as well calculated as any for the religious exercises of a school is this:

1. In the morning, open the school with a very short prayer, resembling in its object and length the opening prayer in the morning at Congregational churches. The posture which, from some considerable experience, I would recommend at this exercise, is sitting with the head reclined upon the desk. The prayer, besides being short, should be simple in its language and specific in its petitions. A degree of particularity and familiarity which would be improper elsewhere is not only allowable here, but necessary to the production of the proper effect. That the reader may understand to what extent I mean to be understood to recommend this, I will subjoin a form, such as in spirit I suppose such a prayer ought to be.

"Our Father in Heaven, who hast kindly preserved the pupils and the teacher of this school during the past night, come and grant us a continuance of thy protection and blessing during this day. We can not spend the day prosperously and happily without thee. Come, then, and be in this school-room during this day, and help us all to be faithful and successful in duty.

"Guide the teacher in all that he may do. Give him wisdom, and patience, and faithfulness. May he treat all his pupils with kindness; and if any of them should do any thing that is wrong, wilt thou help him, gently but firmly, to endeavor to bring him back to duty. May he sympathize with the difficulties and trials of all, and promote the present happiness as well as the intellectual progress of all who are committed to his care.

"Take care of the pupils too. May they spend the day pleasantly and happily together. Wilt thou, who didst originally give us all our powers, direct and assist us all, this day, in the use and improvement of them. Remove difficulties from our path, and give us all fidelity and patience in every duty. Let no one of us destroy our peace and happiness this day by breaking any of thy commands, or encouraging our companions in sins, or neglecting, in any respect, our duty. We ask all in the name of our great Redeemer. Amen."

Of course the prayer of each day will be varied, unless in special cases the teacher prefers to read some form like the above. But let every one be *minute and particular*, relating especially to school—to school temptations, and trials, and difficulties. Let every one be filled with expressions relating to school, so that it will bear upon every sentence the impression that it is the petition of a teacher and his pupils at the throne of grace.

2. If the pupils can sing, there may be a single verse, or sometimes two verses, of some well-known hymn sung after the prayer at the opening of the school. Teachers will find it much easier to introduce this practice than it would at first be supposed. In almost every school there are enough who can sing to begin, especially if the first experiment is made in a recess, or before or after school; and the beginning once made, the difficulty is over. If but few tunes are sung, a very large proportion of the scholars will soon learn them.

3. Let there be no other regular exercise until the close of the afternoon school. When that hour has arrived, let the teacher devote a very short period, five minutes perhaps, to religious *instruction*, given in various ways. At one time he may explain and illustrate some important truth. At another, read and comment upon a very short portion of Scripture. At another, relate an anecdote or fact which will tend to interest the scholars in the performance of duty. The teacher should be very careful not to imitate on these occasions the formal style of exhortation from the pulpit. Let him use no cant and hackneyed phrases, and never approach the subject of personal piety, or speak of such feelings as pen-

itence for sin, trust in God, and love for the Savior, unless his own heart is really at the time warmed by the emotions which he wishes to awaken in others. Children very easily detect hypocrisy. They know very well when a parent or teacher is talking to them on religious subjects merely as a matter of course for the sake of effect, and such constrained and formal efforts never do any good.

Let, then, every thing which you do in reference to this subject be done with proper regard to the character and condition of the youthful mind, and in such a way as shall be calculated to *interest* as well as to *instruct*. A cold and formal exhortation, or even an apparently earnest one, delivered in a tone of affected solemnity, will produce no good effect. Perhaps I ought not to say it will produce *no* good effect, for good does sometimes result as a sort of accidental consequence from almost any thing. I mean it will have no effectual *tendency* to do good. You must vary your method, too, in order to interest your pupils. Watch their countenances when you are addressing them, and see if they look interested. If they do not, be assured that there is something wrong, or at least something ill-judged or inefficient in your manner of explaining the truths which you wish to have produce an effect upon their minds.

That you may be prepared to bring moral and religious truths before their minds in the way I have described, your own mind must take a strong interest in this class of truths. You must habituate yourself to look at the moral and religious aspects and relations of all that you see and hear. When you are reading, notice such facts and remember such narratives as you can turn to good account in this way. In the same way, treasure up in your mind such occurrences as may come under your own personal observation when traveling, or when mixing with society.

That the spirit and manner of these religious exercises may be the more distinctly understood, I will give some examples.

Let us suppose, then, that the hour for closing school has come. The books are laid aside; the room is still; the boys expect the few words which the teacher is accustomed to address to them, and, looking up to him, they listen to hear what he has to say.

"You may take your Bibles."

The boys, by a simultaneous movement, open their desks, and take from them their copies of the sacred volume.

"What is the first book of the New Testament?"

"Matthew," they all answer at once.

"The second?" "Mark." "The third?" "Luke." "The next?" "John." "The next?" "The Acts." "The next?"

Many answer, "Romans."

"The next?"

A few voices say faintly, and with hesitation, "First of Corinthians."

"I perceive your answers become fainter and fainter. Do you know what is the last book of the New Testament?"

The boys answer promptly, "Revelations."

"Do you know what books are between the Acts and the book of Revelation?"

Some say "No, sir;" some begin to enumerate such books as occur to them, and some, perhaps, begin to name them promptly and in their regular order.

"I do not mean," interrupts the teacher, "the *names* of the books, but the *kinds* of books."

The boys hesitate.

"They are epistles or letters. Do you know who wrote the letters?"

"Paul," "Peter," answer many voices at once.

"Yes, there were several writers. Now the point which I wish to bring before you is this; do you know in what order, I mean on what principles, the books are arranged?"

"No, sir," is the universal reply.

"I will tell you. First come all Paul's epistles. If you turn over the leaves of the Testament, you will see that Paul's letters are all put together after the book of the Acts; and what I wish you to notice is, that they are arranged in the *order* of *their length.* The longest comes first, and then the next, and so on to the shortest, which is the epistle to Philemon. This, of course, comes last—no, I am wrong in saying it is the last of Paul's epistles; there is one more to the Hebrews; and this comes after all the others, for there has been a good deal of dispute whether it was really written by Paul. You will see that his name is not at the beginning of it, as it is in his other epistles: so it was put last.

"Then comes the Epistle of James. Will you see whether it is longer than any that come after it?" The boys, after a minute's examination, answer, "Yes, sir;" "Yes, sir."

"What comes next?"

"The epistles of Peter."

"Yes; and you will see that the longest of Peter's epistles is next in length to that of James's; and, indeed, all his are arranged in the order of their length."

"Yes, sir."

"What comes next?"

"John's."

"Yes; and they are arranged in the order of their length. Do you now understand the principle of the arrangement of the epistles?"

"Yes, sir."

"I should like to have any of you who are interested in it to try to express this principle in a few sentences, on paper, and lay it on my desk to-morrow, and I will read what you write. You will find it very difficult to express it. Now you may lay aside your books. It will be pleasanter for you if you do it silently."

Intelligent children will be interested even in so simple a point as this—much more interested than a maturer mind, unacquainted with the peculiarities of children, would suppose. By bringing up from time to time some such literary inquiry as this, they will be led insensibly to regard the Bible as opening a field for interesting intellectual research, and will more easily be led to study it.

At another time the teacher spends his five minutes in aiming to accomplish a very different object. I will suppose it to be one of those afternoons when all has gone smoothly and pleasantly in school. There has been nothing to excite strong interest or emotion; and there has been (as every teacher knows there sometimes will be), without any assignable cause which he can perceive, a calm, and quiet, and happy spirit diffused over the minds and countenances of the little assembly. His evening communication should accord with this feeling, and he should make it the occasion to promote those pure and hallowed emotions in which every immortal mind must find its happiness, if it is to enjoy any worth possessing.

When all is still, the teacher addresses his pupils as follows:

"I have nothing but a simple story to tell you to-night. It is true, and the fact interested me very much when I witnessed it, but I do not know that it will interest you now merely to hear it repeated. It is this:

"Last vacation, I was traveling in a remote and thinly-settled country, among the mountains, in another state. I was riding with a gentleman on an almost unfrequented road. Forests were all around us, and the houses were small and very few.

"At length, as we were passing an humble and solitary dwelling, the gentleman said to me, 'There is a young woman sick in this house; should you like to go in and see her?' 'Yes, sir,' said I, 'very much. She can have very few visitors, I think, in this lonely place, and if you think she would like to see us, I should like to go.'

"'We turned our horses toward the door, and as we were riding up, I asked what was the matter with the young woman.

"'Consumption,' the gentleman replied; 'and I suppose she will not live long.'

"At that moment we dismounted and entered the house. It was a very pleasant summer afternoon, and the door was open. We entered, and were received by an elderly lady, who seemed glad to see us. In one corner of the room was a bed, on which was lying the patient whom we had come to visit. She was pale and thin in her countenance, but there was a very calm and happy expression beaming in her eye. I went up to her bedside, and asked her how she did.

"I talked with her some time, and found that she was a Christian. She did not seem to know whether she would get well again or not, and, in fact, she did not appear to care much about it. She was evidently happy then, and she believed that she should continue so. She had been penitent for her sins, and had sought and obtained forgiveness, and enjoyed, in her loneliness, not only the protection of God, but also his presence in her heart, diffusing peace and happiness there. When I came into the house, I said to myself, 'I pity, I am sure, a person who is confined by sickness in this lonely place, with nothing to interest or amuse her;' but when I came out, I said to myself, 'I do not pity her at all.'"

Never destroy the effect of such a communication as this by attempting to follow it up with an exhortation, or with general remarks, vainly attempting to strengthen the impression.

Never, do I say? Perhaps there may be some exceptions. But children are not reached by formal exhortations; their hearts are touched and affected in other ways. Sometimes you must reprove, sometimes you must condemn; but indiscriminate and perpetual harangues about the guilt of impenitence, and earnest entreaties to begin a life of piety, only harden the hearts they are intended to soften, and consequently confirm those who hear them in the habits of sin.

In the same way a multitude of other subjects, infinite in number and variety, may be brought before your pupils at stated seasons for religious instruction. It is unnecessary to give any more particular examples, but still it may not be amiss to suggest a few general principles, which ought to guide those who are addressing the young on every subject, and especially on the subject of religion.

1. *Make no effort to simplify language when addressing the young.* Children always observe this, and are always displeased with it, unless they are very young; and it is not necessary. They can understand ordinary language well enough, if the *subject* is within their comprehension, and treated in a manner adapted to their powers. If you doubt whether children can understand language, tell such a story as this, with ardor of tone and proper gesticulation, to a child only two or three years old:

"I saw an enormous dog in the street the other day. He was sauntering along slowly, until he saw a huge piece of meat lying down on the ground. He grasped it instantly between his teeth, and ran away with all speed, until he disappeared around a corner so that I could see him no more."

In such a description there is a large number of words which such a child would not understand if they stood alone, but the whole description would be perfectly intelligible. The reason is, the *subject* is simple; the facts are such as a very little child would be interested in; and the connection of each new word, in almost every instance, explains its meaning. That is the way by which children learn all language. They learn the meaning of words, not by definitions, but by their connection in the sentences in which they hear them; and, by long practice, they acquire an astonishing facility of doing this. It is true they sometimes mistake, but not often, and the teacher of children of almost any age need not be afraid that he shall not be understood. There is no danger from his using the *language* of men, if his subject, and the manner in which he treats it, and the form and structure of his sentences, are what they ought to be. Of course there may be cases, in fact there often will be cases, where particular words will require special explanation, but they will be comparatively few, and instead of making efforts to avoid them, it will be better to let them come. The pupils will be interested and profited by the explanation.

Perhaps some may ask what harm it will do to simplify language when talking to children. "It certainly can do no injury," they may say, "and it diminishes all possibility of being misunderstood." It does injury in at least three ways:

(1.) It disgusts the young persons to whom it is addressed, and prevents their being interested in what is said. I once met two children, twelve years of age, who had just returned from hearing a very able discourse, delivered before a number of Sabbath-schools assembled on some public occasion. "How did you like the discourse?" said I.

"Very well indeed," they replied; "only," said one of them, smiling, "he talked to us as if we were all little children."

Girls and boys, however young, never consider themselves little children, for they can always look down upon some younger than themselves. They are mortified when treated as though they could not understand what is really within the reach of their faculties. They do not like to have their powers underrated, and they are right in this feeling. It is common to all, old and young.

(2.) Children are kept back in learning language if their teacher makes effort to *come down*, as it is called, to their comprehension in the use of words. Notice that I say *in the use of words;* for, as I shall show presently, it is absolutely necessary to come down to the comprehension of children in some other respects. If, however, in the use of words, those who address children confine themselves to such words as children already understand, how are they to make progress in that most important of all studies, the knowledge of language? Many a mother keeps back her child, in this way, to a degree that is hardly conceivable, thus doing all in her power to perpetuate in the child an ignorance of its mother tongue.

Teachers ought to make constant efforts to increase their scholars' stock of words by using new ones from time to time, taking care to explain them when the connection does not do it for them; so that, instead of *coming down* to the language of childhood, they ought rather to go as far away from it as they can, without leaving their pupils behind them.

(3.) But perhaps the greatest evil of this practice is, it satisfies the teacher. He thinks he addresses his pupils in the right manner, and overlooks altogether the real peculiarities in which the power to interest the young depends. He talks to them in simple language, and wonders why they are not interested. He certainly is *plain* enough. He is vexed with them for not attending to what he says, attributing it to their dullness or regardlessness of all that is useful or good, instead of perceiving that the great difficulty is his own want of skill. These three evils are sufficient to deter the teacher from the practice.

2. Present your subject, not in its *general views*, but in its *minute details*. This is the great secret of interesting the young. Present it in its details and in its practical exemplifications; do this with any subject whatever, and children will always be interested.

To illustrate this, let us suppose two teachers wishing to explain to their pupils the same subject, and taking the following opposite methods of doing it. One, at the close of school, addresses his charge as follows:

"The moral character of any action, that is, whether it is right or wrong, depends upon the *motives* with which it is performed. Men look only at the outward conduct, but God looks at the heart. In order, now, that any action should be pleasing to God, it is necessary it should be performed from the motive of a desire to please him.

"Now there are a great many other motives of action which prevail among mankind besides this right one. There is love of praise, love of money, affection for friends, and many others."

By the time the teacher has proceeded thus far, he finds, as he looks around the room, that the countenances of his pupils are assuming a listless and inattentive air. One is restless in his seat, evidently paying no attention. Another has reclined his head upon his desk, lost in a reverie, and others are looking round the room at one another, or at the door, restless and impatient, hoping that the dull lecture will soon be over.

The other teacher says:

"I have thought of an experiment I might try, which would illustrate to you a very important subject. Suppose I should call one of the boys, A, to me, and should say to him, 'I wish you to go to your seat, and transcribe a piece of poetry as handsomely as you can. If it is written as well as you can possibly write it, I will give you a quarter of a dollar. Suppose I say this to him privately, so that none of the rest of the boys can hear, and he goes to take his seat and begins to work. You perceive that I have presented to him a motive to exertion."

"Yes, sir," say the boys, all looking with interest at the teacher, wondering how this experiment is going to end.

"Well, what would that motive be?"

"Money." "The quarter of a dollar." "Love of money," or perhaps other answers, are heard from the various parts of the room.

"Yes, love of money it is called. Now suppose I should call another boy, one with whom I was particularly acquainted, and who I should know would make an effort to please me, and should say to him, 'For a particular reason, I want you to copy this poetry'—giving him the same—'I wish you to copy it handsomely, for I wish to send it away, and have not time to copy it myself. Can you do it for me?'

"Suppose the boy should say he could, and should take it to his seat and begin, neither of the boys knowing what the other was doing. I should now have offered to this second boy a motive. Would it be the same with the other?"

"No, sir."

"What was the other?"

"Love of money."

"What is this?"

The boys hesitate.

"It might be called," continues the teacher, "friendship. It is the motive of a vast number of the actions which are performed in this world.

"Do you think of any other common motive of action besides love of money and friendship?"

"Love of honor," says one; "fear," says another.

"Yes," continues the teacher, "both these are common motives. I might, to exhibit them, call two more boys, one after the other, and say to the one, 'I will thank you to go and copy this piece of poetry as well as you can. I want to send it to the school committee as a specimen of improvement made in this school.'

"To the other I might say, 'You have been a careless boy to-day; you have not got your lessons well. Now take your seat and copy this poetry. Do it carefully. Unless you take pains, and do it as well as you possibly can, I shall punish you severely before you go home.'

"How many motives have I got now? Four, I believe."

"Yes, sir," say the boys.

"Love of money, friendship, love of honor, and fear. We called the first boy A; let us call the others B, C, and D;

no, we shall remember better to call them by the name of their motives. We will call the first M, for money; the second, F, for friendship; the third, H, for honor; and the last, F—we have got an F already; what shall we do? On the whole, it is of no consequence; we will have two F's, but we will take care not to confound them.

"But there are a great many other motives entirely distinct from these. For example, suppose I should say to a fifth boy, 'Will you copy this piece of poetry? It belongs to one of the little boys in school: he wants a copy of it, and I told him I would try to get some one to copy it for him.' This motive, now, would be benevolence; that is, if the boy who was asked to copy it was not particularly acquainted with the other, and did it chiefly to oblige him. We will call this boy B, for Benevolence.

"Now suppose I call a sixth boy, and say to him, 'I have set four or five boys to work copying this piece of poetry; now I wish you to sit down, and see if you can not do it better than any of them. After all are done, I will compare them, and see if yours is not the best.' This would be trying to excite emulation. We must call this boy, then, E. But the time I intended to devote to talking with you on this subject for to-day is expired. Perhaps to-morrow I will take up the subject again."

The reader now will observe that the grand peculiarity of the instructions given by this last teacher, as distinguished from those of the first, consists in this, that the parts of the subject are presented *in detail*, and in *particular exemplification.* In the first case, the whole subject was dispatched in a single, general, and comprehensive description; in the latter, it is examined minutely, one point being brought forward at a time. The discussions are enlivened, too, by meeting and removing such little difficulties as will naturally come up in such an investigation. Boys and girls will take an interest in such a lecture; they will regret to have it come to a conclusion, and will give their attention when the subject is again brought forward on the following day. Let us suppose the time for continuing the exercise to have arrived. The teacher resumes the discussion thus:

"I was talking to you yesterday about the motives of action. How many had I made?"

Some say "Four," some "Five," some "Six."

"Can you name any of them?"

The boys attempt to recollect them, and they give the names in the order in which they accidentally occur to the various individuals. Of course the words Fear, Emulation, Honor, Friendship, and others, come in confused and irregular sounds from every part of the school-room.

"You do not recollect the order," says the teacher, "and it is of no consequence, for the order I named was only accidental. Now to go on with my account: suppose all these boys to sit down and go to writing, each one acting under the impulse of the motive which had been presented to him individually. But, in order to make the supposition answer my purpose, I must add two other cases. I will imagine that one of these boys is called away a few minutes, and leaves his paper on his desk, and that another boy, of an ill-natured and morose disposition, happening to pass by and see his paper, thinks he will sit down and write upon it a few lines, just to tease and vex the one who was called away. We will also suppose that I call another boy to me, who I have reason to believe is a sincere Christian, and say to him, 'Here is a new duty for you to perform this afternoon. This piece of poetry is to be copied; now do it carefully and faithfully. You know that this morning you committed yourself to God's care during the day; now remember that he has been watching you all the time thus far, and that he will be noticing you all the time you are doing this; he will be pleased if you do your duty faithfully.'

"The boys thus all go to writing. Now suppose a stranger should come in, and, seeing them all busy, should say to me,

"'What are all these boys doing?'

"'They are writing.'

"'What are they writing?'

"'They are writing a piece of poetry.'

"'They seem to be very busy; they are very industrious, good boys.'

"'Oh no! it is not by any means certain that they are *good* boys.'

"'I mean that they are good boys *now;* that they are doing right at *this time.*'

"'*That* is not certain; some of them are doing right and some are doing very wrong, though they are all writing the same piece of poetry.'

"The stranger would perhaps look surprised while I said this, and would ask an explanation, and I might properly reply as follows:

"'Whether the boys are at this moment doing right or wrong depends not so much upon what they are doing as upon the feelings of the heart with which they are doing it. I acknowledge that they are all doing the same thing outwardly; they are all writing the same extract, and they are all doing it attentively and carefully, but they are thinking of very different things.'

"'What are they thinking of?'

"'Do you see that boy?' I might say, pointing to one of them. 'His name is M. He is writing for money. He is saying to himself all the time, "I hope I shall get the quarter of a dollar." He is calculating what he shall buy with it, and every good or bad letter that he makes, he is considering the chance whether he shall succeed or fail in obtaining it.'

"'What is the next boy to him thinking of?'

"'His name is B. He is copying to oblige a little fellow whom he scarcely knows, and is trying to make his copy handsome, so as to give him pleasure. He is thinking how gratified his schoolmate will be when he receives it, and is forming plans to get acquainted with him.

"'Do you see that boy in the back seat? He has maliciously taken another boy's place just to spoil his work. He knows, too, that he is breaking the rules of the school in being out of his place, but he stays notwithstanding, and is delighting himself with thinking how disappointed and sad his schoolmate will be when he comes in and finds his work spoiled by having another handwriting in it, when he was depending on doing it all himself.'

"'I see,' the stranger might say by this time, 'that there is a great difference among these boys; have you told me about them all?'

"'No,' I might reply, 'there are several others. I will only mention one more. He sits in the middle of the second desk. He is writing carefully, simply because he wishes to do his duty and please God. He thinks that God is present, and loves him, and takes care of him, and he is obedient and grateful in return. I do not mean that he is all the time thinking of God, but love to him is his motive of effort.'

"Do you see now, boys, what I mean to teach you by this long supposition?"

"Yes, sir."

"I presume you do. Perhaps it would be difficult for you to express it in words; I can express it in general terms thus:

"*Our characters depend, not on what we do, but on the spirit and motive with which we do it.* What I have been saying throws light upon one important verse in the Bible, which I should like to have read. James, have you a Bible in your desk?"

"Yes, sir."

"Will you turn to 1 Samuel, xvi., 7, and then rise and read it? Read it loud, so that all the school can hear."

James read as follows:

"MAN LOOKETH ON THE OUTWARD APPEARANCE, BUT GOD LOOKETH ON THE HEART."

This is the way to reach the intellect and the heart of the young. Go *into detail.* Explain truth and duty, not in an abstract form, but exhibit it *in actual and living examples.*

(3.) Be very cautious how you bring in the awful sanctions of religion to assist you directly in the discipline of your school. You will derive a most powerful indirect assistance from the influence of religion in the little community which you govern, but this will be through the prevalence of its spirit in the hearts of your pupils, and not from any assistance which you can usually derive from it in managing particular cases of transgression. Many teachers make great mistakes in this respect. A bad boy, who has done something openly and directly subversive of the good order of the school, or the rights of his companions, is called before the master, who thinks that the most powerful weapon to wield against him is the Bible. So, while the trembling culprit stands before him, he administers to him a reproof, which consists of an almost ludicrous mixture of scolding, entreaty, religious instruction, and threatening of punishment. But such an occasion as this is no time to touch a bad boy's heart. He is steeled at such a moment against any thing but mortification and the desire to get out of the hands of the master, and he has an impression that the teacher appeals to religious principles only to assist him to sustain his own authority. Of course, religious truth, at such a time, can make no good impression. There may be exceptions to this rule. There doubtless are. I have found some; and every successful teacher who reads this will probably call to mind some which have occurred in the course of his own experience. I am only speaking of what ought to be the general rule, which is to reserve religious truths for moments of a different character altogether. Bring the principles of the Bible forward when the mind is calm, when the emotions are quieted, and all within is at rest; and in exhibiting them, be actuated, not by a desire to make your duties of government easier, but to promote the real and permanent happiness of your charge.

(4.) Do not be eager to draw from your pupils an expression of their personal interest in religious truth. Lay before them, and enforce, by all the means in your power, the principles of Christian duty, but do not converse with them for the purpose of gratifying your curiosity in regard to their piety, or your spiritual pride by counting up the numbers of those who have been led to piety by your influence. Beginning to act from Christian principle is the beginning of a new life, and it may be an interesting subject of inquiry to you to ascertain how many of your pupils have experienced the change; but, in many cases, it would merely gratify curiosity to know. There is no question, too, that, in very many instances, the faint glimmering of religious interest, which would have kindled into a bright flame, is extinguished at once, and perhaps forever, by the rough inquiries of a religious friend. Besides, if you make inquiries, and form a definite opinion of your pupils, they will know that this is your practice, and many a one will repose in the belief that you consider him or her a Christian, and you will thus increase the number, already unfortunately too large, of those who maintain the form and pretenses of piety without its power; whose hearts are filled with self-sufficiency and spiritual pride, and perhaps zeal for the truths and external duties of religion, while the real spirit of piety has no place there. They trust to some imaginary change, long since passed by, and which has proved to be spurious by its failing of its fruits. The best way—in fact, the only way—to guard against this danger, especially with the young, is to show, by your manner of speaking and acting on this subject at all times, that you regard a truly religious life as the only evidence of piety, and that, consequently, however much interest your pupils may apparently take in religious instruction, they can not know, and you can not know, whether Christian principle reigns within them in any other way than by following them through life, and observing how, and with what spirit, the various duties which devolve upon them are performed.

There are very many fallacious indications of piety, so fallacious and so plausible that there are very few, even among intelligent Christians, who are not often greatly deceived. "By their fruits ye shall know them," said the Savior; a direction sufficiently plain, one would think, and pointing to a test sufficiently easy to be applied. But it is slow and tedious work to wait for fruits, and we accordingly seek a criterion which will help us quicker to a result. You see your pupil serious and thoughtful. It is well; but it is not proof of piety. You see him deeply interested when you speak of his obligations to his Maker, and the duties he owes to Him. This is well, but it is no proof of piety. You know he reads his Bible daily, and offers his morning and evening prayers. When you speak to him of God's goodness, and of his past ingratitude, his bosom heaves with emotion, and the tear stands in his eye. It is all well. You may hope that he is going to devote his life to the service of God; but you can not know, you can not even believe with any great confidence. These appearances are not piety. They are not conclusive evidences of it. They are only, in the young, faint grounds of hope that the genuine fruits of piety will appear.

I am aware that there are many persons so habituated to judging with confidence of the piety of others from some such indications as I have described, that they will think I carry my cautions to the extreme. Perhaps I do; but the Savior said, "By their fruits ye shall know them," and it is safest to follow his direction.

By the word "fruits," however, our Savior unquestionably does not mean the mere moral virtues of this life. The fruits to be looked at are the fruits of *piety*, that is, indications of permanent attachment to the Creator, and a desire to obey his commands. We must look for these.

There is no objection to your giving particular individuals special instruction adapted to their wants and circumstances. You may do this by writing or in other ways, but do not lead them to make up their minds fully that they are Christians in such a sense as to induce them to feel that the work is done. Let them understand that becoming a Christian is *beginning* a work, not *finishing* it. Be cautious how you form an opinion even yourself on the question of the genuineness of their piety. Be content not to know. You will be more faithful and watchful if you consider it uncertain, and they will be more faithful and watchful too.

(5.) Bring very fully and frequently before your pupils the practical duties of religion in all their details, especially their duties at home, to their parents, and to their brothers and sisters. Do not, however, allow them to mistake morality for religion. Show them clearly what piety is in its essence, and this you can do most successfully by exhibiting its effects.

(6.) Finally, let me insert as the keystone of all that I have been saying in this chapter, be sincere, and ardent, and consistent in your own piety. The whole structure which I have been attempting to build will tumble into ruins without this. Be constantly watchful and careful, not only to maintain intimate communion with God, and to renew it daily in your seasons of retirement, but to guard your conduct. Let piety control and regulate it. Show your pupils that it makes you amiable, patient, forbearing, benevolent in little things as well as in great things, and your example will co-operate with your instructions, and allure your pupils to walk in the paths which you tread. But no clearness and faithfulness in religious teaching will atone for the injury which a bad example will effect. Conduct speaks louder than words, and no persons are more shrewd than the young to discover the hollowness of empty professions, and the heartlessness of mere pretended interest in their good.

I am aware that this book may fall into the hands of some who may take little interest in the subject of this chapter. To such I may perhaps owe an apology for having thus fully discussed a topic in which only a part of my readers can be supposed to be interested. My apology is this: It is obvious and unquestionable that we all owe allegiance to the Supreme. It is so obvious and unquestionable as to be entirely beyond the necessity of proof, for it is plain that nothing but such a bond of union can keep the peace among the millions of distinct intelligences with which the creation is filled. It is therefore the plain duty of every man to establish that connection between himself and his Maker which the Bible requires, and to do what he can to bring others to the peace and happiness of piety. These truths are so plain that they admit of no discussion and no denial, and it seems to me highly unsafe for any man to neglect or to postpone the performance of the duty which arises from them. A still greater hazard is incurred when such a man, having forty or fifty fellow-beings almost entirely under his influence, leads them, by his example, away from their Maker, and so far that he must, in many cases, hopelessly confirm the separation. With these views, I could not, when writing on the duties of a teacher of the young, refrain from bringing distinctly to view this which has so imperious a claim.

CHAPTER VI.

THE MOUNT VERNON SCHOOL.

PERHAPS there is no way by which teachers can, in a given time, do more to acquire a knowledge of their art, and an interest in it, than by visiting each others' schools.

It is not always the case that any thing is observed by the visitor which he can directly and wholly introduce into his own school, but what he sees suggests to him modifications or changes, and it gives him, at any rate, renewed strength and resolution in his work to see how similar objects are accomplished, or similar difficulties removed by others. I have often thought that there ought, on this account, to be far greater freedom and frequency in the interchange of visits than there is.

Next, however, to a visit to a school, comes the reading of a vivid description of it. I do not mean a cold, theoretical exposition of the general principles of its management and instruction, for these are essentially the same in all good schools. I mean a minute account of the plans and arrangements by which these general principles are applied. Suppose twenty of the most successful teachers in New England would write such a description, each of his own school, how valuable would be the volume which should contain them!

With these views, I have concluded to devote one chapter to the description of a school which was for several years under my care.* The account was originally prepared and *printed*, but not published, for the purpose of distribution among the scholars, simply because this seemed to be the easiest and surest method of making them, on their admission to the school, acquainted with its arrangements and plans. It is addressed, therefore, throughout to a pupil, and I preserve its original form, as, by its being addressed to pupils, and intended to influence them, it is an example of the mode of address and the kind of influence recommended in this work. It was chiefly designed for new scholars; a copy of it was presented to each on the day of her admission to the school, and it was made her first duty to read it attentively.

The system which it describes is one which gradually grew up in the institution under the writer's care. The school was commenced with a small number of pupils, and without any system or plan whatever, and the one here described was formed insensibly and by slow degrees, through the influence of various and accidental circumstances. I have no idea that it is superior to the plans of government and instruction adopted in many other schools. It is true that there must necessarily be *some* system in every large institution; but various instructors will fall upon different principles of organization, which will naturally be such as are adapted to the habits of thought and manner of instruction of their respective authors, and consequently each will be best for its own place. While, therefore, some system—some methodical arrangement is necessary in all schools, it is not necessary that it should be the same in all. It is not even desirable that it should be. I consider this plan as only one among a multitude of others, each of which will be success-

* The author was still connected with this school at the time when this work was written.

ful, not by the power of its intrinsic qualities, but just in proportion to the ability and faithfulness with which it is carried into effect.

There may be features of this plan which teachers who may read it may be inclined to adopt. In other cases, suggestions may occur to the mind of the reader, which may modify in some degree his present plans. Others may merely be interested in seeing how others effect what they, by other methods, are equally successful in effecting.

It is in these and similar ways that I have often myself been highly benefited in visiting schools and in reading descriptions of them, and it is for such purposes that I insert the account here.

TO A NEW SCHOLAR ON HER ADMISSION TO THE MOUNT VERNON SCHOOL.

As a large school is necessarily somewhat complicated in its plan, and as new scholars usually find that it requires some time and gives them no little trouble to understand the arrangements they find in operation here, I have concluded to write a brief description of these arrangements, by help of which you will, I hope, the sooner feel at home in your new place of duty. That I may be more distinct and specific, I shall class what I have to say under separate heads.

I. YOUR PERSONAL DUTY.

Your first anxiety as you come into the school-room, and take your seat among the busy multitude, if you are conscientiously desirous of doing your duty, will be, lest, ignorant as you are of the whole plan and of all the regulations of the institution, you should inadvertently do what will be considered wrong. I wish first, then, to put you at rest on this score. There is but one rule of this school. That you can easily keep.

You will observe on one side of my desk a clock upon the

wall, and not far from it a piece of apparatus that is probably new to you. It is a metallic plate, upon which are marked, in gilded letters, the words "*Study Hours.*" This is upright, but it is so attached by its lower edge to its support by means of a hinge that it can fall over from above, and thus be in a *horizontal* position; or it will rest in an *inclined* position—*half down*, as it is called. It is drawn up and let down by a cord passing over a pulley. When it passes either way, its upper part touches a bell, which gives all in the room notice of its motion.

Now when this "*Study Card*,"* as the scholars call it, is *up*, so that the words "STUDY HOURS" are presented to the view of the school, it is the signal for silence and study. THERE IS THEN TO BE NO COMMUNICATION AND NO LEAVING OF SEATS EXCEPT AT THE DIRECTION OF TEACHERS. When it is *half down*, each scholar may leave her seat and whisper, but she must do nothing which will disturb others. When it is *down*, all the duties of school are suspended, and scholars are left entirely to their liberty.

As this is the only rule of the school, it deserves a little more full explanation; for not only your progress in study, but your influence in promoting the welfare of the school, and, consequently, your peace and happiness while you are a member of it, will depend upon the strictness with which you observe it.

Whenever, then, the study card goes up, and you hear the sound of its little bell, immediately and instantaneously stop, whatever you are saying. If you are away from your seat, go directly to it and there remain, and forget in your own silent and solitary studies, so far as you can, all that are around you. You will remember that all *communication* is forbidden. Whispering, making signs, writing upon paper or a slate, bowing to any one, and, in fact, *every* possible way by which one person may have any sort of mental intercourse

* This apparatus has been previously described. See p. 47.

with another, is wrong. A large number of the scholars take a pride and pleasure in carrying this rule into as perfect an observance as possible. They say that as this is the only rule with which I trouble them, they ought certainly to observe this faithfully. I myself, however, put it upon other ground. I am satisfied that it is better and pleasanter for you to observe it most rigidly, if it is attempted to be enforced at all.

You will ask, "Can not we obtain permission of you or of the teachers to leave our seats or to whisper if it is necessary?" The answer is "No." You must never ask permission of me or of the teachers. You can leave seats or speak at the *direction* of the teachers, that is, when they of their own accord ask you to do it, but you are never to ask their permission. If you should, and if any teachers should give you permission, it would be of no avail. I have never given them authority to grant any permissions of the kind.

You will then say, "Are we never, on any occasion whatever, to leave our seats in study hours?" Yes, you are. There are two ways:

1. *At the direction of teachers.*—Going to and from recitations is considered as at the *direction* of teachers. So, if a person is requested by a teacher to transact any business, or is elected to a public office, or appointed upon a committee, leaving seats or speaking, so far as is really necessary for the accomplishing such a purpose, is considered as at the direction of teachers, and is consequently right. In the same manner, if a teacher should ask you individually, or give general notice to the members of a class, to come to her seat for private instruction, or to go to any part of the school-room for her, it would be right to do it. The distinction, you observe, is this: the teacher may, *of her own accord,* direct any leaving of seats which she may think necessary to accomplish the objects of the school. She must not, however, *at the request of an individual,* for the sake of her mere private conve-

nience, give her permission to speak or to leave her seat. If, for example, a teacher should say to you in your class, "As soon as you have performed a certain work you may bring it to me," you would, in bringing it, be acting under her *direction*, and would consequently do right. If, however, you should want a pencil, and should ask her to give you leave to borrow it, even if she should give you leave you would do wrong to go, for you would not be acting at her *direction*, but simply by her *consent*, and she has no authority to grant consent.

2. The second case in which you may leave your seat is when some very uncommon occurrence takes place, which is sufficient reason for suspending all rules. If your neighbor is faint, you may speak to her, and, if necessary, lead her out. If your mother or some other friend should come into the school-room, you can go and sit with her upon the sofa, and talk about the school.* And so in many other similar cases. Be very careful not to abuse this privilege, and make slight causes the grounds of your exceptions. It ought to be a very clear case. If a young lady is unwell in a trifling degree, so as to need no assistance, you would evidently do wrong to talk to her. The rule, in fact, is very similar to that which all well-bred people observe at church. They never speak or leave their seats unless some really important cause, such as sickness, requires them to break over all rules and go out. You have, in the same manner, in really important cases, such as serious sickness in your own case or in that of your companions, or the coming in of a stranger, or any thing else equally extraordinary, power to lay aside any rule, and to act as the emergency may require. In using this discretion, however, be sure to be on the safe side. In such cases, never ask permission. You must act on your own responsibility.

Reasons for this rule.—When the school was first estab-

* A sofa was placed against the wall, by the side of the teachers' desk, for the accommodation of visitors.

lished, there was no absolute prohibition of whispering. Each scholar was allowed to whisper in relation to her studies. They were often, very often, enjoined to be conscientious and faithful, but, as might have been anticipated, the experiment failed. It was almost universally the practice to whisper more or less about subjects entirely foreign to the business of the school. This all the scholars repeatedly acknowledged; and they almost unanimously admitted that the good of the school required the prohibition of all communication during certain hours. I gave them their choice, either always to ask permission when they wished to speak, or to have a certain time allowed for the purpose, during which free intercommunication might be allowed to all the school, with the understanding, however, that, out of this time, no permission should ever be asked or granted. They very wisely chose the latter plan, and the Study Card was constructed and put up, to mark the times of free communication and of silent study. The card was at first down every half hour for one or two minutes. The scholars afterward thinking that their intellectual habits would be improved and the welfare of the school promoted by their having a longer time for uninterrupted study, of their own accord, without any influence from me, proposed that the card should be down only once an hour. This plan was adopted by them by vote. I wish it to be understood that it was not *my* plan, but *theirs;* and that I am at any time willing to have the Study Card down once in half an hour, whenever a majority of the scholars, voting by ballot, desire it.

You will find that this system of having a distinct time for whispering, when all may whisper freely, all communication being entirely excluded at other times, will at first give you some trouble. It will be hard for you, if you are not accustomed to it, to learn conscientiously and faithfully to comply. Besides, at first you will often need some little information or desire to ask for an article which you might obtain in a moment, but which you can not innocently ask for till the card is down, and this might keep you waiting an hour. You will, however, after a few such instances, soon learn to make your preparations beforehand, and if you are a girl of enlarged views and elevated feelings, you will good-humoredly acquiesce in suffering a little inconvenience yourself for the sake of helping to preserve those *distinct* and well *defined* lines by which all boundaries must be marked in a large establishment, if order and system are to be preserved at all.

Though at first you may experience a little inconvenience, you will soon take pleasure in the scientific strictness of the plan. It will gratify you to observe the profound stillness of the room where a hundred are studying. You will take pleasure in observing the suddèn transition from the silence of study hours to the joyful sounds and the animating activity of recess when the Study Card goes down; and then when it rises again at the close of the recess, you will be gratified to observe how suddenly the sounds which have filled the air, and made the room so lively a scene, are hushed into silence by the single and almost inaudible touch of that little bell. You will take pleasure in this; for young and old always take pleasure in the strict and rigid operation of *system* rather than in laxity and disorder. I am convinced, also, that the scholars do like the operation of this plan, for I do not have to make any efforts to sustain it. With the exception that occasionally, usually not oftener than once in several months, I allude to the subject, and that chiefly on account of a few careless and unfaithful individuals, I have little to say or to do to maintain the authority of the Study Card. Most of the scholars obey it of their own accord, implicitly and cordially. And I believe they consider this faithful monitor not only one of the most useful, but one of the most agreeable friends they have. We should not only regret its services, but miss its company if it should be taken away.

This regulation then, namely, to abstain from all communication with one another, and from all leaving of seats, at certain times which are marked by the position of the Study Card, is the only one which can properly be called a *rule* of the school. There are a great many arrangements and plans relating to the *instruction* of the pupils, but no other specific *rules* relating to *their conduct.* You are, of course, while in the school, under the same moral obligations which rest upon you elsewhere. You must be kind to one another, respectful to superiors, and quiet and orderly in your deportment. You must do nothing to encroach upon another's rights, or to interrupt and disturb your companions in their pursuits. You must not produce disorder, or be wasteful of the public property, or do any thing else which you might know is in itself wrong. But you are to avoid these things, not because there are any rules in this school against them, for there are none, but because they are in *themselves wrong*—in all places and under all circumstances, wrong. The universal and unchangeable principles of duty are the same here as elsewhere. I do not make rules pointing them out, but expect that you will, through your own conscience and moral principle, discover and obey them.

It is wrong, for instance, for you to speak harshly or unkindly to your companions, or to do any thing to wound their feelings unnecessarily, in any way. But this is a universal principle of duty, not a rule of school.

So it is wrong for you to be rude and noisy, and thus disturb others who are studying, or to brush by them carelessly, so as to jostle them at their writing or derange their books. But to be careful not to do injury to others in the reckless pursuit of our own pleasures is a universal principle of duty, not a rule of school.

Such a case as this, for example, once occurred. A number of little girls began to amuse themselves in recess with running about among the desks in pursuit of one another, and they told me, in excuse for it, when I called them to account, that they did not know that it was "*against the rule.*"

"It is not against the rule," said I; "I have never made any rule against running about among the desks."

"Then," asked they, "did we do wrong?"

"Do you think it would be a good plan," I inquired, "to have it a common amusement in the recess for the girls to hunt each other among the desks?"

"No, sir," they replied, simultaneously.

"Why not? There are some reasons. I do not know, however, whether you will have the ingenuity to think of them."

"We may start the desks from their places," said one.

"Yes," said I, "they are fastened down very slightly, so that I may easily alter their position."

"We might upset the inkstands," said another.

"Sometimes," added a third, "we run against the scholars who are sitting in their seats."

"It seems, then, you have ingenuity enough to discover

the reasons. Why did not these reasons prevent your doing it?"

"We did not think of them before."

"True; that is the exact state of the case. Now, when persons are so eager to promote their own enjoyment as to forget the rights and the comforts of others, it is *selfishness.* Now is there any rule in this school against selfishness?"

"No, sir."

"You are right. There is not. But selfishness is wrong, very wrong, in whatever form it appears, here and every where else, and that whether I make any rules against it or not."

You will see, from this anecdote, that, though there is but one rule of the school, I by no means intend to say that there is only *one way of doing wrong here.* That would be very absurd. You *must not do any thing which you may know, by proper reflection, to be in itself wrong.* This, however, is a universal principle of duty, not a *rule* of the Mount Vernon School. If I should attempt to make rules which would specify and prohibit every possible way by which you might do wrong, my laws would be innumerable, and even then I should fail of securing my object, unless you had the disposition to do your duty. No legislation can enact laws as fast as a perverted ingenuity can find means to evade them.

You will perhaps ask what will be the consequence if we transgress either the single rule of the school or any of the great principles of duty. In other words, What are the punishments which are resorted to in the Mount Vernon School? The answer is, there are no punishments. I do not say that I should not, in case all other means should fail, resort to the most decisive measures to secure obedience and subordination. Most certainly I should do so, as it would plainly be my duty to do it. If you should at any time be so unhappy as to violate your obligations to yourself, to your companions, or to me—should you misimprove your time, or exhibit an unkind or a selfish spirit, or be disrespectful or insubordinate to your teachers, I should go frankly and openly, but kindly to you, and endeavor to convince you of your fault. I should very probably do this by addressing a note to you, as I suppose this would be less unpleasant to you than a conversation. In such a case, I shall hope that you will as frankly and openly reply, telling me whether you admit your fault and are determined to amend, or else informing me of the contrary. I shall wish you to be *sincere*, and then I shall know what course to take next. But as to the consequences which may result to you if you should persist in what is wrong, it is not necessary that you should know them beforehand. They who wander from duty always plunge themselves into troubles which they do not anticipate; and if you do what, at the time you are doing it, you know to be wrong, it will not be unjust that you should suffer the consequences, even if they were not beforehand understood and expected. This will be the case with you all through life, and it will be the case here.

I say it *will* be the case here; I ought rather to say that it will be the case should you be so unhappy as to do wrong and to persist in it. Such persistance, however, never occurs —at least it occurs so seldom, and at intervals so great, that every thing of the nature of punishment, that is, the depriving a pupil of any enjoyment, or subjecting her to any disgrace, or giving her pain in any way in consequence of her faults, except the simple pain of awakening conscience in her bosom, is almost entirely unknown. I hope that you will always be ready to confess and forsake your faults, and endeavor, while you remain in school, to improve in character, and attain, as far as possible, every moral excellence.

I ought to remark, before dismissing this topic, that I place very great confidence in the scholars in regard to their moral conduct and deportment, and they fully deserve it. I have no care and no trouble in what is commonly called *the gov-*

ernment of the school. Neither myself nor any one else is employed in any way in watching the scholars, or keeping any sort of account of them. I should not at any time hesitate to call all the teachers into an adjoining room, leaving the school alone for half an hour, and I should be confident that, at such a time, order, and stillness, and attention to study would prevail as much as ever. The scholars would not look to see whether I was in my desk, but whether the Study Card was up. The school was left in this way, half an hour every day, during a quarter, that we might have a teachers' meeting, and the studies went on generally quite as well, to say the least, as when the teachers were present. One or two instances of irregular conduct occurred. I do not now recollect precisely what they were. They were, however, fully acknowledged and not repeated, and I believe the scholars were generally more scrupulous and faithful then than at other times. They would not betray the confidence reposed in them. This plan was continued until it was found more convenient to have the teachers' meetings in the afternoons.

When any thing wrong is done in school, I generally state the case, and request the individuals who have done it to let me know who they are. They inform me sometimes by notes and sometimes in conversation; but they always inform me. The plan *always* succeeds. The scholars all know that there is nothing to be feared from confessing faults to me; but that, on the other hand, it is a most direct and certain way to secure returning peace and happiness.

I can illustrate this by describing a case which actually occurred, though the description is not to be considered so much an accurate account of what took place in a particular instance as an illustration of the *general spirit and manner* in which such cases are disposed of. I accidentally understood that some of the younger scholars were in the habit, during recesses and after school, of ringing the door-bell and then running away, to amuse themselves with the perplexity of their companions who should go to the door and find no one there. I explained in a few words, one day, to the school, that this was wrong.

"How many," I then asked, "have ever been put to the trouble to go to the door when the bell has thus been rung? They may rise."

A very large number of scholars stood up. Those who had done the mischief were evidently surprised at the extent of the trouble they had occasioned.

"Now," I continued, "I think all will be convinced that the trouble which this practice has occasioned to the fifty or sixty young ladies, who can not be expected to find amusement in such a way, is far greater than the pleasure it can have given to the few who are young enough to have enjoyed it. Therefore it was wrong. Do you think that the girls who rang the bell might have known this by proper reflection?"

"Yes, sir," the school generally answered.

"I do not mean," said I, "if they had set themselves formally at work to think about the subject, but with such a degree of reflection as ought reasonably to be expected of little girls in the hilarity of recess and of play."

"Yes, sir," was still the reply, but fainter than before.

"There is one way by which I might ascertain whether you were old enough to know that this was wrong, and that is by asking those who have refrained from doing this, because they supposed it would be wrong, to rise. Then, if some of the youngest scholars in school should stand up, as I have no doubt they would, it would prove that all might have known, if they had been equally conscientious. But if I ask those to rise who have *not* rung the bell, I shall make known to the whole school who they are that have done it, and I wish that the exposure of faults should be private, unless it is *necessary* that it should be public. I will, therefore, not do it. I have myself, however, no doubt that all might have known that it was wrong.

"There is," continued I, "another injury which must grow out of such a practice. This I should not have expected the little girls could think of. In fact, I doubt whether any in school will think of it. Can any one tell me what it is?"

No one replied.

"I should suppose that it would lead you to disregard the bell when it rings, and that consequently a gentleman or lady might sometimes ring in vain, the scholars near the door saying, 'Oh, it is only the little girls.'"

"Yes, sir," was heard from all parts of the room.

I found, from farther inquiry, that this had been the case, and I closed by saying,

"I am satisfied that those who have inadvertently fallen into this practice are sorry for it, and that if I should leave it here, no more cases of it would occur, and this is all I wish. At the same time, they who have done this will feel more effectually relieved from the pain which having done wrong must necessarily give them, if they individually acknowledge it to me. I wish, therefore, that all who have thus rung the bell in play would write me notes stating the facts. If any one does not do it, she will punish herself severely, for she will feel for many days to come that while her companions were willing to acknowledge their faults, she wished to conceal and cover hers. Conscience will reproach her bitterly for her insincerity, and, whenever she hears the sound of the door-bell, it will remind her not only of her fault, but of what is far worse, *her willingness to appear innocent when she was really guilty.*"

Before the close of the school I had eight or ten notes acknowledging the fault, describing the circumstances of each case, and expressing promises to do so no more.

It is by such methods as this, rather than by threatening and punishment, that I manage the cases of discipline which from time to time occur; but even such as this, slight as it is, occur very seldom. Weeks and weeks sometimes elapse without one. When they do occur, they are always easily settled by confession and reform. Sometimes I am asked to *forgive* the offense. But I have no power to forgive. God must forgive you when you do wrong, or the burden must remain. My duty is to take measures to prevent future transgression, and to lead those who have been guilty of it to God for pardon. If they do not go to Him, though they may satisfy me, as principal of a school, by not repeating the offence, they must remain *unforgiven.* I can *forget,* and I do forget. For example, in this last case I have not the slightest recollection of any individual who was engaged in it. The evil was entirely removed, and had it not afforded me a convenient illustration here, perhaps I should never have thought of it again; still, it may not yet be *forgiven.* It may seem strange that I should speak so seriously of God's forgiveness for such a trifle as that. Does He notice a child's ringing a door-bell in play? He notices when a child is willing to yield to temptation to do what she knows to be wrong, and to act even in the slightest trifle from a selfish disregard for the convenience of others. This spirit He always notices, and though I may stop any particular form of its exhibition, it is for Him alone to forgive it and to purify the heart from its power. But I shall speak more particularly on this subject under the head of Religious Instruction.

II. ORDER OF DAILY EXERCISES.

There will be given you, when you enter the school, a blank schedule, in which the divisions of each forenoon for one week are marked, and in which your own employments for every half hour are to be written. (A copy of this is inserted on page 222.)

This schedule, when filled up, forms a sort of a map for the week, in which you can readily find what are your duties for any particular time. The following description will enable you better to understand it.

Opening of the School.

The first thing which will call your attention as the hour for the commencement of the school approaches in the morning is the ringing of a bell five minutes before the time arrives by the regulator, who sits at the curtained desk before the Study Card. One minute before the time the bell is rung again, which is the signal for all to take their seats and prepare for the opening of the school. When the precise moment arrives, the Study Card is drawn up, and at the sound of its little bell, all the scholars recline their heads upon their desks, and unite with me in a very short prayer for God's protection and blessing during the day. I adopted the plan of allowing the scholars to sit, because I thought it would be pleasanter for them, and they have, in return, been generally, so far as I know, faithful in complying with my wish that they would all assume the posture proposed, so that the school may present the uniform and serious aspect which is proper when we are engaged in so solemn a duty. If you move your chair back a little, you will find the posture not inconvenient; but the only reward you will have for faithfully complying with the general custom is the pleasure of doing your duty, for no one watches you, and you would not be called to account should you neglect to conform to the usage of the school.

I hope, however, that you will conform to it. Indeed, all truly refined and well-bred people make it a universal rule of life to conform to the innocent religious usages of those around them, wherever they may be.

After the prayer we sing one or two verses of a hymn. The music is led by a piano, and we wish all to join in it who can sing. The exercises which follow are exhibited to the eye by the diagram on the next page.

MOUNT VERNON SCHOOL.

SCHEDULE OF STUDIES. 1833.

Miss

	First Hour.		Second Hour.				Third Hour.				Fourth Hour.	
	Evening Lessons.		Languages.		G.	R.	Mathematics.		G.	R.	Sections.	
Monday . . .												
Tuesday . . .												
Wednesday												
Thursday . .												
Friday												
Saturday . .												

I now proceed to describe in detail the several hours, as represented in the diagram.

First Hour.—Evening Lessons.

The first hour of the day, as you will see by the schedule, is marked evening lessons, because most, though not all, of the studies assigned to it are intended to be prepared out of school. These studies are miscellaneous in their character, comprising Geography, History, Natural and Intellectual Philosophy, and Natural History. This hour, like all the other hours for study, is divided into two equal parts, some classes reciting in the first part, and others in the second. A bell is always rung *five minutes before* the time for closing the recitation, to give the teachers notice that their time is nearly expired, and then again *at the time*, to give notice to new classes to take their places. Thus you will observe that five minutes before the half hour expires the bell will ring, soon after which the classes in recitation will take their seats. Precisely at the end of the half hour it will ring again, when new classes will take their places. In the same manner, notice is given five minutes before the second half of the hour expires, and so in all the other three hours.

At the end of the first hour the Study Card will be let half down five minutes, and you will perceive that the sound of its bell will immediately produce a decided change in the whole aspect of the room. It is the signal, as has been before explained, for universal permission to whisper and to leave seats, though not for loud talking or play, so that those who wish to continue their studies may do so without interruption. When the five-minute period has expired the card goes up again, and its sound immediately restores silence and order.

Second Hour.—Languages.

We then commence the second hour of the school. This

is devoted to the study of the languages. The Latin, French, and English classes recite at this time. By English classes I mean those studying the English *as a language*, that is, classes in Grammar, Rhetoric, and Composition. The hour is divided as the first hour is, and the bell is rung in the same way, that is, at the close of each half hour, and also five minutes before the close, to give the classes notice that the time for recitation is about to expire.

First General Exercise.

You will observe, then, that there follows upon the schedule a quarter of an hour marked G. That initial stands for General Exercise, and when it arrives each pupil is to lay aside her work, and attend to any exercise which may be proposed. This quarter of an hour is appropriated to a great variety of purposes. Sometimes I give a short and familiar lecture on some useful subject connected with science or art, or the principles of duty. Sometimes we have a general reading lesson. Sometimes we turn the school into a Bible class. Again, the time is occupied in attending to some *general* business of the school. The bell is rung one minute before the close of the time, and when the period appropriated to this purpose has actually expired, the Study Card, for the first time in the morning, is let entirely down, and the room is at once suddenly transformed into a scene of life, and motion, and gayety.

First Recess.

The time for the recess is a quarter of an hour, and, as you will see, it is marked R. on the schedule. We have various modes of amusing ourselves, and finding exercise and recreation in recesses. Sometimes the girls bring their battledores to school. Sometimes they have a large number of soft balls with which they amuse themselves. A more common amusement is marching to the music of the piano. For this purpose a set of signals by the whistle has been devised, by which commands are communicated to the school.

In these and similar amusements the recesses pass away, and one minute before it expires the bell is rung to give notice of the approach of study hours.

At this signal the scholars begin to prepare for a return to the ordinary duties of school, and when, at the full expiration of the recess, the Study Card again goes up, silence, and attention, and order is immediately restored.

Third Hour.—Mathematics.

There follows next, as you will see by reference to the schedule, an hour marked Mathematics. It is time for studying and reciting Arithmetic, Algebra, Geometry, and similar studies. It is divided, as the previous hours were, into two equal parts, and the bell is rung, as has been described, five minutes before the close, and also precisely at the close of each half hour.

Second General Exercise.—Business.

Then follow two quarter hours, appropriated like those heretofore described, the first to a General Exercise, the second to a recess. At the first of these the general business of the school is transacted. As this business will probably appear new to you, and will attract your attention, I will describe its nature and design.

At first you will observe a young lady rise at the secretary's desk to read a journal of what was done the day before. The notices which I gave, the arrangements I made, the subjects discussed and decided, and, in fact, every thing important and interesting in the business or occurrences of the preceding day, is recorded by the secretary of the school, and read at this time. This journal ought not to be a mere dry record of votes and business, but, as far as possible, an interesting description, in a narrative style, of the occurrences of the day. The secretary must keep a memorandum, and ascertain that every thing important really finds a place in the record, but she may employ any good writer in school to prepare, from her minutes, the full account.

After the record is read, you will observe me take from a little red morocco wrapper which has been brought to my desk a number of narrow slips of paper, which I am to read aloud. In most assemblies, it is customary for any person wishing it to rise in his place and propose any plan, or, as it is called, "make any motion" that he pleases. It would be unpleasant for a young lady to do this in presence of a hundred companions, and we have consequently resorted to another plan. The red wrapper is placed in a part of the room accessible to all, and any one who pleases writes upon a narrow slip of paper any thing she wishes to lay before the school, and deposits it there, and at the appointed time the whole are brought to me. These propositions are of various kinds. I can, perhaps, best give you an idea of them by such specimens as occur to me.

"A. B. resigns her office of copyist, as she is about to leave school."

"Proposed that a class in Botany be formed. There are many who would like to join it."

"When will vacation commence?"

"Proposed that a music committee be appointed, so that we can have some marching in recess."

"Proposed that school begin at nine o'clock."

"Mr. Abbott, will you have the goodness to explain to us what is meant by the Veto Message?"

"Proposed that we have locks upon our desks."

You see that the variety is very great, and there are usually from four or five to ten or fifteen of such papers daily. You will be at liberty to make in this way any suggestion or inquiry, or to propose any change you please in any part of the instruction or administration of the school. If any thing dissatisfies you, you ought not to murmur at it in private, or complain of it to your companions, thus injuring to no purpose both your own peace and happiness and theirs, but you ought immediately to bring up the subject in the way above described, that the evil may be removed. I receive some of the most valuable suggestions in this way from the older and most reflecting pupils. These suggestions are read. Sometimes I decide the question that arises myself. Sometimes I say that the pupils may decide it. Sometimes I ask their opinion and wishes, and then, after taking them into consideration, come to a conclusion.

For example, I will insert a few of these propositions, as these papers are called, describing the way in which they would be disposed of. Most of them are real cases.

"Mr. Abbott, the first class in Geography is so large that we have not room in the recitation seats. Can not we have another place?"

After reading this, I should perhaps say,

"The class in Geography may rise and be counted."

They rise. Those in each division are counted by the proper officer, as will hereafter be explained, and the numbers are reported aloud to me. It is all done in a moment.

"How many of you think you need better accommodations?"

If a majority of hands are raised, I say,

"I wish the teacher of that class would ascertain whether any other place of recitation is vacant, or occupied by a smaller class at that time, and report the case to me."

"Proposed that we be allowed to walk upon the common in the recesses."

"I should like to have some plan formed by which you can walk on the common in recesses, but there are difficulties. If all should go out together, it is probable that some would be rude and noisy, and that others would come back tardy and out of breath. Besides, as the recess is short, so many would be in haste to prepare to go out, that there would be a great crowd and much confusion in the ante-room and passage-ways. I do not mention these as insuperable objections, but only as difficulties which there must be some plan to avoid. Perhaps, however, they can not be avoided. Do any of you think of any plan?"

I see, perhaps, two or three hands raised, and call upon the individuals by name, and they express their opinions. One says that a part can go out at a time. Another proposes that those who are tardy one day should not go out again, &c.

"I think it possible that a plan can be formed on these or some such principles. If you will appoint a committee who will prepare a plan, and mature its details, and take charge of the execution of it, you may try the experiment. I will allow it to go on as long as you avoid the evils I have above alluded to."

A committee is then raised, to report in writing at the business hour of the following day.

"Proposed that the Study Card be down every half hour."

"You may decide this question yourselves. That you may vote more freely, I wish you to vote by ballot. The boxes will be open during the next recess. The vote-receivers will write the question and place it upon the boxes. All who feel interested in the subject may carry in their votes, Aye or Nay. When the result is reported to me I will read it to the school."

In this and similar ways the various business brought up is disposed of. This custom is useful to the scholars, for it exercises and strengthens their judgment and their reflecting powers more than almost any thing besides; so that, if interesting them in this way in the management of the school were of no benefit to me, I should retain the practice as most valuable to them. But it is most useful to me and to the school. I think that nothing has contributed more to its prosperity than the active interest which the scholars have always taken in its concerns, and the assistance they have rendered me in carrying my plans into effect.

You will observe that in transacting this business very little is actually done by myself, except making the ultimate decision. All the details of business are assigned to teachers, or to officers and committees appointed for the purpose. By this means we dispatch business very rapidly. The system of offices will be explained in another place; but I may say here that all appointments and elections are made in this quarter hour, and by means of the assistance of these officers the transaction of business is so facilitated that much more can sometimes be accomplished than you would suppose possible. I consider this period as one of the most important in the whole morning.

Second Recess.

After the expiration of the quarter hour above described, the Study Card is dropped, and a recess succeeds.

Fourth Hour.—Sections.

In all the former part of the day the scholars are divided into *classes*, according to their proficiency in particular branches of study, and they resort to their *recitations* for *instruction*. They now are divided into six *sections*, as we call them, and placed under the care of *superintendents*, not for instruction, but for what may be called supervision. *Teaching* a pupil is not all that is necessary to be done for her in school. There are many other things to be attended to, such as supplying her with the various articles necessary for her use, seeing that her desk is convenient, that her time is well arranged, that she has not too much to do nor too little, and that no difficulty which can be removed obstructs her progress in study or her happiness in school. The last hour is appropriated to this purpose, with the understanding, however, that such a portion of it as is not wanted by the superintendent is to be spent in study. You will see, then, when the last hour arrives, that all the scholars go in various directions to the

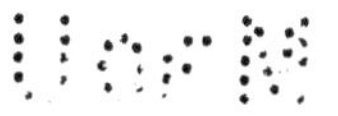

meetings of their respective sections. Here they remain as long as the superintendent retains them. Sometimes they adjourn almost immediately, perhaps after having simply attended to the distribution of pens for the next day; at other times they remain during the hour, attending to such exercises as the superintendent may plan. The design, however, and nature of this whole arrangement I shall explain more fully in another place.

Close of the School.

As the end of the hour approaches, five minutes' notice is given by the bell, and when the time arrives the Study Card is half dropped for a moment before the closing exercises. When it rises again the room is restored to silence and order. We then sing a verse or two of a hymn, and commend ourselves to God's protection in a short prayer. As the scholars raise their heads from the posture of reverence which they have assumed, they pause a moment till the regulator lets down the Study Card, and the sound of its bell is the signal that our duties at school are ended for the day.

III. INSTRUCTION AND SUPERVISION OF PUPILS.

For the instruction of the pupils the school is divided into *classes*, and for their general supervision into *sections*, as has been intimated under the preceding caption. The head of a *class* is called a *teacher*, and the head of a *section* a *superintendent*. The same individual may be both the teacher of a class and the superintendent of a section. The two offices are, however, entirely distinct in their nature and design. As you will perceive by recalling to mind the daily order of exercises, the classes meet and recite during the first three hours of the school, and the sections assemble on the fourth and last. We shall give each a separate description.

1. CLASSES.

The object of the division into classes is *instruction*. Whenever it is desirable that several individuals should pursue a particular study, a list of their names is made out, a book selected, a time for recitation assigned, a teacher appointed, and the exercises begin. In this way a large number of classes have been formed, and the wishes of parents, or the opinion of the principal, and, in many cases, that of the pupil, determines how many and what shall be assigned to each individual. A list of these classes, with the average age of the members, the name of the teacher, and the time of recitation, is posted in a conspicuous place, and public notice is given whenever a new class is formed. You will therefore have the opportunity to know all the arrangements of school in this respect, and I wish you to exercise your own judgment and discretion a great deal in regard to your studies. I do not mean I expect you to *decide*, but to *reflect* upon them. Look at the list, and consider what are most useful for you. Propose to me or to your parents changes, whenever you think they are necessary; and when you finish one study, reflect carefully, yourself, on the question what you shall next commence.

The scholars prepare their lessons when they please. They are expected to be present and prepared at the time of recitation, but they make the preparation when it is most convenient. The more methodical and systematic of the young ladies mark the times of *study* as well as of *recitation* upon their schedules, so that the employment of their whole time at school is regulated by a systematic plan. You will observe, too, that by this plan of having a great many classes reciting through the first three hours of the morning, every pupil can be employed as much or as little as her parents desire. In a case of ill health, she may, as has often been done in such cases at the request of parents, join one or two classes only, and occupy the whole forenoon in preparing for them, and be entirely free from school duties at home. Or she may, as is much more frequently the case, choose to join a great many classes, so as to fill up, perhaps, her whole schedule with recitations, in which case she must prepare all her lessons at home. It is the duty of teachers to take care, however, when a pupil pleads want of time as a reason for being unprepared in any lesson, that the case is fully examined, in order that it may be ascertained whether the individual has joined too many classes, in which case some one should be dropped, and thus the time and the employments of each individual should be so adjusted as to give her constant occupation *in school*, and as much more as her parents may desire. By this plan of the classes, each scholar advances just as rapidly in her studies as her time, and talents, and health will allow. No one is kept back by the rest. Each class goes on regularly and systematically, all its members keeping exactly together in that study; but the various members of it will have joined a greater or less number of other classes, according to their age, or abilities, or progress in study, so that all will or may have full employment for their time.

When you first enter the school, you will, for a day or two, be assigned to but few classes, for your mind will be distracted by the excitement of new scenes and pursuits, and the intellectual effort necessary for *joining* a class is greater than that requisite for *going on* with it after being once under way. After a few days you will come to me and say, perhaps (for this is ordinarily the process),

"Mr. Abbott, I think I have time for some more studies."

"I will thank you to bring me your schedule," I say in reply, "so that I can see what you have now to do."

By glancing my eye over the schedule in such a case, I see in a moment what duties have been already assigned you, and from my general schedule, containing all the studies of the school, I select what would be most suitable for you after conferring with you about your past pursuits, and your own wishes or those of your parents in regard to your future course. Additions are thus made until your time is fully occupied.

The manner of recitation in the classes is almost boundlessly varied. The design is not to have you commit to memory what the book contains, but to understand and digest it—to incorporate it fully into your own mind, that it may come up in future life in such a form as you wish it for use. Do not then, in ordinary cases, endeavor to fix *words*, but *ideas* in your minds. Conceive clearly—paint distinctly to your imagination what is described—contemplate facts in all their bearings and relations, and thus endeavor to exercise the judgment, and the thinking and reasoning powers, rather than the mere memory, upon the subjects which will come before you.

2. SECTIONS.

In describing the order of daily exercises, I alluded to the *sections* which assemble in the last hour of the school. It is necessary that I should fully describe the system of sections, as it constitutes a very important part of the plan of the school.

Besides giving the scholars the necessary intellectual instruction, there are, as I have already remarked, a great many other points which must receive attention in order to promote their progress, and to secure the regular operation and general welfare of the school. These various points have something common in their nature, but it is difficult to give them a common name. They are such as supplying the pupils with pens and paper, and stationery of other kinds; becoming acquainted with each individual; ascertaining that she has enough and not too much to do; arranging her work so that no one of her duties shall interfere with another; assisting her to discover and correct her faults, and removing any sources of difficulty or causes of discontent which may gradually come in her way. These, and a multitude of similar points, constituting what may be called the general *administration* of the school, become, when the number of pupils is large, a most important branch of the teacher's duty.

To accomplish these objects more effectually, the school is divided into SIX SECTIONS, arranged, not according to proficiency in particular studies, as the several classes are, but according to *age and general maturity of mind.* Each one of these sections is assigned to the care of a superintendent. These superintendents, it is true, during most of school hours, are also teachers. Their duties, however, as *Teachers* and as *Superintendents,* are entirely distinct. I shall briefly enumerate the duties which devolve upon her in the latter capacity.

1. A superintendent ought to prepare an exact list of the members of her section, and to become intimately acquainted with them, so as to be as far as possible their friend and confidante, and to feel a stronger interest in their progress in study and their happiness in school, and a greater personal attachment to them than to any other scholars.

2. She is to superintend the preparation of their schedules; to see that each one has enough and not too much to do, by making known to me the necessity of a change, where such necessity exists; to see that the schedules are submitted to the parents, and that their opinion or suggestions, if they wish to make any, are reported to me.

3. She is to take care that all the daily wants of her section are supplied—that all have pens and paper, and desks of suitable height. If any are new scholars, she ought to interest herself in assisting them to become acquainted in school; if they are friendless and alone, to find companions for them, and to endeavor in every way to make their time pass pleasantly and happily.

4. To watch the characters of the members of her section.

To inquire of their several teachers as to the progress they make in study, and the faithfulness and punctuality with which they prepare their lessons. She ought to ascertain whether they are punctual at school and regular in their habits—whether their desks are neat and well arranged, and their exercises carefully executed. She ought to correct, through her own influence, any evils of this kind she may find, or else immediately to refer the cases where this can not be done to me.

The better and the more pleasantly to accomplish the object of exerting a favorable influence upon the characters of the members of their section, the superintendents ought often to bring up subjects connected with moral and religious duty in section meetings. This may be done in the form of subjects assigned for composition, or proposed for free discussion in writing or conversation, or the superintendents may write themselves, and read to the section the instructions they wish to give.

When subjects for written composition are thus assigned, they should be so presented to the pupils as to lead their minds to a very practical mode of regarding them. For example, instead of simply assigning the subject *Truth* as the theme of an abstract moral essay, bring up definite points of a practical character, such especially as are connected with the trials and temptations of early life. "I wish you would all give me your opinions," the teacher might say in such a case, "on the question, What is the most frequent inducement that leads children to tell falsehoods? Also, do you think it is right to tell untruths to very little children, as many persons do, or to people who are sick? Also, whether it would be right to tell a falsehood to an insane man in order to manage him?"

Sometimes, instead of assigning a subject of composition *verbally*, the superintendent exhibits an engraving, and the several members of the class then write any thing they please which is suggested to them by the engraving. For example, suppose the picture thus exhibited were to represent a girl sewing in an attic. The compositions to which it would give

rise might be very various. One pupil would perhaps simply give an account of the picture itself, describing the arrangements of the room, and specifying the particular articles of furniture contained in it. Another would give a soliloquy supposed to be spoken by the sewing-girl as she sits at her work. Another would narrate the history of her life, of course an imaginary one. Another would write an essay on the advantages of industry and independence.

This is a very good way of assigning subjects of composition, and, if well managed, it may be the means of awakening a great interest in writing among almost all the pupils of a school.

5. Though the superintendents, as such, have, necessarily speaking, no *teaching* to do, still they ought particularly to secure the progress of every pupil in what may be called the *essential* studies, such as reading, writing, and spelling. For this purpose, they either see that their pupils are going on successfully in classes in school in these branches, or they may attend to them in the section, provided that they never allow such instruction to interfere with their more appropriate and important duties.

In a word, the superintendents are to consider the members of their sections as pupils confided to their care, and they are not merely to discharge mechanically any mere routine of duty, such as can be here pointed out, but to exert all their powers, their ingenuity, their knowledge of human character, their judgment and discretion, in every way, to secure for each of those committed to their care the highest benefits which the institution to which they belong can afford. They are to keep a careful and faithful record of their plans and of the history of their respective sections, and to endeavor as faithfully and as diligently to advance the interests of the members of them as if the sections were separate and independent schools of their own.

A great responsibility is thus evidently intrusted to them, but not a great deal of *power*. They ought not to make changes, except in very plain cases, without referring the subject to me. They ought not to make rash experiments, or even to try many new plans, without first obtaining my approval of them. They ought to refer all cases which they can not easily manage to my care. They ought to understand the distinction between *seeing that a thing is done* and *doing it*. For example, if a superintendent thinks that one of her section is in too high a class in Arithmetic, her duty is not to undertake, by her own authority, to remove her to a lower one, for, as superintendent, she has no authority over Arithmetic classes, nor should she go to the opposite extreme of saying, "I have no authority over Arithmetic classes, and therefore I have nothing to do with this case." She ought to go to the teacher of the class to which her pupil had been unwisely assigned, converse with her, obtain her opinion, then find some other class more suited to her attainments, and after fully ascertaining all the facts in the case, bring them to me, that I may make the change. This is *superintendence—looking over* the condition and progress of the scholar. The superintendents have thus great responsibility, and yet, comparatively, little power. They accomplish a great deal of good, and, in its ordinary course, it is by their direct personal efforts; but in making changes, and remedying defects and evils, they act generally in a different way.

The last hour of school is devoted to the sections. No classes recite then, but the sections meet, if the superintendents wish, and attend to such exercises as they provide. Each section has its own organization, its own officers and plans. These arrangements of course vary in their character according to the ingenuity and enterprise of the superintendents, and more especially according to the talents and intellectual ardor of the members of the section.

The two upper sections are called senior, the next two middle, and the two younger junior. The senior sections are distinguished by using paper for section purposes with a light blue tinge. To the middle sections is assigned a light straw color; and to the junior, pink. These colors are used for the schedules of the members, and for the records and other documents of the section.

This account, though it is brief, will be sufficient to explain to you the general principles of the plan. You will soon become acquainted with the exercises and arrangements of the particular section to which you will be assigned, and by taking an active interest in them, and endeavoring to co-operate with the superintendent in all her measures, and to comply with her wishes, you will very materially add to her happiness, and do your part toward elevating the character of the circle to which you will belong.

IV. OFFICERS.

In consequence of the disposition early manifested by the scholars to render me every assistance in their power in carrying into effect the plans of the school and promoting its prosperity, I gradually adopted the plan of assigning to various officers and committees a number of specific duties relating to the general business of the school. These officers have gradually multiplied as the school has increased and as business has accumulated. The system has, from time to time, been revised, condensed, and simplified, and at the present time it is thus arranged. The particular duties of each officer are minutely described to the individuals themselves at the time of their election; all I intend here is to give a general view of the plan, such as is necessary for the scholars at large.

There are, then, *five departments* of business intrusted to officers of the school. The names of the officers, and a brief exposition of their duties, are as follows:

[I omit the particular explanation of the duties of the officers, as the arrangement must vary in different schools, and the details of any one plan can only be useful in the school-room to which it belongs. It will be sufficient to name the officers of each department, with their duties, in general terms.]

1. REGULATORS.—To assist in the ordinary routine of business in school: ringing the bells; managing the Study Card; distributing and collecting papers; counting votes, &c.

2. SECRETARIES.—Keeping the records, and executing writing of various kinds.

3. ACCOUNTANTS.—Keeping a register of the scholars, and various other duties connected with the accounts.

4. LIBRARIANS.—To take charge of books and stationery.

5. CURATORS.—To secure neatness and good order in the apartments.

The secretaries and accountants are appointed by the principal, and will generally be chosen from the teachers. The first in each of the other departments are chosen by ballot, by the scholars. Each one thus chosen nominates the second in her department, and they two the assistants. These nominations must be approved at a teachers' meeting; for, if a scholar is inattentive to her studies, disorderly in her desk, or careless and troublesome in her manners, she evidently ought not to be appointed to public office. No person can hold an office in two of these departments. She can, if she pleases, however, resign one to accept another. Each of these departments ought often to assemble and consult together, and form plans for carrying into effect with greater efficiency the objects intrusted to them. They are to keep a record of all their proceedings, the head of the department acting as secretary for this purpose.

The following may be given as an example of the manner in which business is transacted by means of these officers. On the day that the above description of their duties was written, I wished for a sort of directory to assist the collector employed to receive payments for the bills, and, to obtain it, I took the following steps:

At the business quarter hour I issued the following order:

"Before the close of school, I wish the distributors to leave upon each of the desks a piece of paper" (the size I described). "It is for a purpose which I shall then explain."

Accordingly, at some leisure moment before the close of school, each one of the regulators went with her box to the stationery shelves, which you will see in the corners of the room, where a supply of paper of all the various sizes used in school is kept, and, taking out a sufficient number, they supplied all the desks in their respective divisions.

When the time for closing school arrived, I requested each young lady to write the name of her parent or guardian upon the paper, and opposite to it his place of business. This was done in a minute or two.

"All those whose parent's or guardian's name begins with a letter above *m* may rise."

They rose.

"The distributors may collect the papers."

The officers then passed round in regular order, each through her own division, and collected the papers.

"Deliver them at the accountants' desk."

They were accordingly carried there, and received by the accountants.

In the same manner, the others were collected and received by the accountants, but kept separate.

"I wish now the second accountant would copy these in a little book I have prepared for the purpose, arranging them alphabetically, referring all doubtful cases again to me."

The second accountant then arranged the papers, and prepared them to go into the book, and the writer who belongs to the department copied them fairly.

I describe this case, because it was one which occurred at the time I was writing the above description, and not because there is any thing otherwise peculiar in it. Such cases are continually taking place, and by the division of labor above illustrated, I am very much assisted in a great many of the duties which would otherwise consume a great portion of my time.

Any of the scholars may at any time make suggestions in writing to any of these officers or to the whole school; and if an officer should be partial, or unfaithful, or negligent in her duty, any scholar may propose her impeachment. After hearing what she chooses to write in her defense, a vote is taken on sustaining the impeachment. If it is sustained, she is deprived of the office, and another appointed to fill her place.

V. THE COURT.

I have already described how all serious cases of doing wrong or neglect of duty are managed in the school. I manage them myself, by coming as directly and as openly as I can to the heart and conscience of the offender. There are, however, a number of little transgressions, too small to be individually worthy of serious attention, but which are yet troublesome to the community when frequently repeated. These relate chiefly to *order in the school-rooms.* These misdemeanors are tried, half in jest and half in earnest, by a sort of *court,* whose forms of process might make a legal gentleman smile. They, however, fully answer our purpose. I can best give you an idea of the court by describing an actual trial. I ought, however, first to say that any young lady who chooses to be free from the jurisdiction of the court can signify that wish to me, and she is safe from it. This, however, is never done. They all see the useful influence of it, and wish to sustain it.

Near the close of school, I find, perhaps, on my desk a paper, of which the following may be considered a copy. It is called the indictment.

We accuse Miss A. B. of having waste papers in the aisle opposite her desk, at 11 o'clock, on Friday, Oct. 12.

C. D. } Witnesses.
E. F. }

I give notice after school that a case is to be tried. Those interested, twenty or thirty perhaps, gather around my desk, while the sheriff goes to summon the accused and the witnesses. A certain space is marked off as the precincts of the court, within which no one must enter in the slightest degree, on pain of imprisonment, that is, confinement to her seat until court adjourns.

"Miss A. B., you are accused of having an untidy floor about your desk. Have you any objection to the indictment?"

While she is looking over the indictment to discover a mis-spelled word, or an error in the date, or some other latent flaw, I appoint any two of the by-standers jury. The jury come forward to listen to the cause.

The accused returns the indictment, saying she has no objection, and the witnesses are called upon to present their testimony.

Perhaps the prisoner alleges in defense that the papers were out *in the aisle*, not *under her desk*, or that she did not put them there, or that they were too few or too small to deserve attention.

My charge to the jury would be somewhat as follows:

"You are to consider and decide whether she was guilty of disorder, taking into view the testimony of the witnesses and also her defense. It is considered here that each young lady is responsible not only for the appearance of the carpet *under her desk*, but also for *the aisle opposite to it*, so that her first ground of defense must be abandoned. So, also, with the second, that she did not put them there. She ought not to *have* them there. Each scholar must keep her own place in a proper condition; so that if disorder is found there, no matter who made it, she is responsible if she only had time to remove it. As to the third, you must judge whether enough has been proved by the witnesses to make out real disorder." The jury write *guilty* or *not guilty* upon the paper, and it is returned to me. If sentence is pronounced, it is usually confinement to the seat during a recess, or part of a recess, or something that requires a slight effort or sacrifice for the public good. The sentence is always something *real*, though always *slight*, and the court has a great deal of influence in a double way—making amusement and preserving order.

The cases tried are very various, but none of the serious business of the school is intrusted to it. Its sessions are always held out of school hours, and, in fact, it is hardly considered by the scholars as a constituent part of the arrangements of the school; so much so, that I hesitated much about inserting an account of it in this description.

VI. RELIGIOUS INSTRUCTION.

In giving you this account, brief as it is, I ought not to omit to speak of one feature of our plan, which we have always intended should be one of the most prominent and distinctive characteristics of the school. The gentlemen who originally interested themselves in its establishment had mainly in view the exertion, by the principal, of a decided moral and religious influence over the hearts of the pupils. Knowing, as they did, how much more dutiful and affectionate at home you would be, how much more successful in your studies at school, how much happier in your intercourse with each other, and in your prospects for the future both here and hereafter, if your hearts could be brought under the influence of Christian principle, they were strongly desirous that the school should be so conducted that its religious influence, though gentle and alluring in its character, should be frank, and open, and decided. I need not say that I myself entered very cordially into these views. It has been my constant effort, and one of the greatest sources of my enjoyment, to try to win my pupils to piety, and to create such an atmosphere in school that conscience, and moral principle, and affection for the unseen Jehovah should reign here. You can easily see how much pleasanter it is for me to have the school controlled by such influence, than if it were necessary for me to hire you to diligence in duty by prizes or rewards, or to deter you from neglect or from transgression by reproaches, and threatenings, and punishments.

The influence which the school has thus exerted has always been cordially welcomed by my pupils, and approved, so far as I have known, by their parents, though four or five denominations, and fifteen or twenty different congregations, have been from time to time represented in the school. There are few parents who would not like to have their children *Christians*—sincerely and practically so; for every thing which a parent can desire in a child is promoted just in proportion as she opens her heart to the influence of the spirit of piety. But that you may understand what course is taken, I shall describe, first, what I wish to effect in the hearts of my pupils, and then what means I take to accomplish the object.

1. A large number of young persons of your age, and in circumstances similar to those in which you are placed, perform with some fidelity their various outward duties, *but maintain no habitual and daily communion with God.* It is very wrong for them to live thus without God, but they do not see, or, rather, do not feel the guilt of it. They only think of their accountability to *human beings* like themselves; for example, their parents, teachers, brothers and sisters, and friends. Consequently, they think most of their *external* conduct, which is all that human beings can see. Their *hearts* are neglected, and become very impure, full of evil thoughts, and desires, and passions, which are not repented of, and consequently not forgiven. Now what I wish to accomplish in regard to all my pupils is, that they should begin to *feel their accountability to God*, and to act according to it; that they should explore their *hearts*, and ask God's forgiveness for all their past sins, through Jesus Christ, who died for them that they might be forgiven; and that they should from this time try to live *near to God*, feel his presence, and enjoy that solid peace and happiness which flows from a sense of his protection. When such a change takes place, it relieves the mind from that constant and irritating uneasiness which the great mass of mankind feel as a constant burden; the ceaseless forebodings of a troubled conscience reproaching them for their past accumulated guilt, and warning them of a judgment to come. The change which I endeavor to promote relieves the heart both of the present suffering and of the future danger.

After endeavoring to induce you to begin to act from Christian principle, I wish to explain to you your various duties to yourselves, your parents, and to God.

2. The measures to which I resort to accomplish these objects are three:

First, *Religious Exercises in School.*—We open and close the school with a very short prayer and one or two verses of a hymn. Sometimes I occupy ten or fifteen minutes at one of the general exercises, or at the close of the school, in giving instruction upon practical religious duty. The subjects are sometimes suggested by a passage of Scripture read for the purpose, but more commonly in another way.

You will observe often, at the close of the school or at an appointed general exercise, that a scholar will bring to my desk a dark-colored morocco wrapper containing several small strips of paper, upon which questions relating to moral or religious duty, or subjects for remarks from me, or anecdotes, or short statements of facts, giving rise to inquiries of various kinds, are written. This wrapper is deposited in a place accessible to all the scholars, and any one who pleases deposits in it any question or suggestion on religious subjects which may occur to her. You can at any time do this yourself, thus presenting any doubt, or difficulty, or inquiry which may at any time occur to you.

Secondly, *Religious Exercise on Saturday afternoon.*—In order to bring up more distinctly and systematically the subject of religious duty, I established, a long time ago, a religious meeting on Saturday afternoon. It is intended for those who feel interested in receiving such instruction, and who can conveniently attend at that time. If you have no other engagements, and if your parents approve of it, I should be happy to have you attend. There will be very little to interest you except the subject itself, for I make all the instructions which I give there as plain, direct, and practical as is in my power.

A considerable number of the scholars usually attend, and frequently bring with them many of their female friends. You can at any time invite any one whom you please to come to the meeting. It commences at half past three, and continues about half an hour.

Thirdly, *Personal Religious Instruction.*—In consequence of the large number of my pupils, and the constant occupation of my time in school, I have scarcely any opportunity of religious conversation with them, even with those who particularly desire it. The practice has therefore arisen, and gradually extended itself almost universally in school, of writing to me on the subject. These communications are usually brief notes, expressing the writer's interest in the duties of piety, or bringing forward her own peculiar practical difficulties, or making specific inquiries, or asking particular instruction in regard to some branch of religious duty. I answer in a similar way, very briefly and concisely, however, for the number of notes of this kind which I receive is very large, and the time which I can devote to such a correspondence necessarily limited. I should like to receive such communications from all my pupils; for advice or instruction communicated in reply, being directly personal, is far more likely to produce effect. Besides, my remarks, being in writing, can be read a second time, and be more attentively considered and reconsidered than when words are merely spoken. These communications must always be begun by the pupil. I never (unless there may be occasional exceptions in some few very peculiar cases) commence. I am prevented from doing this both by my unwillingness to obtrude such a subject personally upon those who might not welcome it, and by want of time. I have scarcely time to write to all those who are willing first to write to me. Many cases have occurred where individuals have strongly desired some private communication with me, but have hesitated long, and shrunk reluctantly from the first step. I hope it will not be so with you.

Should you ever wish to receive from me any direct religious instruction, I hope you will write immediately and freely. I shall very probably not even notice that it is the first time I have received such a communication from you. So numerous and so frequent are these communications, that I seldom observe, when I receive one from any individual for the first time, that it comes from one who has not written me before.

Such are the means to which I resort in endeavoring to lead my pupils to God and to duty, and you will observe that the whole design of them is to win and to allure, not to compel. The regular devotional exercises of school are all which you will *necessarily* witness. These are very short, occupying much less time than many of the pupils think desirable. The rest is all private and voluntary. I never make any effort to urge any one to attend the Saturday meeting, nor do I, except in a few rare and peculiar cases, ever address any one personally, unless she desires to be so addressed. You will be left, therefore, in this school, unmolested, to choose your own way. If you should choose to neglect religious duty, and to wander away from God, I shall still do all in my power to make you happy in school, and to secure for you in future life such a measure of enjoyment as can fall to the share of one over whose prospects in another world there hangs so gloomy a cloud. I shall never reproach you, and perhaps may not even know what your choice is. Should you, on the other hand, prefer the peace and happiness of piety, and be willing to begin to walk in its paths, you will find many, both among the teachers and pupils of the Mount Vernon School, to sympathize with you, and to encourage and help you on your way.

CHAPTER VII.

SCHEMING.

SOME of the best teachers in our country, or, rather, of those who might be the best, lose a great deal of their time, and endanger, or perhaps entirely destroy, their hopes of success by a scheming spirit, which is always reaching forward to something new. One has in his mind some new school-book by which Arithmetic, Grammar, or Geography are to be taught with unexampled rapidity, and his own purse to be filled in a much more easy way than by waiting for the rewards of patient industry. Another has the plan of a school, bringing into operation new principles of management or instruction, which he is to establish on some favored spot, and which is to become, in a few years, a second Hofwyl. Another has some royal road to learning, and, though he is trammeled and held down by what he calls the ignorance and stupidity of his trustees or his school committee, yet, if he could fairly put his principles and methods to the test, he is certain of advancing the science of education half a century at least at a single leap.

Ingenuity in devising new ways, and enterprise in following them, are among the happiest characteristics of a new country rapidly filling with a thriving population. Without these qualities there could be no advance; society must be stationary; and from a stationary to a retrograde condition, the progress is inevitable. The disposition to make improvements and changes may, however, be too great. If so, it must be checked. On the other hand, a slavish attachment to old established practices may prevail. Then the spirit of enterprise and experiment must be awakened and encouraged. Which of these two is to be the duty of a writer at any time will of course depend upon the situation of the community at the time when he writes, and of the class of readers for which he takes his pen. Now, at the present time, it is undoubtedly true, that while among the great mass of teachers there may be too little originality and enterprise, there is still among many a spirit of innovation and change to which a caution ought to be addressed. But, before I proceed, let me protect myself from misconception by one or two remarks.

1. There are a few individuals in various parts of our country who, by ingenuity and enterprise, have made real and important improvements in many departments of our science, and are still making them. The science is to be carried forward by such men. Let them not, therefore, understand that any thing which I shall say applies at all to those real improvements which are from time to time brought before the public. As examples of this, there might easily be mentioned, were it necessary, several new modes of study, and new text-books, and literary institutions on new plans, which have been brought forward within a few years, and have proved, on actual trial, to be of real and permanent value.

These are, or rather they were, when first conceived by the original projectors, new schemes, and the result has proved that they were good ones. Every teacher, too, must hope that such improvements will continue to be made. Let nothing, therefore, which shall be said on the subject of scheming in this chapter be interpreted as intended to condemn real improvements of this kind, or to check those which may now be in progress by men of age or experience, or of sound judgment, who are capable of distinguishing between a real improvement and a whimsical innovation which can never live any longer than it is sustained by the enthusiasm of the original inventor.

2. There are a great many teachers in our country who make their business a mere dull and formal routine, through which they plod on, month after month, and year after year, without variety or change, and who are inclined to stigmatize with the appellation of idle scheming all plans, of whatever kind, to give variety or interest to the exercises of the school. Now whatever may be said in this chapter against unnecessary innovation and change does not apply to efforts to secure variety in the details of daily study, while the great leading objects are steadily pursued. This subject has already been discussed in the chapter on Instruction, where it has been shown that every wise teacher, while he pursues the same great object, and adopts in substance the same leading measures at all times, will exercise all the ingenuity he possesses, and bring all his inventive powers into requisition to give variety and interest to the minute details.

To explain now what is meant by such scheming as is to be condemned, let us suppose a case which is not very uncommon. A young man, while preparing for college, takes a school. When he first enters upon the duties of his office, he is diffident and timid, and walks cautiously in the steps which precedent has marked out for him. Distrusting himself, he seeks guidance in the example which others have set for him, and, very probably, he imitates precisely, though it may be insensibly and involuntarily, the manners and the plans of his own last teacher. This servitude soon, however, if he is a man of natural abilities, passes away; he learns to try one experiment after another, until he insensibly finds that a plan may succeed, even if it was not pursued by his former teacher. So far it is well. He throws greater interest into his school, and into all its exercises, by the spirit with which he conducts them. He is successful. After the period of his services has expired, he returns to the pursuit of his studies, encouraged by his success, and anticipating farther triumphs in his subsequent attempts.

He goes on through college, we will suppose, teaching from time to time in the vacations, as opportunity occurs, taking more and more interest in the employment, and meeting with greater and greater success. This success is owing in a very great degree to the *freedom* of his practice, that is, to his escape from the thraldom of imitation. So long as he leaves the great objects of the school untouched, and the great features of its organization unchanged, his many plans for accomplishing these objects in new and various ways awaken interest and spirit both in himself and in his scholars, and all goes on well.

Now in such a case as this, a young teacher, philosophizing upon his success and the causes of it, will almost invariably make this mistake, namely, he will attribute to something essentially excellent in his plans the success which, in fact, results from the novelty of them.

When he proposes something new to a class, they all take an interest in it because it is *new*. He takes, too, a special interest in it because it is an experiment which he is trying, and he feels a sort of pride and pleasure in securing its success. The new method which he adopts may not be, *in itself*, in the least degree better than old methods, yet it may succeed vastly better in his hands than any old method he had tried before. And why? Why, because it is new. It awakens interest in his class, because it offers them variety; and it awakens interest in him, because it is a plan which he has devised, and for whose success, therefore, he feels that his credit is at stake. Either of these circumstances is abundantly sufficient to account for its success. Either of these would secure success, unless the plan was a very bad one indeed.

This may easily be illustrated by supposing a particular case. The teacher has, we will imagine, been accustomed to teach spelling in the usual way, by assigning a lesson in the spelling-book, which the scholars, after studying it in their seats, recite by having the words put to them individually in the class. After some time, he finds that one class has lost its interest in this study. He can compel them to study the lesson, it is true, but he perceives, perhaps, that it is a weary task to them. Of course, they proceed with less alacrity, and consequently with less rapidity and success. He thinks, very justly, that it is highly desirable to secure cheerful, not forced, reluctant efforts from his pupils, and he thinks of trying some new plan. Accordingly, he says to them,

"Boys, I am going to try a new plan for this class."

The mere annunciation of a new plan awakens universal attention. The boys all look up, wondering what it is to be.

"Instead of having you study your lessons in your seats, as heretofore, I am going to let you all go together into one corner of the room, and choose some one to read the lesson to you, spelling all the words aloud. You will all listen, and endeavor to remember how the difficult ones are spelled. Do you think you can remember?"

"Yes, sir," say the boys. Children always think they *can* do every thing which is proposed to them as a new plan or experiment, though they are very often inclined to think they *can not* do what is required of them as a task.

"You may have," continues the teacher, "the words read to you once or twice, just as you please. Only, if you have them read but once, you must take a shorter lesson."

He pauses and looks round upon the class. Some say "Once," some "Twice."

"I am willing that you should decide this question. How many are in favor of having shorter lessons, and having them read but once? How many prefer longer lessons, and having them read twice?"

After comparing the numbers, it is decided according to the majority, and the teacher assigns or allows them to assign a lesson.

"Now," he proceeds, "I am not only going to have you study in a different way, but recite in a different way too. You may take your slates with you, and after you have had time to hear the lesson read slowly and carefully twice, I shall come and dictate to you the words aloud, and you will all write them from my dictation. Then I shall examine your slates, and see how many mistakes are made."

Any class of boys, now, would be exceedingly interested in such a proposal as this, especially if the master's ordinary principles of government and instruction had been such as to interest the pupils in the welfare of the school and in their own progress in study. They will come together in the place assigned, and listen to the one who is appointed to read the words to them, with every faculty aroused, and their whole souls engrossed in the new duties assigned them. The teacher, too, feels a special interest in his experiment. Whatever else he may be employed about, his eye turns instinctively to this group with an intensity of interest which an experienced teacher who has long been in the field, and who has tried experiments of this sort a hundred times, can scarcely conceive; for let it be remembered that I am describing the acts and feelings of a new beginner, of one who is commencing his work with a feeble and trembling step, and perhaps this is his first step away from the beaten path in which he has been accustomed to walk.

This new plan is continued, we will suppose, for a week, during which time the interest of the pupils continues. They get longer lessons and make fewer mistakes than they did by the old method. Now, in speculating on this subject, the teacher reasons very justly that it is of no consequence whether the pupil receives his knowledge through the eye or through the ear; whether they study in solitude or in company. The point is to secure their progress in learning to spell the words of the English language, and as this point is secured far more rapidly and effectually by his new method, the inference is to his mind very obvious, that he has made a great improvement—one of real and permanent value. Perhaps he will consider it an extraordinary discovery.

But the truth is, that in almost all such cases as this, the secret of the success is not that the teacher has discovered a *better* method than the ordinary ones, but that he has discovered a *new* one. The experiment will succeed in producing more successful results just as long as the novelty of it continues to excite unusual interest and attention in the class, or the thought that it is a plan of the teacher's own invention leads him to take a peculiar interest in it. And this may be a month, or perhaps a quarter; and precisely the same effects would have been produced if the whole had been reversed, that is, if the plan of dictation had been the old one, which in process of time had, in this supposed school, lost its interest, and the teacher, by his ingenuity and enterprise, had discovered and introduced what is now the common mode.

"Very well," perhaps my reader will reply, "it is surely something gained to awaken and continue interest in a dull study for a quarter, or even a month. The experiment is worth something as a pleasant and useful change, even if it is not permanently superior to the other."

It is indeed worth something. It is worth a great deal; and the teacher who can devise and execute such plans, *understanding their real place and value, and adhering steadily through them all to the great object which ought to engage his attention*, is in the almost certain road to success as an instructor. What I wish is not to discourage such efforts; they ought to be encouraged to the utmost; but to have their real nature and design, and the real secret of their success fully understood, and to have the teacher, above all, take good care that all his new plans are made, not the substitutes for the great objects which he ought to keep steadily in view, but only the means by which he may carry them into more full and complete effect.

In the case we are supposing, however, we will imagine that the teacher does not do this. He fancies that he has made an important discovery, and begins to inquire whether the *principle*, as he calls it, can not be applied to some other studies. He goes to philosophizing upon it, and can find many reasons why knowledge received through the ear makes a more ready and lasting impression than when it comes through the eye. He attempts to apply the method to Arithmetic and Geography, and in a short time is forming plans for the complete metamorphosis of his school. When engaged in hearing a recitation, his mind is distracted with his schemes and plans, and instead of devoting his attention fully to the work he may have in hand, his thoughts are wandering continually to new schemes and fancied improvements, which agitate and perplex him, and which elude his efforts to give them a distinct and definite form. He thinks he must, however, carry out his *principle*. He thinks of its applicability to a thousand other cases. He revolves over and over again in his mind plans for changing the whole arrangement of his school. He is again and again lost in perplexity, his mind is engrossed and distracted, and his present duties are performed with no interest, and consequently with little spirit or success.

Now his error is in allowing a new idea, which ought only to have suggested to him an agreeable change for a time in one of his classes, to swell itself into undue and exaggerated importance, and to draw off his mind from what ought to be the objects of his steady pursuit.

Perhaps some teacher of steady intellectual habits and a well-balanced mind may think that this picture is fanciful, and that there is little danger that such consequences will ever actually result from such a cause. But, far from having exaggerated the results, I am of opinion that I might have gone much farther. There is no doubt that a great many instances have occurred in which some simple idea like the one I have alluded to has led the unlucky conceiver of it, in his eager pursuit, far deeper into the difficulty than I have here supposed. He gets into a contention with the school committee, that formidable foe to the projects of all scheming teachers; and it would not be very difficult to find many actual cases where the individual has, in consequence of some such idea, quietly planned and taken measures to establish some new institution, where he can carry on unmolested his plans, and let the world see the full results of his wonderful discoveries.

We have in our country a very complete system of literary institutions, so far as external organization will go, and the prospect of success is far more favorable in efforts to carry these institutions into more complete and prosperous operation, than in plans for changing them, or substituting others in their stead. Were it not that such a course would be unjust to individuals, a long and melancholy catalogue might easily be made out of abortive plans which have sprung up in the minds of young men in the manner I have described, and which, after perhaps temporary success, have resulted in partial or total failure. These failures are of every kind. Some are school-books on a new plan, which succeeds in the inventor's hand chiefly on account of the spirit which carried it into effect, but which in ordinary hands, and under ordinary circumstances, and especially after long-continued use, have failed of exhibiting any superiority. Others are institutions, commenced with great zeal by the projectors, and which prosper just as long as that zeal continues. Zeal will make any thing succeed for a time. Others are new plans of instruction or government, generally founded on some good principle carried to an extreme, or made to grow into exaggerated and disproportionate importance. Examples almost innumerable of these things might be particularized, if it were proper, and it would be found, upon examination, that the amount of ingenuity and labor wasted upon such attempts would have been sufficient, if properly expended, to have elevated very considerably the standard of education, and to have placed existing institutions in a far more prosperous and thriving state than they now exhibit.

The reader will perhaps ask, Shall we make no efforts at improvement? Must every thing in education go on in a uniform and monotonous manner, and, while all else is advancing, shall our cause alone stand still? By no means. It must advance; but let it advance mainly by the industry and fidelity of those who are employed in it; by changes slowly and cautiously made; not by great efforts to reach forward to brilliant discoveries, which will draw off the attention from essential duties, and, after leading the projector through perplexities and difficulties without number, end in mortification and failure.

Were I to give a few concise and summary directions in regard to this subject to a young teacher, they would be the following:

1. Examine thoroughly the system of public and private schools as now constituted in most of the states of this Union, until you fully understand it and appreciate its excellences and its completeness; see how fully it provides for the wants of the various classes of our population.

By this I mean to refer only to the completeness of the *system*, as a system of organization. I do not refer at all to the internal management of these institutions; this last is, of course, a field for immediate and universal effort at progress and improvement.

2. If, after fully understanding this system as it now exists, you are of opinion that something more is necessary; if you think some classes of the community are not fully provided for, or that some of our institutions may be advantageously exchanged for others, the plan of which you have in mind, consider whether your age, and experience, and standing as an instructor are such as to enable you to place confidence in your opinion.

I do not mean by this that a young man may not make a useful discovery, but only that he may be led away by the ardor of early life to fancy that essential and important which is really not so. It is important that each one should determine whether this is not the case with himself, if his mind is revolving some new plan.

3. Perhaps you are contemplating only a single new institution, which is to depend for its success on yourself and some coadjutors whom you have in mind and whom you well know. If this is the case, consider whether the establishment you are contemplating can be carried on, after you shall have left it, by such men as can ordinarily be obtained. If the plan is founded on some peculiar notions of your own, which would enable you to succeed in it when others, who might also be interested in such a scheme, would probably fail, consider whether there may not be danger that your plan may be imitated by others who can not carry it into successful operation, so that it may be the indirect means of doing injury. A man is, in some degree, responsible for his example and for the consequences which may indirectly flow from his course, as well as for the immediate results which he produces. The Fellenberg school at Hofwyl was perhaps, by its direct results, as successful for a time as any other institution in the world; but there is a great offset to the good which it has thus done to be found in the history of the thousand wretched imitations of it which have been started only to linger a little while and die, and in

which a vast amount of time, and talent, and money have been wasted.

4. Consider the influence you may have upon the other institutions of our country, by attaching yourself to some one under the existing organization. If you take an academy or a private school, constituted and organized like other similar institutions, success in your own will give you influence over others. A successful teacher of an academy raises the general standard of academic instruction. A college professor, if he brings extraordinary talents to bear upon the regular duties of that office, throws light, universally, upon the whole science of college discipline and instruction, and thus aids in infusing a continually renewed life and vigor into those venerable seats of learning that might otherwise sink into de-

crepitude and decay. By going, however, to some new field, establishing some new and fanciful institution, you take yourself from such a sphere; you exert no influence over others, except upon feeble imitators, who fail in their attempts, and bring discredit upon your plans by the awkwardness with which they attempt to adopt them. How much more service, then, to the cause of education will a man of genius render, by falling in with the regularly organized institutions of the country and elevating them, than if in early life he were to devote his powers to some magnificent project of an establishment to which his talents would unquestionably have given temporary success, but which would have taken him away from the community of teachers, and confined the results of his labors to the more immediate effects which his daily duties might produce.

5. Perhaps, however, your plan is not the establishment of some new institution, but the introduction of some new study or pursuit into the one with which you are connected. Before, however, you interrupt the regular arrangements of your school to make such a change, consider carefully what is the real and appropriate object of your institution. Every thing is not to be done in school. The principles of division of labor apply with peculiar force to this employment; so that you must not only consider whether the branch which you are now disposed to introduce is important, but whether it is really such an one as it is on the whole best to include among the objects to be pursued in such an institution. Many teachers seem to imagine that if any thing is in itself important, and especially if it is an important branch of education, the question is settled of its being a proper object of attention in school. But this is very far from being the case. The whole work of education can never be intrusted to the teacher. Much must of course remain in the hands of the parent; it ought so to remain. The object of a school is not to take children out of the parental hands, substituting the watch and guardianship of a stranger for the natural care of father and mother. Far from it. It is only the association of the children for those purposes which can be more successfully accomplished by association. It is a union for few, specific, and limited objects, for the accomplishment of that

part (and it is comparatively a small part of the general objects of education) which can be most successfully effected by public institutions and in assemblies of the young.

6. If the branch which you are desiring to introduce appears to you to be an important part of education, and if it seems to you that it can be most successfully attended to in schools, then consider whether the introduction of it, *and of all the other branches having equal claims*, will or will not give to the common schools too great a complexity. Consider whether it will succeed in the hands of ordinary teachers. Consider whether it will require so much time and effort as will draw off in any considerable degree, the attention of the teacher from the more essential parts of his duty. All will admit that it is highly important that every school should be simple in its plan—as simple as its size and general circumstances will permit, and especially that the public schools in every town and village of our country should never lose sight of what is and must be, after all, their great design—*teaching the whole population to read, write, and calculate.*

7. If it is a school-book which you are wishing to introduce, consider well before you waste your time in preparing it, and your spirits in the vexatious work of getting it through the press; whether it is, *for general use*, so superior to those already published as to induce teachers to make a change in favor of yours. I have italicized the words *for general use*, for no delusion is more common than for a teacher to suppose that because a text-book which he has prepared and uses in manuscript is better for *him* than any other work which he can obtain, it will therefore be better for *general circulation*. Every man, if he has any originality of mind, has of course some peculiar method of his own, and he can of course prepare a text-book which will be better adapted to this method than those ordinarily in use. The history of a vast number of text-books, Arithmetics, Geographies, and Grammars, is this: A man of somewhat ingenious mind,

adopts some peculiar mode of instruction in one of these branches, and is quite successful, not because the method has any very peculiar excellence, but simply because he takes a greater interest in it, both on account of its novelty and also from the fact that it is his own invention. He conceives the plan of writing a text-book to develop and illustrate this method. He hurries through the work. By some means or other he gets it printed. In due time it is regularly advertised. The journals of education give notice of it; the author sends a few copies to his friends, and that is the end of it. Perhaps a few schools may make a trial of it, and if, for any reason, the teachers who try it are interested in the work, probably in their hands it succeeds. But it does not succeed so well as to attract general attention, and consequently does not get into general circulation. The author loses his time and his patience. The publisher, unless, unfortunately, it was published on the author's account, loses his paper, and in a few months scarcely any body knows that such a book ever saw the light.

It is in this way that the great multitude of school-books which are now constantly issuing from the press take their origin. Far be it from me to discourage the preparation of good school-books. This department of our literature offers a fine field for the efforts of learning and genius. What I contend against is the endless multiplicity of useless works, hastily conceived and carelessly executed, and which serve no purpose but to employ uselessly talents which, if properly applied, might greatly benefit both the community and the possessor.

8. If, however, after mature deliberation, you conclude that you have the plan of a school-book which you ought to try to mature and execute, be slow and cautious about it. Remember that so great is now the competition in this branch, nothing but superior excellence or very extraordinary exertions will secure the favorable reception of a work. Examine all that your predecessors have done before you.

Obtain, whatever may be the trouble and expense, all other text-books on the subject, and examine them thoroughly. If you see that you can make a very decided advance on all that has been done, and that the public will probably submit to the inconvenience and expense of a change to secure the result of your labors, go forward slowly and carefully in your work, no matter how much investigation, how much time and labor it may require. The more difficulty you may find in gaining the eminence, the less likely will you be to be followed by successful competitors.

9. Consider, in forming your text-book, not merely the whole subject on which you are to write, but also look extensively and thoroughly at the institutions throughout the country, and consider carefully the character of the teachers by whom you expect it to be used. Sometimes a man publishes a text-book, and when it fails on trial, he says "it is because they did not know how to use it. The book in itself was good. The whole fault was in the awkwardness and ignorance of the teacher." How absurd! As if, to make a good text-book, it was not as necessary to adapt it to teachers as to scholars. A *good text-book, which the teachers for whom it was intended did not know how to use!!* In other words, a good contrivance, but entirely unfit for the purpose for which it was intended.

10. Lastly, in every new plan, consider carefully whether its success in your hands, after you have tried it and found it successful, be owing to its novelty and to your own special interest in it, or to its own innate and intrinsic superiority. If the former, use it so long as it will last, simply to give variety and interest to your plans. Recommend it in conversation or in other ways to teachers with whom you are acquainted, not as a wonderful discovery, which is going to change the whole science of education, but as one method among others which may be introduced from time to time to relieve the monotony of the teacher's labors.

In a word, do not go away from the established institutions of our country, or deviate from the great objects which are at present, and ought continually to be pursued by them, without great caution, circumspection, and deliberate inquiry. But, within these limits, exercise ingenuity and invention as much as you will. Pursue steadily the great objects which demand the teacher's attention. They are simple and few. Never lose sight of them, nor turn to the right or to the left to follow any ignis fatuus which may arise to allure you away, but exercise as much ingenuity and enterprise as you please in giving variety and interest to the modes by which these objects are pursued.

If planning and scheming are confined within these limits, and conducted on these principles, the teacher will save all the agitating perplexity and care which will otherwise be his continual portion. He can go forward peaceably and quietly, and while his own success is greatly increased, he may be of essential service to the cause in which he is engaged, by making known his various experiments and plans to others. For this purpose, it seems to me highly desirable that every teacher should KEEP A JOURNAL of all his plans. In these should be carefully entered all his experiments; the new methods he adopts; the course he takes in regard to difficulties which may arise, and any interesting incidents which may occur which it would be useful for him to refer to at some future time. These, or the most interesting of them, should be made known to other teachers. This may be done in several ways:

(1.) By publishing them in periodicals devoted to education. Such contributions, furnished by judicious men, would be among the most valuable articles in such a work. They would be far more valuable than any general speculations, however well conceived or expressed.

(2.) In newspapers intended for general circulation. There

are very few editors whose papers circulate in families who would not gladly receive articles of this kind to fill a teacher's department in their columns. If properly written, they would be read with interest and profit by multitudes of parents, and would throw much light on family government and instruction.

(3.) By reading them in teachers' meetings. If half a dozen teachers who are associated in the same vicinity would meet once a fortnight, simply to hear each other's journals, they would be amply repaid for their time and labor. Teachers' meetings will be interesting and useful, when those who come forward in them will give up the prevailing practice of delivering orations, and come down at once to the scenes and to the business of the school-room.

There is one topic connected with the subject of this chapter which deserves a few paragraphs. I refer to the rights of the committee, or the trustees, or patrons in the control of the school. The right to such control, when claimed at all, is usually claimed in reference to the teacher's new plans, which renders it proper to allude to the subject here; and it ought not to be omitted, for a great many cases occur in which teachers have difficulties with the trustees or committee of their school. Sometimes these difficulties result at last in an open rupture; at other times in only a slight and temporary misunderstanding, arising from what the teacher calls an unwise and unwarrantable interference on the part of the committee or the trustees in the arrangements of the school. Difficulties of some sort very often arise. In fact, a right understanding of this subject is, in most cases, absolutely essential to the harmony and co-operation of the teacher and the representatives of his patrons.

There are then, it must be recollected, three different parties connected with every establishment for education: the parents of the scholars, the teacher, and the pupils themselves. Sometimes, as, for example, in a common private school, the parents are not organized, and whatever influence they exert they must exert in their individual capacity. At other times, as in a common district or town school, they are by law organized, and the school committee chosen for this purpose are their legal representatives. In other instances, a board of trustees are constituted by the appointment of the founders of the institution, or by the Legislature of a state, to whom is committed the oversight of its concerns, and who are consequently the representatives of the founders and patrons of the school.

There are differences between these various modes of organization which I shall not now stop to examine, as it will be sufficiently correct for my purpose to consider them all as only various ways of organizing the *employers* in the contract by which the teacher is employed. The teacher is the agent; the patrons represented in these several ways are the principals. When, therefore, in the following paragraphs I use the word *employers*, I mean to be understood to speak of the committee, or the trustees, or the visitors, or the parents themselves, as the case in each particular institution may be; that is, the persons for whose purpose and at whose expense the institution is maintained, or their representatives.

Now there is a very reasonable and almost universally established rule, which teachers are very frequently prone to forget, namely, *the employed ought always to be responsible to the employers, and to be under their direction.* So obviously reasonable is this rule, and, in fact, so absolutely indispensable in the transaction of all the business of life, that it would be idle to attempt to establish and illustrate it here. It has, however, limitations, and it is applicable to a much greater extent, in some departments of human labor than in others. It is *applicable* to the business of teaching, and though I confess that it is somewhat less absolute and imperious here, still it is obligatory, I believe, to a far greater extent than teachers have been generally willing to admit.

A young lady, I will imagine, wishes to introduce the study of Botany into her school. The parents or the committee object; they say that they wish the children to confine their attention exclusively to the elementary branches of education. "It will do them no good," says the chairman of the committee, "to learn by heart some dozen or two of learned names. We want them to read well, to write well, and to calculate well, and not to waste their time in studying about pistils, and stamens, and nonsense."

Now what is the duty of the teacher in such a case? Why, very plainly her duty is the same as that of the governor of a state, where the people, through their representatives, regularly chosen, negative a proposal which he considers calculated to promote the public good. It is his duty to submit to the public will; and, though he may properly do all in his power to present the subject to his employers in such a light as to lead them to regard it as he does, he must still, until they do so regard it, bow to their authority; and every magistrate who takes an enlarged and comprehensive view of his duties as the executive of a republican community, will do this without any humiliating feelings of submission to unauthorized interference with his plans. He will, on the other hand, enjoy the satisfaction of feeling that he confines himself to his proper sphere, and leave to others the full possession of rights which properly pertain to them.

It is so with every case where the relation of employer and employed subsists. You engage a carpenter to erect a house for you, and you present your plan; instead of going to work and executing your orders according to your wishes, he falls to criticising and condemning it; he finds fault with this, and ridicules that, and tells you you ought to make such and such an alteration in it. It is perfectly right for him to give his opinion, in the tone and spirit of *recommendation or suggestion*, with a distinct understanding that with his employer rests the power and the right to decide. But how many teachers take possession of their school-room as though it was an empire in which they are supreme, who resist every interference of their employers as they would an attack upon their personal freedom, and who feel that in regard to every thing connected with school they have really no actual responsibility.

In most cases, the employers, knowing how sensitive teachers very frequently are on this point, acquiesce in it, and leave them to themselves. Whenever, in any case, they think that the state of the school requires their interference, they come cautiously and fearfully to the teacher, as if they were encroaching upon his rights, instead of advancing with the confidence and directness with which employers have always a right to approach the employed; and the teacher, with the view he has insensibly taken of the subject, being perhaps confirmed by the tone and manner which his employers use, makes the conversation quite as often an occasion of resentment and offense as of improvement. He is silent, perhaps, but in his heart he accuses his committee or his trustees of improper interference in *his* concerns, as though it was no part of *their* business to look after work which is going forward for their advantage, and for which they pay.

Perhaps some individuals who have had some collision with their trustees or committee will ask me if I mean that a teacher ought to be entirely and immediately under the supervision and control of the trustees, just as a mechanic is when employed by another man. By no means. There are various circumstances connected with the nature of this employment, such as the impossibility of the employers fully understanding it in all its details, and the character and the standing of the teacher himself, which always will, in matter of fact, prevent this. The employers always will, in a great many respects, place more confidence in the teacher and in his views than they will in their own. But still, the ultimate power is theirs. Even if they err, if they wish to have a course pursued which is manifestly inexpedient and wrong, *they still have a right to decide.* It is their work ; it is going on at their instance and at their expense, and the power of ultimate decision on all disputed questions must, from the very nature of the case, rest with them. The teacher may, it is true, have his option either to comply with their wishes or to seek employment in another sphere ; but while he remains in the employ of any persons, whether in teaching or in any other service, he is bound to yield to the wishes of his employers when they insist upon it, and to submit good-humoredly to their direction when they shall claim their undoubted right to direct.

This is to be done, it must be remembered, when they are wrong as well as when they are right. The obligation of the teacher is not founded upon *the superior wisdom* of his employers in reference to the business for which they have engaged him, for they are very probably his inferiors in this respect, but *upon their right as employers* to determine *how their own work shall be done.* A gardener, we will suppose, is engaged by a gentleman to lay out his grounds. The gardener goes to work, and, after a few hours, the gentleman comes out to see how he goes on and to give directions. He proposes something which the gardener, who, to make the case stronger, we will suppose knows better than the proprietor of the grounds, considers ridiculous and absurd ; nay, we will suppose *it is* ridiculous and absurd. Now what can the gardener do ? There are obviously two courses. He can say to the proprietor, after a vain attempt to convince him he is wrong, "Well, sir, I will do just as you say. The grounds are yours : I have no interest in it or responsibility, except to accomplish your wishes." This would be right. Or he might say, "Sir, you have a right to direct upon your own grounds, and I do not wish to interfere with your plans ; but I must ask you to obtain another gardener. I have a reputation at stake, and this work, if I do it even at your direction, will be considered as a specimen of my taste and of my planning, so that I must, in justice to myself, decline remaining in your employment." This, too, would be right, though probably, both in the business of gardening and of teaching, the case ought to be a strong one to render it expedient.

But it would not be right for him, after his employer should have gone away, to say to himself, with a feeling of resentment at the imaginary *interference*, "I shall not follow any such directions; I understand my own trade, and shall receive no instructions in it from him;" and then, disobeying all directions, go on and do the work contrary to the orders of his employer, who alone has a right to decide.

And yet a great many teachers take a course as absurd and unjustifiable as this would be. Whenever the parents, or the committee, or the trustees express, however mildly and properly, their wishes in regard to the manner in which they desire to have their own work performed, their pride is at once aroused. They seem to feel it an indignity to act in any other way than just in accordance with their own will and pleasure; and they absolutely refuse to comply, resenting the interference as an insult; or else, if they apparently yield, it is with mere cold civility, and entirely without any honest desire to carry the wishes thus expressed into actual effect.

Parents may, indeed, often misjudge. A good teacher will, however, soon secure their confidence, and they may acquiesce in his opinion. But they ought to be watchful, and the teacher ought to feel and acknowledge their authority on all questions connected with the education of their children. They have originally entire power in regard to the course which is to be pursued with them. Providence has made the parents responsible, and wholly responsible, for the manner in which their children are prepared for the duties of this life, and it is interesting to observe how very cautious the laws of society are about interfering with the parent's wishes in regard to the education of the child. There are many cases in which enlightened governments might make arrangements which would be better than those made by the parents if they are left to themselves. But they will not do it; they ought not to do it. God has placed the responsibility in the hands of the father and mother, and unless the manner in which it is exercised is calculated to endanger or to injure the community, there can rightfully be no interference except that of argument and persuasion.

It ought also to be considered that upon the parents will come the consequences of the good or bad education of their children, and not upon the teacher, and consequently it is right that they should direct. The teacher remains, perhaps, a few months with his charge, and then goes to other places, and perhaps hears of them no more. He has thus very little at stake. The parent has every thing at stake; and it is manifestly unjust to give one man the power of deciding, while he escapes all the consequences of his mistakes, if he makes any, and to take away all the *power* from those upon whose heads all the suffering which will follow an abuse of the power must descend.

CHAPTER VIII.

REPORTS OF CASES.

THERE is, perhaps, no way by which a writer can more effectually explain his views on the subject of education than by presenting a great variety of actual cases, whether real or imaginary, and describing particularly the course of treatment which he would recommend in each. This method of communicating knowledge is very extensively resorted to in the medical profession, where writers detail particular cases, and report the symptoms and the treatment for each succeeding day, so that the reader may almost fancy himself actually a visitor at the sick-bed, and the nature and effects of the various prescriptions become fixed in the mind with almost as much distinctness and permanency as actual experience would give.

This principle has been kept in view, the reader may perhaps think, too closely in all the chapters of this volume, almost every point brought up having been illustrated by anecdotes and narratives. I propose, however, devoting one chapter now to presenting a number of miscellaneous cases, without any attempt to arrange them. Sometimes the case will be merely stated, the reader being left to draw the inference; at others, such remarks will be added as the case suggests.

All will, however, be intended to answer some useful purpose, either to exhibit good or bad management and its consequences, or to bring to view some trait of human nature, as it exhibits itself in children, which it may be desirable for the teacher to know. Let it be understood, however, that these cases are not selected with reference to their being strange or extraordinary. They are rather chosen because they are common; that is, they, or cases similar, will be constantly occurring to the teacher, and reading such a chapter will be the best substitute for experience which the teacher can have. Some are descriptions of literary exercises or plans which the reader can adopt in classes or with a whole school; others are cases of discipline, good or bad management, which the teacher can imitate or avoid. The stories are from various sources, and are the results of the experience of several individuals.

1. Hats and Bonnets.—The master of a district school was accidentally looking out of the window one day, and he saw one of the boys throwing stones at a hat, which was put up for that purpose upon the fence. He said nothing about it at the time, but made a memorandum of the occurrence, that he might bring it before the school at the proper time. When the hour set apart for attending to the general business of the school had arrived, and all were still, he said,

"I saw one of the boys throwing stones at a hat to-day: did he do right or wrong?"

There were one or two faint murmurs which sounded like "*Wrong*," but the boys generally made no answer.

"Perhaps it depends a little upon the question whose hat it was. Do you think it does depend upon that?"

"Yes, sir."

"Well, suppose then it was not his own hat, and he was throwing stones at it without the owner's consent, would it be plain in that case whether he was doing right or wrong?"

"Yes, sir; wrong," was the universal reply.

"Suppose it was his own hat, would he have been right? Has a boy a right to do what he pleases with his own hat?"

"Yes, sir," "Yes, sir;" "No, sir," "No, sir," answered the boys, confusedly.

"I do not know whose hat it was. If the boy who did it is willing to rise and tell me, it will help us to decide this question."

The boy, knowing that a severe punishment was not in such a case to be anticipated, and, in fact, apparently pleased with the idea of exonerating himself from the blame of willfully injuring the property of another, rose and said,

"I suppose it was I, sir, who did it, and it was my own hat."

"Well," said the master, "I am glad that you are willing to tell frankly how it was; but let us look at this case. There are two senses in which a hat may be said to belong to any person. It may belong to him because he bought it and paid for it, or it may belong to him because it fits him and he wears it. In other words, a person may have a hat as his property, or he may have it only as a part of his dress. Now you see that, according to the first of these senses, all the hats in this school belong to your fathers. There is not, in fact, a single boy in this school who has a hat of his own."

The boys laughed.

"Is not this the fact?"

"Yes, sir."

"It certainly is so, though I suppose James did not consider it. Your fathers bought your hats. They worked for them and paid for them. You are only the wearers, and consequently every generous boy, and, in fact, every honest boy, will be careful of the property which is intrusted to him, but which, strictly speaking, is not his own.

2. Mistakes.—A wide difference must always be made

between mistakes arising from carelessness, and those resulting from circumstances beyond control, such as want of sufficient data, and the like. The former are always censurable; the latter never; for they may be the result of correct reasoning from insufficient data, and it is the reasoning only for which the child is responsible.

"What do you suppose a prophet is?" said a teacher to a class of little boys. The word occurred in their reading lesson.

The scholars all hesitated; at last one ventured to reply:

"If a man should sell a yoke of oxen, and get more for them than they are worth, he would be a prophet."

"Yes," said the instructor, "that is right; that is one kind of *profit*, but this is another and a little different," and he proceeded to explain the word, and the difference of the spelling.

This child had, without doubt, heard of some transaction of the kind which he described, and had observed that the word *profit* was applied to it. Now the care which he had exercised in attending to it at the time, and remembering it when the same word (for the difference in the spelling he of course knew nothing about) occurred again, was really commendable. The fact, which is a mere accident, that we affix very different significations to the same sound, was unknown to him. The fault, if any where, was in the language and not in him, for he reasoned correctly from the data he possessed, and he deserved credit for it.

The teacher should always discriminate carefully between errors of this kind, and those that result from culpable carelessness.

3. Tardiness.—"My duty to this school," said a teacher to his pupils, "demands, as I suppose you all admit, that I should require you all to be here punctually at the time appointed for the commencement of the school. I have done nothing on this subject yet, for I wished to see whether you

would not come early on principle. I wish now, however, to inquire in regard to this subject, and to ascertain how many have been tardy, and to consider what must be done hereafter."

He made the inquiries, and ascertained pretty nearly how many had been tardy, and how often within a week.

The number was found to be so great that the scholars admitted that something ought to be done.

"What shall I do?" asked he. "Can any one propose a plan which will remedy the difficulty?"

There was no answer.

"The easiest and pleasantest way to secure punctuality is for the scholars to come early of their own accord, upon principle. It is evident, from the reports, that many of you do so, but some do not. Now there is no other plan which will not be attended with very serious difficulty, but I am willing to adopt the one which will be most agreeable to yourselves, if it will be likely to accomplish the object. Has any one any plan to propose?"

There was a pause.

"It would evidently," continued the teacher, "be the easiest for me to leave this subject, and do nothing about it. It is of no personal consequence to me whether you come early or not, but as long as I hold this office I must be faithful, and I have no doubt the school committee, if they knew how many of you were tardy, would think I ought to do something to diminish the evil.

"The best plan that I can think of is that all who are tardy should lose their recess."

The boys looked rather anxiously at one another, but continued silent.

"There is a great objection to this plan from the fact that a boy is sometimes necessarily absent, and by this rule he will lose his recess with the rest, so that the innocent will be punished with the guilty."

"I should think, sir," said William, "that those who are *necessarily* tardy might be excused."

"Yes, I should be very glad to excuse them, if I could find out who they are."

The boys seemed to be surprised at this remark, as if they thought it would not be a difficult matter to decide.

"How can I tell?" asked the master.

"You can hear their excuses, and then decide."

"Yes," said the teacher: "but here are fifteen or twenty boys tardy this morning; now how long would it take me to hear their excuses, and understand each case thoroughly, so that I could really tell whether they were tardy from good reasons or not?"

No answer.

"Should you not think it would take a minute apiece?"

"Yes, sir."

"It would, undoubtedly, and even then I could not in many cases tell. It would take fifteen minutes, at least. I can not do this in school hours, for I have not time, and if I do it in recess it will consume the whole of every recess. Now I need the *rest* of a recess as well as you, and it does not seem to me to be just that I should lose the whole of mine every day, and spend it in a most unpleasant business, when I take pains myself to come punctually every morning. Would it be just?"

"No, sir."

"I think it would be less unjust to deprive all those of their recess who are tardy; for then the loss of a recess by a boy who had not been to blame would not be very common, and the evil would be divided among the whole; but in the plan of my hearing the excuses it would all come upon one."

After a short pause one of the boys said that they might be required to bring written excuses.

"Yes, that is another plan," said the teacher; "but there are objections to it. Can any of you think what they are? I suppose you have all been, either at this school or at some other, required to bring written excuses, so that you have seen the plan tried. Now have you never noticed any objection to it?"

One boy said that it gave the parents a great deal of trouble at home.

"Yes," said the teacher, "this is a great objection; it is often very inconvenient to write. But that is not the greatest difficulty; can any of you think of any other?"

There was a pause.

"Do you think that these written excuses are, after all, a fair test of the real reasons for tardiness? I understand that sometimes boys will tease their fathers or mothers for an excuse when they do not deserve it, 'Yes, sir,' and sometimes they will loiter about when sent of an errand before school, knowing that they can get a written excuse, when they might easily have been punctual."

"Yes, sir," "Yes, sir," said the boys.

"Well, now, if we adopt this plan, some unprincipled boy would always contrive to have an excuse, whether necessarily tardy or not; and, besides, each parent would have a different principle and a different opinion as to what was a reasonable excuse, so that there would be no uniformity, and, consequently, no justice in the operation of the system."

The boys admitted the truth of this, and, as no other plan was presented, the rule was adopted of requiring all those who were tardy to remain in their seats during the recess, whether they were necessarily tardy or not. The plan very soon diminished the number of loiterers.

4. HELEN'S LESSON.—The possibility of being inflexibly firm in measures, and, at the same time, gentle and mild in manners and language, is happily illustrated in the following description, which is based on an incident narrated by Mrs. Sherwood:

"Mrs. M. had observed, even during the few days that

Helen had been under her care, that she was totally unaccustomed to habits of diligence and application. After making all due allowance for long-indulged habits of indolence and inattention, she one morning assigned an easy lesson to her pupil, informing her at the same time that she should hear it immediately before dinner. Helen made no objections to the plan, but she silently resolved not to perform the required task. Being in some measure a stranger, she thought her aunt would not insist upon perfect obedience, and besides, in her estimation, she was too old to be treated like a child.

"During the whole morning Helen exerted herself to be mild and obliging; her conduct toward her aunt was uncommonly affectionate. By these and various other artifices she endeavored to gain her first victory. Meanwhile Mrs. M. quietly pursued her various avocations, without apparently noticing Helen's conduct. At length dinner-hour arrived; the lesson was called for, but Helen was unprepared. Mrs. M. told Helen she was sorry that she had not learned the lesson, and concluded by saying that she hoped she would be prepared before tea-time.

"Helen, finding she was not to come to the table, began to be a little alarmed. She was acquainted in some measure with the character of her aunt, still she hoped to be allowed to partake of the dessert, as she had been accustomed to on similar occasions at home, and soon regained her wonted composure. But the dinner-cloth was removed, and there sat Helen, suffering not a little from hunger; still she would not complain; she meant to convince her aunt that she was not moved by trifles.

"A walk had been proposed for the afternoon, and as the hour drew near, Helen made preparations to accompany the party. Mrs. M. reminded her of her lesson, but she just noticed the remark by a toss of the head, and was soon in the green fields, apparently the gayest of the gay. After her return from the excursion she complained of a head-ache, which in fact she had. She threw herself languidly on the sofa, sighed deeply, and took up her History.

"Tea was now on the table, and most tempting looked the white loaf. Mrs. M. again heard the pupil recite, but was sorry to find the lesson still imperfectly prepared. She left her, saying she thought half an hour's additional study would conquer all the difficulties she found in the lesson.

"During all this time Mrs. M. appeared so perfectly calm, composed, and even kind, and so regardless of sighs and doleful exclamations, that Helen entirely lost her equanimity, and let her tears flow freely and abundantly. Her mother was always moved by her tears, and would not her aunt relent? No. Mrs. M. quietly performed the duties of the table, and ordered the tea-equipage to be removed. This latter movement brought Helen to reflection. It is useless to resist, thought she; indeed, why should I wish to? Nothing too much has been required of me. How ridiculous I have made myself appear in the eyes of my aunt, and even of the domestics!

"In less than an hour she had the satisfaction of reciting her lesson perfectly; her aunt made no comments on the occasion, but assigned her the next lesson, and went on sewing. Helen did not expect this; she had anticipated a refreshing cup of tea after the long siege. She had expected that even something nicer than usual would be necessary to compensate her for her past sufferings. At length, worn out by long-continued watching and fasting, she went to the closet, provided herself with a cracker, and retired to bed to muse deliberately on the strange character of her aunt.

"Teachers not unfrequently threaten their pupils with some proper punishment, but, when obliged to put the threat into execution, contrive in some indirect way to abate its rigor, and thus destroy all its effects. For example, a mother was in the habit, when her little boy ran beyond his prescribed play-ground, of putting him into solitary confinement. On such occasions, she was very careful to have some amusing book or diverting plaything in a conspicuous part of the room, and not unfrequently a piece of gingerbread was given to solace the runaway. The mother thought it very strange her little boy should so often transgress, when he knew what to expect from such a course of conduct. The boy was wiser than the mother; he knew perfectly well how to manage the business. He could play with the boys beyond the garden gate, and if detected, to be sure he was obliged to spend a quiet hour in the pleasant parlor. But this was not intolerable as long as he could expect a paper of sugar-plums, a cake, or at least something amply to compensate him for the loss of a game at marbles."

5. Complaints of Long Lessons.—A college officer assigned lessons which the idle and ignorant members of the class thought too long. They murmured for a time, and at last openly complained. The other members of the class could say nothing in behalf of the professor, awed by the greatest of all fears to a collegian, the fear of being called a "*fisher*" or a "*blueskin.*" The professor paid no attention to the petitions and complaints which were poured in upon him, and which, though originated by the idle, all were compelled to vote for. He coldly, and with uncompromising dignity, went on; the excitement in the class increased, and what is called a college rebellion, with all its disastrous consequences to the infatuated rebels, ensued.

Another professor had the dexterity to manage the case in a different way. After hearing that there was dissatisfaction, he brought up the subject as follows:

"I understand, gentlemen, that you consider your lessons too long. Perhaps I have overrated the abilities of the class, but I have not intended to assign you more than you can accomplish. I feel no other interest in the subject than the pride and pleasure it would give me to have my class stand high, in respect to the amount of ground it has gone over, when you come to examination. I propose, therefore, that you appoint a committee, in whose abilities and judgment you can confide, and let them examine this subject and report. They might ascertain how much other classes have done, and how much is expedient for this class to attempt; and then, by estimating the number of recitations assigned to this study, they can easily determine what should be the length of the lessons."

The plan was adopted, and the report put an end to the difficulty.

6. English Composition.—The great prevailing fault of writers in this country is an affectation of eloquence. It is almost universally the fashion to aim, not at striking thoughts, simply and clearly expressed, but at splendid language, glowing imagery, and magnificent periods. It arises, perhaps, from the fact that public speaking is the almost universal object of ambition, and, consequently, both at school and at college, nothing is thought of but oratory. Vain attempts at oratory result, in nine cases out of ten, in grandiloquence and empty verbiage—common thoughts expressed in pompous periods.

The teacher should guard against this, and assign to children such subjects as are within the field of childish observation. A little skill on his part will soon determine the question which kind of writing shall prevail in his school. The following specimens, both written with some skill, will illustrate the two kinds of writing alluded to. Both were written by pupils of the same age, twelve; one a boy, the other a girl. The subjects were assigned by the teacher. I need not say that the following was the writer's first attempt at composition, and that it is printed without alteration.

The Pains of a Sailor's Life.

The joyful sailor embarks on board of his ship, the sails are spread to catch the playful gale, swift as an arrow he cuts the rolling wave. A few days thus sporting on the briny wave, when suddenly the sky is overspread with clouds, the rain descends in torrents, the sails are lowered, the gale begins, the vessel is carried with great velocity, and the shrouds, unable to support the tottering mast, gives way to the furious tempest; the vessel is drove among the rocks, is sprung aleak; the sailor works at the pumps till, faint and weary, is heard from below, six feet of water in the hold; the boats are got ready, but, before they are into them, the vessel is dashed against a reef of rocks; some, in despair, throw themselves into the sea; others get on the rocks without any clothes or provisions, and linger a few days, perhaps weeks or months, living on shell fish, or perhaps taken up by some ship; others get on pieces of the wreck, and perhaps be cast on some foreign country, where perhaps he may be taken by the natives, and sold into slavery where he never more returns.

In regard to the following specimen, it should be stated that when the subject was assigned, the pupil was directed to see how precisely she could imitate the language and conversation which two little children really lost in the woods would use. While writing, therefore, her mind was in pursuit of the natural and the simple, not of the eloquent.

Two Children lost in the Woods.

Emily. Look here! see how many berries I've got. I don't believe you've got so many.

Charles. Yes, I'm sure I have. My basket's almost full; and if we hurry, we shall get ever so many before we go home. So pick away as fast as you can, Emily.

Emily. There, mine is full. Now we'll go and find some flowers for mother. You know somebody told us there were some red ones close to that rock.

Charles. Well, so we will. We'll leave our baskets here, and come back and get them.

Emily. But if we can't find our way back, what shall we do?

Charles. Poh! I can find the way back. I only want a quarter to seven years old, and I sha'n't lose myself, I know.

Emily. Well, we've got flowers enough, and now I'm tired and want to go home.

Charles. I don't; but, if you are tired, we'll go and find our baskets.

Emily. Where do you think they are? We've been looking a great while for them. I know we are lost, for when we went after the flowers we only turned once, and coming back we have turned three times.

Charles. Have we? Well, never mind, I guess we shall find them.

Emily. I'm afraid we sha'n't. Do let's run.

Charles. Well, so do. Oh, Emily! here's a brook, and I am sure we didn't pass any brook going.

Emily. Oh dear! we must be lost. Hark! Charles, didn't you hear that dreadful noise just now? Wasn't it a bear?

Charles. Poh! I should love to see a bear here. I guess, if he should come near me, I would give him one good slap that would make him feel pretty bad. I could kill him at the first hit.

Emily. I should like to see you taking hold of a bear. Why, didn't you know bears were stronger than men? But only see how dark it grows; we sha'n't see ma to-night, I'm afraid.

Charles. So am I: do let's run some more.

Emily. Oh, Charles, do you believe we shall ever find the way out of this dreadful long wood?

Charles. Let's scream, and see if somebody won't come.

Emily. Well (screaming), ma! ma!

Charles (screaming also). Pa! pa!

Emily. Oh dear! there's the sun setting. It will be dreadfully dark by-and-by, won't it?

We have given enough for a specimen. The composition, though faulty in many respects, illustrates the point we had in view.

7. Insincere Confession.—An assistant in a school informed the principal that she had some difficulty in preserving order in a certain class composed of small children. The principal accordingly went into the class, and something like the following dialogue ensued:

"Your teacher informs me," said the principal, "that there is not perfect order in the class. Now if you are satisfied that there has not been order, and wish to help me discover and correct the fault, we can do it very easily. If, on the other hand, you do not wish to co-operate with me, it will be a little more difficult for me to correct it, and I must take a different course. Now I wish to know, at the outset, whether you do or do not wish to help me?"

A faint "Yes, sir," was murmured through the class.

"I do not wish you to assist me unless you really and honestly desire it yourselves; and if you undertake to do it, you must do it honestly. The first thing which will be necessary will be an open and thorough exposure of all which has been wrong, and this, you know, will be unpleasant. But I will put the question to vote by asking how many are willing that I should know, entirely and fully, all that they have done in this class that has been wrong?"

Very nearly all the hands were raised at once, promptly, and the others were gradually brought up, though with more or less of hesitation.

"Are you willing not only to tell me yourselves what you have done, but also, in case any one has forgotten something which she has done, that others should tell me of it?"

The hands were all raised.

After obtaining thus from the class a distinct and universal expression of willingness that all the facts should be made known, the principal called upon all those who had any thing to state to raise their hands, and those who raised them had opportunity to say what they wished. A great number of very trifling incidents were mentioned, such as could not have produced any difficulty in the class, and, consequently, could not have been the real instances of disorder alluded to. Or at least it was evident, if they were, that in the statement they must have been so palliated and softened that a really honest confession had not been made. This result might, in such a case, have been expected. Such is human nature, that in nine cases out of ten, unless such a result had been particularly guarded against, it would have inevitably followed.

Not only will such a result follow in individual cases like this, but, unless the teacher watches and guards against it, it will grow into a habit. I mean, boys will get a sort of an idea that it is a fine thing to confess their faults, and by a show of humility and frankness will deceive their teacher, and perhaps themselves, by a sort of acknowledgment, which in fact exposes nothing of the guilt which the transgressor professes to expose. A great many cases occur where teachers are pleased with the confession of faults, and scholars perceive it, and the latter get into the habit of coming to the teacher when they have done something which they think may get them into difficulty, and make a sort of half confession, which, by bringing forward every palliating circumstance, and suppressing every thing of different character, keeps entirely out of view all the real guilt of the transgression. The criminal is praised by the teacher for the frankness and honesty of the confession, and his fault is freely forgiven. He goes away, therefore, well satisfied with himself, when, in fact, he has been only submitting to a little mortification, voluntarily, to avoid the danger of a greater; much in the same spirit with that which leads a man to receive the small-pox by inoculation, to avoid the danger of taking it in the natural way.

The teacher who accustoms his pupils to confess their faults voluntarily ought to guard carefully against this danger. When such a case as the one just described occurs, it will afford a favorable opportunity of showing distinctly to pupils the difference between an honest and a hypocritical confession. In this instance the teacher proceeded thus:

"Now there is one more question which I wish you all to answer by your votes honestly. It is this. Do you think that the real disorder which has been in this class—that is, the real cases which you referred to when you stated to me that you thought that the class was not in good order—have been now really exposed, so that I honestly and fully understand the case? How many suppose so?"

Not a single hand was raised.

"How many of you think, and are willing to avow your opinion, that I have *not* been fully informed of the case?"

A large proportion held up their hands.

"Now it seems the class pretended to be willing that I

should know all the affair. You pretended to be willing to tell me the whole, but when I call upon you for the information, instead of telling me honestly, you attempt to amuse me by little trifles, which in reality made no disturbance, and you omit the things which you know were the real objects of my inquiries. Am I right in my supposition?"

They were silent. After a moment's pause, one perhaps raised her hand, and began now to confess something which she had before concealed.

The teacher, however, interrupted her by saying,

"I do not wish to have the confession made now. I gave you all time to do that, and now I should rather not hear any more about the disorder. I gave an opportunity to have it acknowledged, but it was not honestly improved, and now I should rather not hear. I shall probably never know.

"I wished to see whether this class would be honest—really honest, or whether they would have the insincerity to pretend to be confessing when they were not doing so honestly, so as to get the credit of being frank and sincere, when in reality they are not so. Now am I not compelled to conclude that this latter is the case?"

Such an example will make a deep and lasting impression. It will show that the teacher is upon his guard; and there are very few so hardened in deception that they would not wish that they had been really sincere rather than rest under such an imputation.

8. Court.—A pupil, quite young (says a teacher), came to me one day with a complaint that one of her companions had got her seat. There had been some changes in the seats by my permission, and probably, from some inconsistency in the promises which I had made, there were two claimants for the same desk. The complainant came to me, and appealed to my recollection of the circumstance.

"I do not recollect any thing about it," said I.

"Why, Mr. B.!" replied she, with astonishment.

"No," said I; "you forget that I have, every day, arrangements, almost without number, of such a kind to make, and as soon as I have made one I immediately forget all about it."

"Why, don't you remember that you got me a new baize?"

"No; I ordered a dozen new baizes at that time, but I do not remember who they were for."

There was a pause; the disappointed complainant seemed not to know what to do.

"I will tell you what to do. Bring the case into court, and I will try it regularly."

"Why, Mr. B., I do not like to do any thing like that about it; besides, I do not know how to write an indictment."

"Oh," I answered, "the scholars will like to have a good trial, and this will make a new sort of case. All our cases thus far have been for *offenses*—that is what they call criminal cases—and this will be only an examination of the conflicting claims of two individuals to the same property, and it will excite a good deal of interest. I think you had better bring it into court."

She went slowly and thoughtfully to her seat, and presently returned with an indictment.

"Mr. B., is this right?"

It was as follows:

I accuse Miss A. B. of coming to take away my seat—the one Mr. B. gave me.

Witnesses, { C. D. / E. T. }

"Why—yes—that will do; and yet it is not exactly right. You see this is what they call a *civil* case."

"I don't think it is very *civil*."

"No, I don't mean it was civil to take your seat, but this is not a case where a person is prosecuted for having done any thing wrong."

The plaintiff looked a little perplexed, as if she could not understand how it could be otherwise than wrong for a girl to usurp her seat.

"I mean, you do not bring it into court as a case of wrong. You do not want her to be punished, do you?"

"No, I only want her to give me up my seat; I don't want her to be punished."

"Well, then, you see that, although she may have done wrong to take your seat, it is not in that point of view that you bring it into court. It is a question about the right of property, and the lawyers call such cases *civil* cases, to distinguish them from cases where persons are tried for the purpose of being punished for doing wrong. These last are called criminal cases."

The aggrieved party still looked perplexed. "Well, Mr. B.," she continued, "what shall I do? How shall I write it? I can not say any thing about *civil* in it, can I?"

A form was given her which would be proper for the purpose, and the case was brought forward, and the evidence on both sides examined. The irritation of the quarrel was soon dissipated in the amusement of a semi-serious trial, and both parties good-humoredly acquiesced in the decision.

9. Teachers' Personal Character.—Much has been said within a few years, by writers on the subject of education in this country, on the desirableness of raising the business of teaching to the rank of a learned profession. There is but one way of doing this, and that is raising the personal characters and attainments of the teachers themselves. Whether an employment is elevated or otherwise in public estimation, depends altogether on the associations connected with it in the public mind, and these depend altogether on the characters of the individuals who are engaged in it. Franklin, by the simple fact that he was a printer himself, has done more toward giving dignity and respectability to the employment of

printing, than a hundred orations on the intrinsic excellence of the art. In fact, all mechanical employments have, within a few years, risen in rank in this country, not through the influence of efforts to impress the community directly with a sense of their importance, but simply because mechanics themselves have risen in intellectual and moral character. In the same manner, the employment of the teacher will be raised most effectually in the estimation of the public, not by the individual who writes the most eloquent oration on the intrinsic dignity of the art, but by the one who goes forward most successfully in the exercise of it, and who, by his general attainments and public character, stands out most fully to the view of the public as a well-informed, liberal-minded, and useful man.

If this is so—and it can not well be denied—it furnishes to every teacher a strong motive to exertion for the improvement of his own personal character. But there is a stronger motive still in the results which flow directly to himself from such efforts. No man ought to engage in any business which, as mere business, will engross all his time and attention. The Creator has bestowed upon every one a mind, upon the cultivation of which our rank among intelligent beings, our happiness, our moral and intellectual power, every thing valuable to us, depend; and after all the cultivation which we can bestow, in this life, upon this mysterious principle, it will still be in embryo. The progress which it is capable of making is entirely indefinite. If by ten years of cultivation we can secure a certain degree of knowledge and power, by ten more we can double, or more than double it, and every succeeding year of effort is attended with equal success. There is no point of attainment where we must stop, or beyond which effort will bring in a less valuable return.

Look at that teacher, and consider for a moment his condition. He began to teach when he was twenty years of age, and now he is forty. Between the ages of fifteen and twenty he made a vigorous effort to acquire such an education as would fit him for these duties. He succeeded, and by these efforts he raised himself from being a mere laborer, receiving for his daily toil a mere daily subsistence, to the respectability and the comforts of an intellectual pursuit. But this change once produced, he stops short in his progress. Once seated in his desk, he is satisfied, and for twenty years he has been going through the same routine, without any effort to advance or to improve. He does not reflect that the same efforts, which so essentially altered his condition and prospects at twenty, would have carried him forward to higher and higher sources of influence and enjoyment as long as he should continue them. His efforts ceased when he obtained a situation as teacher at fifty dollars a month, and, though twenty years have glided away, he is now exactly what he was then.

There is probably no employment whatever which affords so favorable an opportunity for personal improvement—for steady intellectual and moral progress, as that of teaching. There are two reasons for this:

First, there is time for it. With an ordinary degree of health and strength, the mind can be vigorously employed at least ten hours a day. As much as this is required of students in many literary institutions. In fact, ten hours to study, seven to sleep, and seven to food, exercise, and recreation, is perhaps as good an arrangement as can be made; at any rate, very few persons will suppose that such a plan allows too little under the latter head. Now six hours is as much as is expected of a teacher under ordinary circumstances, and it is as much as ought ever to be bestowed; for, though he may labor four hours out of school in some new field, his health and spirits will soon sink under the burden, if, after his weary labors during the day in school, he gives up his evenings to the same perplexities and cares. And it is not necessary. No one who knows any thing of the nature of the human mind, and who will reflect a moment on the subject, can doubt that a man can make a better school by expending six hours labor upon it with alacrity and ardor, than he can by driving himself on to ten. Every teacher, therefore, who is commencing his work, should begin with the firm determination of devoting only six hours daily to the pursuit. Make as good a school, and accomplish as much for it as you can in six hours, and let the rest go. When you come from your school-room at night, leave all your perplexities and cares behind you. No matter what unfinished business or unsettled difficulties remain, dismiss them till another sun shall rise, and the hour of duty for another day shall come. Carry no school-work home with you, and do not even talk of your school-work at home. You will then get refreshment and rest. Your mind, during the evening, will be in a different world from that in which you have moved during the day. At first this will be difficult. It will be hard for you, unless your mind is uncommonly well disciplined, to dismiss all your cares; and you will think, each evening, that some peculiar emergency demands your attention *just at that time*, and that as soon as you have passed the crisis you will confine yourself to what you admit are generally reasonable limits; but if you once allow school, with its perplexities and cares, to get possession of the rest of the day, it will keep possession. It will intrude itself into all your waking thoughts, and trouble you in your dreams. You will lose all command of your powers, and, besides cutting off from yourself all hope of general intellectual progress, you will, in fact, destroy your success as a teacher. Exhaustion, weariness, and anxiety will be your continual portion, and in such a state no business can be successfully prosecuted.

There need be no fear that employers will be dissatisfied if the teacher acts upon this principle. If he is faithful, and enters with all his heart into the discharge of his duties during six hours, there will be something in the ardor, and alacrity, and spirit with which his duties will be performed which parents and scholars will both be very glad to receive in exchange for the languid, and dull, and heartless toil in which the other method must sooner or later result.

If the teacher, then, will confine himself to such a portion of time as is, in fact, all he can advantageously employ, there will be much left which can be devoted to his own private employment—more than is usual in the other avocations of life. In most of these other avocations there is not the same necessity for limiting the hours which a man may devote to his business. A merchant, for example, may be employed nearly all the day at his counting-room, and so may a mechanic. A physician may spend all his waking hours in visiting patients, and feel little more than healthy fatigue. The reason is, that in all these employments, and, in fact, in most of the employments of life, there is so much to diversify, so many little incidents constantly occurring to animate and relieve, and so much bodily exercise, which alternates with and suspends the fatigues of the mind, that the labors may be much longer continued, and with less cessation, and yet the health not suffer. But the teacher, while engaged in his work, has his mind continually on the stretch. There is little relief, little respite, and he is almost entirely deprived of bodily exercise. He must, consequently, limit his hours of attending to his business, or his health will soon sink under labors which Providence never intended the human mind to bear.

There is another circumstance which facilitates the progress of the teacher. It is a fact that all this general progress has a direct and immediate bearing upon his pursuits. A lawyer may read in an evening an interesting book of travels, and find nothing to help him with his case, the next day, in court; but almost every fact which the teacher thus learns will come *at once into use* in some of his recitations at school.

We do not mean to imply by this that the members of the legal profession have not need of a great variety and extent of knowledge; they doubtless have. It is simply in the *directness* and *certainty* with which the teacher's knowledge may be applied to his purpose that the business of teaching has the advantage over every other pursuit.

This fact, now, has a very important influence in encouraging and leading forward the teacher to make constant intellectual progress, for every step brings at once a direct reward.

10. The Chestnut Burr.—*A story for school-boys.*—One fine Saturday afternoon, in the fall of the year, the master was taking a walk in the woods, and he came to a place where a number of boys were gathering chestnuts.

One of the boys was sitting upon a bank trying to open some chestnut burrs which he had knocked off from the tree. The burrs were green, and he was attempting to open them by pounding them with a stone.

He was a very impatient boy, and was scolding in a

loud, angry tone against the burrs. He did not see, he said, what in the world chestnuts were made to grow so for. They ought to grow right out in the open air, like apples, and not have such vile porcupine skins on them, just to plague the boys. So saying, he struck with all his might a fine large burr, crushed it to pieces, and then jumped up, using at the same time profane and wicked words. As soon as he turned round he saw the master standing very near him. He felt very much ashamed and afraid, and hung down his head.

"Roger," said the master (for this boy's name was Roger), "can you get me a chestnut burr?"

Roger looked up for a moment to see whether the master was in earnest, and then began to look around for a burr.

A boy who was standing near the tree, with a red cap full of burrs in his hand, held out one of them. Roger took the burr and handed it to the master, who quietly put it into his pocket, and walked away without saying a word.

As soon as he was gone, the boy with the red cap said to Roger, "I expected that the master would have given you a good scolding for talking so."

"The master never scolds," said another boy, who was sitting on a log pretty near, with a green satchel in his hand, "but you see if he does not remember it." Roger looked as if he did not know what to think about it.

"I wish," said he, "I knew what he is going to do with that burr."

That afternoon, when the lessons had been all recited, and it was about time to dismiss the school, the boys put away their books, and the master read a few verses in the Bible, and then offered a prayer, in which he asked God to forgive all the sins which any of them had committed that day, and to take care of them during the night. After this he asked the boys all to sit down. He then took his handkerchief out of his pocket and laid it on the desk, and afterward he put his hand into his pocket again, and took out the chestnut burr, and all the boys looked at it.

"Boys," said he, "do you know what this is?"

One of the boys in the back seat said, in a half whisper, "It is nothing but a chestnut burr."

"Lucy," said the master to a bright-eyed little girl near him, "what is this?"

"It is a chestnut burr, sir," said she.

"Do you know what it is for?"

"I suppose there are chestnuts in it."

"But what is this rough, prickly covering for?"

Lucy did not know.

"Does any body here know?" said the master.

One of the boys said that he supposed it was to hold the chestnuts together, and keep them up on the tree.

"But I heard a boy say," replied the master, "that they ought not to be made to grow so. The nut itself, he thought, ought to hang alone on the branches, without any prickly covering, just as apples do."

"But the nuts themselves have no stems to be fastened by," answered the same boy.

"That is true; but I suppose this boy thought that God could have made them grow with stems, and that this would have been better than to have them in burrs."

After a little pause the master said that he would explain to them what the chestnut burr was for, and wished them all to listen attentively.

"How much of the chestnut is good to eat, William?" asked he, looking at a boy before him.

"Only the meat."

"How long does it take the meat to grow?"

"All summer, I suppose, it is growing."

"Yes; it begins early in the summer, and gradually swells and grows until it has become of full size, and is ripe, in the fall. Now suppose there was a tree out here near the school-house, and the chestnut meats should grow upon it without any shell or covering; suppose, too, that they should taste like good ripe chestnuts at first, when they were very small. Do you think they would be safe?"

William said "No; the boys would pick and eat them before they had time to grow."

"Well, what harm would there be in that? Would it not be as well to have the chestnuts early in the summer as to have them in the fall?"

William hesitated. Another boy who sat next to him said,

"There would not be so much meat in the chestnuts if they were eaten before they had time to grow."

"Right," said the master; "but would not the boys know this, and so all agree to let the little chestnuts stay, and not eat them while they were small?"

William said he thought they would not. If the chestnuts were good, he was afraid they would pick them off and eat them if they were small.

All the rest of the boys in the school thought so too.

"Here, then," said the master, "is one reason for having prickles around the chestnuts when they are small. But then it is not necessary to have all chestnuts guarded from boys in this way; a great many of the trees are in the woods, which the boys do not see; what good do the burrs do in these trees?"

The boys hesitated. Presently the boy who had the green satchel under the tree with Roger, who was sitting in one corner of the room, said,

"I should think they would keep the squirrels from eating them.

"And besides," continued he, after thinking a moment, "I should suppose, if the meat of the chestnut had no covering, the rain would wet it and make it rot, or the sun might dry and wither it."

"Yes," said the master, "these are very good reasons why the nut should be carefully guarded. First the meats are packed away in a hard brown shell, which the water can not get through; this keeps it dry, and away from dust and other things which might injure it. Then several nuts thus protected grow closely together inside this green, prickly covering, which spreads over them and guards them from the larger animals and the boys. Where the chestnut gets its full growth and is ripe, this covering, you know, splits open, and the nuts drop out, and then any body can get them and eat them."

The boys were then all satisfied that it was better that chestnuts should grow in burrs.

"But why," asked one of the boys, "do not apples grow so?"

"Can any body answer that question?" asked the master.

The boy with the green satchel said that apples had a smooth, tight skin, which kept out the wet, but he did not see how they were guarded from animals.

The master said it was by their taste. "They are hard and sour before they are full grown, and so the taste is not pleasant, and nobody wishes to eat them, except sometimes a few foolish boys, and these are punished by being made sick. When the apples are full grown, they change from sour to sweet, and become mellow—then they can be eaten. Can you tell me of any other fruits which are preserved in this way?"

One boy answered, "Strawberries and blackberries;" and another said, "Peaches and pears."

Another boy asked why the peach-stone was not outside the peach, so as to keep it from being eaten; but the master said that he would explain this another time. Then he dismissed the scholars, after asking Roger to wait until the rest had gone, as he wished to see him alone.

Several of the articles which follow were communicated

for this work by different teachers, at the request of the author.

11. The Series of Writing Lessons.—Very many pupils soon become weary of the dull and monotonous business of writing, unless some plans are devised to give interest and variety to the exercise; and, on this account, this branch of education, in which improvement may be most rapid, is often the last and most tedious to be acquired.

A teacher, by adopting the following plan, succeeded in awakening a great degree of interest on the subject, and, consequently, of promoting rapid improvement. The plan was this: he prepared, on a large sheet of paper, a series of lessons in coarse-hand, beginning with straight lines, and proceeding to the elementary parts of the various letters, and finally to the letters themselves. This paper was posted up in a part of the room accessible to all.

The writing-books were made of three sheets of foolscap paper, folded into a convenient size, making twenty-four pages in the book. The books were to be ruled by the pupil, for it was thought important that each should learn this art. Every pupil in school, then, being furnished with one of these writing-books, was required to commence this series, and to practice each lesson until he could write it well; then, and not till then, he was permitted to pass to the next. A few brief directions were given under each lesson on the large sheet. For example, under the line of straight marks, which constituted the first lesson, was written as follows:

Straight, equidistant, parallel, smooth, well-terminated.

These directions were to call the attention of the pupil to the excellences which he must aim at, and when he supposed he had secured them, his book was to be presented to the teacher for examination. If approved, the word *Passed*, or, afterward, simply *P.*, was written under the line, and he could then proceed to the next lesson. Other requisites were necessary, besides the correct formation of the letters, to enable one to pass; for example, the page must not be soiled or blotted, no paper must be wasted, and, in no case, a leaf torn out. As soon as *one line* was written in the manner required, the scholar was allowed to pass. In a majority of cases, however, not less than a page would be practiced, and in many instances a sheet would be covered, before one line could be produced which would be approved.

One peculiar excellency of this method was, that although the whole school were working under a regular and systematic plan, individuals could go on independently; that is, the progress of no scholar was retarded by that of his companion; the one more advanced might easily pass the earlier lessons in a few days, while the others would require weeks of practice to acquire the same degree of skill.

During the writing-hour the scholars would practice each at the lesson where he left off before, and at a particular time each day the books were brought from the regular place of deposit and laid before the teacher for examination. Without some arrangement for an examination of all the books together, the teacher would be liable to interruption at any time from individual questions and requests, which would consume much time, and benefit only a few.

When a page of writing could not pass, a brief remark, calling the attention of the pupil to the faults which prevented it, was sometimes made in pencil at the bottom of the page. In other cases, the fault was of such a character as to require full and minute oral directions to the pupil. At last, to facilitate the criticism of the writing, a set of arbitrary marks, indicative of the various faults, was devised and applied, as occasion might require, to the writing-books, by means of red ink.

These marks, which were very simple in their character, were easily remembered, for there was generally some connection between the sign and the thing signified. For example, the mark denoting that letters were too short was simply lengthening them in red ink; a faulty curve was denoted by making a new curve over the old one, &c. The following are the principal criticisms and directions for which marks were contrived:

Strokes rough.	Too tall or too short.
Curve wrong.	Stems not straight.
Bad termination.	Careless work.
Too slanting, and the reverse.	Paper wasted.
Too broad, and the reverse.	Almost well enough to pass.
Not parallel.	Bring your book to the teacher.
Form of the letter bad.	Former fault not corrected.
Large stroke made too fine, and the reverse.	

A catalogue of these marks, with an explanation, was made out and placed where it was accessible to all, and by means of them the books could be very easily and rapidly, but thoroughly criticised.

After the plan had gone on for some time, and its operation was fully understood, the teacher gave up the business of examining the books into the hands of a committee, appointed by him from among the older and more advanced pupils. That the committee might be unbiased in their judgment, they were required to examine and decide upon the books without knowing the names of the writers. Each scholar was, indeed, required to place her name on the right hand upper corner of every page of her writing-book, for the convenience of the distributors; but this corner was turned down when the book was brought in, that it might not be seen by the committee.

This committee was invested with plenary powers, and there was no appeal from their decision. In case they exercised their authority in an improper way, or failed on any account to give satisfaction, they were liable to impeachment, but while they continued in office they were to be strictly obeyed.

This plan went on successfully for three months, and with very little diminution of interest. The whole school went regularly through the lessons in coarse-hand, and afterward through a similar series in fine-hand, and improvement in this branch was thought to be greater than at any former period in the same length of time.

The same principle of arranging the several steps of an art or a study into a series of lessons, and requiring the pupil to pass regularly from one to the other, might easily be applied to other studies, and would afford an agreeable variety.

12. THE CORRESPONDENCE.—A master of a district school was walking through the room with a large rule in his hands, and as he came up behind two small boys, he observed that they were playing with some papers. He struck them once or twice, though not very severely, on the head with the rule which he had in his hand. Tears started from the eyes of one. They were called forth by a mingled feeling of grief, mortification, and pain. The other, who was of "sterner stuff," looked steadily into the master's face, and when his back was turned, shook his fist at him and laughed in defiance.

Another teacher, seeing a similar case, did nothing. The boys, when they saw him, hastily gathered up their playthings and put them away. An hour or two after, a little boy, who sat near the master, brought them a note addressed to them both. They opened it, and read as follows:

"TO EDWARD AND JOHN,—I observed, when I passed you to-day, from your concerned looks, and your hurried manner of putting something into your desk, that you were doing something that you knew was wrong. When you attempt to do any thing whatever which conscience tells you is wrong, you only make yourself uneasy and anxious while you do it, and then you are forced to resort to concealment and deception when you see me coming. You would be a great deal happier if you would always be doing your duty, and then you would never be afraid. Your affectionate teacher, ——— ———."

As the teacher was arranging his papers in his desk at the close of school, he found a small piece of paper neatly folded up in the form of a note, and addressed to him. He read as follows:

"DEAR TEACHER,—We are very much obliged to you for writing us a note. We were making a paper box. We know it was wrong, and are determined not to do so any more. We hope you will forgive us.

"Your pupils, EDWARD,
JOHN."

Which of these teachers understood human nature best?

13. WEEKLY REPORTS.—The plan described by the following article, which was furnished by a teacher for insertion here, was originally adopted, so far as I know, in a school on the Kennebec. I have adopted it with great advantage.

A teacher had one day been speaking to her scholars of certain cases of slight disorder in the school, which, she remarked, had been gradually creeping in, and which, as she thought, it devolved upon the scholars, by systematic efforts, to repress. She enumerated instances of disorder in the arrangement of the rooms, leaving the benches out of their places, throwing waste papers upon the floor, having the desk in disorder inside, spilling water upon the entry floor, irregular deportment, such as too loud talking or laughing in recess, or in the intermission at noon, or when coming to school, and making unnecessary noise in going to or returning from recitations.

"I have a plan to propose," said the teacher, "which I think may be the pleasantest way of promoting a reform in things of this kind. It is this. Let several of your number be chosen a committee to prepare statedly—perhaps as often as once a week—a written report of the state of the school. The report might be read before the school at the close of each week. The committee might consist, in the whole, of seven or eight, or even of eleven or twelve individuals, who should take the whole business into their hands. This committee might appoint individuals of their number to write in turn each week. By this arrangement, it would not be known to the school generally who are the writers of any particular report, if the individuals wish to be anonymous. Two individuals might be appointed at the beginning of the week, who should feel it their business to observe particularly the course of things from day to day with reference to the report. Individuals not members of the committee can render assistance by any suggestions they may present to this committee. These should, however, generally be made in writing.

"Subjects for such a report will be found to suggest themselves very abundantly, though you may not perhaps think so at first. The committee may be empowered not only to state the particulars in which things are going wrong, but the methods by which they may be made right. Let them present us with any suggestions they please. If we do not like them, we are not obliged to adopt them. For instance, it is generally the case, whenever a recitation is attended in the corner yonder, that an end of one of the benches is put against the door, so as to occasion a serious interruption to the exercises when a person wishes to come in or go out. It would come within the province of the committee to attend to such a case as this, that is, to bring it up in the report. The remedy in such a case is a very simple one. Suppose, however, that instead of the *simple* remedy, our committee should propose that the classes reciting in the said corner should be dissolved and the studies abolished? We should know the proposal was an absurd one, but then it would do no hurt; we should have only to reject it.

"Again, besides our faults, let our committee notice the respects in which we are doing particularly well, that we may be encouraged to go on doing well, or even to do better. If they think, for example, that we are deserving of credit for the neatness with which books are kept—for their freedom from blots, or scribblings, or dog's-ears, by which school-books are so commonly defaced, let them tell us so. And the same of any other excellence."

With the plan as thus presented, the scholars were very much pleased. It was proposed by one individual that such a committee should be appointed immediately, and a report prepared for the ensuing week. This was done. The committee were chosen by ballot. The following may be taken as a specimen of their reports:

WEEKLY REPORT.

"The Committee appointed to write the weekly report have noticed several things which they think wrong. In the first place, there have been a greater number of tardy scholars during the past week than usual. Much of this tardiness, we suppose, is owing to the interest felt in building the bower; but we think this business ought to be attended to only in play-hours. If only one or two come in late when we are reading in the morning, or after we have composed ourselves to study at the close of the recess, every scholar must look up from her book—we do not say they ought to do so, but only that they will do so. However, we anticipate an improvement in this respect, as we know 'a word to the wise is sufficient.'

"In the two back rows we are sorry to say that we have noticed whispering. We know that this fact will very much distress our teacher, as she expects assistance, and not trouble, from our older scholars. It is not our business to reprove any one's misconduct, but it is our duty to mention it, however disagreeable it may be. We think the younger scholars, during the past week, have much improved in this respect. Only three cases of whispering among them have occurred to our knowledge.

"We remember some remarks made a few weeks ago by our teacher on the practice of prompting each other in the classes. We wish she would repeat them, for we fear that, by some, they are forgotten. In the class in Geography, particularly in the questions on the map, we have noticed sly whispers, which, we suppose, were the hints of some kind friend designed to refresh the memory of her less attentive companion. We propose that the following question be now put to vote. Shall the practice of prompting in the classes be any longer continued?

"We would propose that we have a composition exercise *this* week similar to the one on Thursday last. It was very interesting, and we think all would be willing to try their thinking powers once more. We would propose, also, that the readers of the compositions should sit near the centre of the room, as last week many fine sentences escaped the ears of those seated in the remote corners.

"We were requested by a very public-spirited individual to mention once more the want of three nails, for bonnets, in the entry. Also, to say that the air from the broken pane of glass on the east side of the room is very unpleasant to those who sit near.

"Proposed that the girls who exhibited so much taste and ingenuity in the arrangement of the festoons of evergreen, and tumblers of flowers around the teacher's desk, be now requested to remove the faded roses and drooping violets. We have gazed on these sad emblems long enough.

"Finally, proposed that greater care be taken by those who stay at noon to place their dinner-baskets in proper places. The contents of more than one were partly strewed upon the entry floor this morning."

If such a measure as this is adopted, it should not be continued uninterrupted for a very long time. Every thing of this sort should be occasionally changed, or it sooner or later becomes only a form.

14. The Shopping Exercise.—I have often, when going a shopping, found difficulty and trouble in making change. I could never calculate very readily, and in the hurry and perplexity of the moment I was always making mistakes. I have heard others often make the same complaint, and I resolved to try the experiment of regularly teaching children to make change. I had a bright little class in Arithmetic, the members of which were always ready to engage with interest in any thing new, and to them I proposed my plan. It was to be called the Shopping Exercise. I first requested each individual to write something upon her slate which she would like to buy, if she was going a shopping, stating the quantity she wished and the price of it. To make the first lesson as simple as possible, I requested no one to go above

ten, either in the quantity or price. When all were ready, I called upon some to read what she had written. Her next neighbor was then requested to tell us how much the purchase would amount to. Then the first one named a bill, which she supposed to be offered in payment, and the second showed what change was needed. A short specimen of the exercise will probably make it clearer than mere description.

Mary. Eight ounces of candy at seven cents.
Susan. Fifty-six cents.
Mary. One dollar.
Susan. Forty-four cents.

Susan. Nine yards of lace at eight cents.
Anna. Seventy-two cents.
Susan. Two dollars.
Anna. One dollar and twenty-eight cents.

Anna. Three pieces of tape at five cents.
Jane. Fifteen cents.
Anna. Three dollars.
Jane. Eighty-five cents.
Several voices. Wrong.
Jane. Two dollars and eighty-five cents.

Jane. Six pictures at eight cents.
Sarah. Forty-two cents.
Several voices. Wrong.
Sarah. Forty-eight cents.
Jane. One dollar.
Sarah. Sixty-two cents.
Several voices. Wrong.
Sarah. Fifty-two cents.

It will be perceived that the same individual who names the article and the price names also the bill which she would give in payment; and the one who sits next her, who calculated the amount, calculated also the change to be returned. She then proposed *her* example to the one next in the line, with whom the same course was pursued, and thus it passed down the class.

The exercise went on for some time in this way, till the pupils had become so familiar with it that I thought it best to allow them to take higher numbers. They were always interested in it, and made great improvement in a short time, and I myself derived great advantage from listening to them.

There is one more circumstance I will add which may contribute to the interest of this account. While the class were confined, in what they purchased, to the number ten, they were sometimes inclined to turn the exercise into a frolic. The variety of articles which they could find costing less than ten cents was so small, that, for the sake of getting something new, they would propose examples really ludicrous, such as these: three meeting-houses at two cents; four pianos at nine cents. But I soon found that if I allowed this at all, their attention was diverted from the main object, and occupied in seeking the most diverting and curious examples.

15. Artifices in Recitations.—The teacher of a small newly-established school had all of his scholars classed together in some of their studies. At recitations he usually sat in the middle of the room, while the scholars occupied the usual places at their desks, which were arranged around the sides. In the recitation in Rhetoric, the teacher, after a time, observed that one or two of the class seldom answered appropriately the questions which came to them, but yet were always ready with some kind of answer—generally an exact quotation of the words of the book. Upon noticing these individuals more particularly, he was convinced that their books were open before them in some concealed situation. Another practice not uncommon in the class was that of *prompting* each other, either by whispers or writing. The teacher took no notice publicly of these practices for some time, until, at the close of an uncommonly good recitation, he remarked, "I think we have had a fine recitation to-day.

It is one of the most agreeable things that I ever do to hear a lesson that is learned as well as this. Do you think it would be possible for us to have as good an exercise every day?" "Yes, sir," answered several, faintly. "Do you think it would be reasonable for me to expect of every member of the class that she should always be able to recite all her lessons without ever missing a single question?" "No, sir," answered all. "I do not expect it," said the teacher. "All I wish is that each of you should be faithful in your efforts to prepare your lessons. I wish you to study from a sense of duty, and for the sake of your own improvement. You know I do not punish you for failures. I have no going up or down, no system of marking. Your only reward, when you have made faithful preparation for a recitation, is the feeling of satisfaction which you will always experience; and when you have been negligent, your only punishment is a sort of uneasy feeling of self-reproach. I do not expect you all to be invariably prepared with every question of your lessons. Sometimes you will be unavoidably prevented from studying them, and at other times, when you have studied them very carefully, you may have forgotten, or you may fail from some misapprehension of the meaning in some cases. Do not, in such a case, feel troubled because you may not have appeared as well as some individual who has not been half as faithful as yourself. If you have done your duty, that is enough. On the other hand, you ought to feel no better satisfied with yourselves when your lesson has not been studied well, because you may have happened to know the parts which came to you. Have I *done* well? should always be the question, not, Have I managed to *appear* well?

"I will say a word here," continued the teacher, "upon a practice which I have known to be very common in some schools, and which I have been sorry to notice occasionally in this. I mean that of prompting, or helping each other along in some way at recitations. Now where a severe punishment is the consequence of a failure, there might seem to be some reasonableness in helping your companions out of difficulty, though even then such tricks are departures from honorable dealing. But, especially where there is no purpose to be served but that of appearing to know more than you do, it certainly must be considered a very mean kind of artifice. I think I have sometimes observed an individual to be prompted where evidently the assistance was not desired, and even where it was not needed. To whisper to an individual the answer to a question is sometimes to pay her rather a poor compliment at least, for it is the same as saying 'I am a better scholar than you are; let me help you along a little.'

"Let us then, hereafter, have only fair, open, honest dealings with each other; no attempts to appear to advantage by little artful manœuvring; no prompting; no peeping into books. Be faithful and conscientious, and then banish anxiety for your success. Do you not think you will find this the best course?" "Yes, sir," answered every scholar. "Are you willing to pledge yourselves to adopt it?" "Yes, sir." "Those who are may raise their hands," said the teacher. Every hand was raised; and the pledge, there was evidence to believe, was honorably sustained.

16. Keeping Resolutions.—The following are notes of a familiar lecture on this subject, given by a teacher at some general exercise in the school. The practice of thus reducing to writing what the teacher may say on such subjects will be attended with excellent effects.

Th' is a subject upon which young persons find much difficulty. The question is asked a thousand times, "How shall I ever learn to keep my resolutions?" Perhaps the great cause of your failures is this. You are not sufficiently *definite* in forming your purposes. You will resolve to do a thing, without knowing with certainty whether it is even possible to do it. Again, you make resolutions which are to run on indefinitely, so that, of course, they can never be fully kept. For instance, one of you will resolve to *rise earlier in the morning*. You fix upon no definite hour, on any definite number of mornings, only you are going to "*rise earlier.*" Morning comes, and finds you sleepy and disinclined to rise. You remember your resolution of rising earlier. "But then it is *very* early," you say. You resolved to rise earlier, but you didn't resolve to rise just then. And this, it may be, is the last of your resolution. Or perhaps you are, for a few mornings, a little earlier; but then, at the end of a week or fortnight, you do not know exactly whether your resolution has been broken or kept, for you had not decided whether to rise earlier for ten days or for ten years.

In the same vague and general manner, a person will resolve to be *more studious* or more diligent. In the case of an individual of a mature and well-disciplined mind, of acquired firmness of character, such a resolution might have effect. The individual will really devote more time and attention to his pursuits. But for one of you to make such a resolution would do no sort of good. It would only be a source of trouble and disquiet. You perceive there is nothing definite—nothing fixed about it. You have not decided what amount of additional time or attention to give to your studies, or when you will begin, or when you will end. There is no one time when you will feel that you are breaking your resolution, because there were no particular times when you were to study more. You waste one opportunity and another, and then, with a feeling of discouragement and self-reproach, conclude to abandon your resolution. "Oh! it does no good to make resolutions," you say; "I never shall keep them."

Now, if you would have the business of making resolutions a pleasant and interesting instead of a discouraging, disquieting one, you must proceed in a different manner. Be definite and distinct in your plan; decide exactly what you will do, and how you will do it—when you will begin, and when you will end. Instead of resolving to "rise earlier," resolve to rise at the ringing of the sunrise bells, or at some other definite time. Resolve to try this, as an experiment, for one morning, or for one week, or fortnight. Decide positively, if you decide at all, and then rise when the time comes, sleepy or not sleepy. Do not stop to repent of your resolution, or to consider the wisdom or folly of it, when the time for acting under it has once arrived.

In all cases, little and great, make this a principle—to consider well before you begin to act, but after you have begun to act, never stop to consider. Resolve as deliberately as you please, but be sure to keep your resolution, whether a wise one or an unwise one, after it is once made. Never allow yourself to reconsider the question of getting up, after the morning has come, except it be for some unforeseen circumstance. Get up for that time, and be more careful how you make resolutions again.

17. Topics.—The plan of the Topic Exercise, as we called it, is this. Six or seven topics are given out, information upon which is to be obtained from any source, and communicated verbally before the whole school, or sometimes before a class formed for this purpose the next day. The subjects are proposed both by teacher and scholars, and if approved, adopted. The exercise is intended to be voluntary, but ought to be managed in a way sufficiently interesting to induce all to join.

At the commencement of the exercise the teacher calls upon all who have any information in regard to the topic assigned—suppose, for example, it is *Alabaster*—to rise. Perhaps twenty individuals out of forty rise. The teacher may perhaps say to those in their seats,

"Do you not know any thing of this subject? Have you neither seen nor heard of alabaster, and had no means of ascertaining any thing in regard to it? If you have, you ought to rise. It is not necessary that you should state a fact altogether new and unheard-of, but if you tell me its color, or some of the uses to which it is applied, you will be complying with my request."

After these remarks, perhaps a few more rise, and possibly the whole school. Individuals are then called upon at random, each to state only one particular in regard to the topic in question. This arrangement is made so as to give all an opportunity to speak. If any scholar, after having mentioned one fact, has something still farther to communicate, she remains standing till called upon again. As soon as an individual has exhausted her stock of information, or if the facts that she intended to mention are stated by another, she takes her seat.

The topics at first most usually selected are the common objects by which we are surrounded—for example, glass, iron, mahogany, and the like. The list will gradually extend itself, until it will embrace a large number of subjects.

The object of this exercise is to induce pupils to seek for general information in an easy and pleasant manner, as by the perusal of books, newspapers, periodicals, and conversation with friends. It induces care and attention in reading, and discrimination in selecting the most useful and important facts from the mass of information. As individuals are called upon, also, to express their ideas *verbally*, they soon acquire by practice the power of expressing them with clearness and force, and communicating with ease and confidence the knowledge they possess.

18. MUSIC.—The girls of our school often amused themselves in recess by collecting into little groups for singing. As there seemed to be a sufficient power of voice, and a respectable number who were willing to join in the performance, it was proposed one day that singing should be introduced as a part of the devotional exercises of the school.

The first attempt nearly resulted in a failure; only a few trembling voices succeeded in singing Old Hundred to the words "Be thou," etc. On the second day Peterborough was sung with much greater confidence on the part of the increased number of singers. The experiment was tried with greater and greater success for several days, when the teacher proposed that a systematic plan should be formed, by which there might be singing regularly at the close of school. It was then proposed that a number of singing-books be obtained, and one of the scholars, who was well acquainted with common tunes, be appointed as chorister. Her duty should be to decide what particular tune may be sung each day, inform the teacher of the metre of the hymn, and take the lead in the exercise. This plan, being approved of by the scholars, was adopted, and put into immediate execution. Several brought copies of the Sabbath School Hymn-Book, which they had in their possession, and the plan succeeded beyond all expectation. The greatest difficulty in the way was to get some one to lead. The chorister, however, was somewhat relieved from the embarrassment which she would naturally feel in making a beginning by the appointment of one or two individuals with herself, who were to act as her assistants. These constituted the *leading* committee, or, as it was afterward termed, *Singing Committee.*

Singing now became a regular and interesting exercise of the school, and the committee succeeded in managing the business themselves.

19. Tabu.—An article was one day read in a school relating to the "Tabu" of the Sandwich Islanders. Tabu is a term with them which signifies consecrated—not to be touched—to be let alone—not to be violated. Thus, according to their religious observances, a certain day will be proclaimed *Tabu;* that is, one upon which there is to be no work or no going out.

A few days after this article was read, the scholars observed one morning a flower stuck up in a conspicuous place against the wall, with the word Tabu in large characters above it. This excited considerable curiosity. The teacher informed them, in explanation, that the flower was a very rare and beautiful specimen, brought by one of the scholars, which he wished all to examine. "You would naturally feel a disposition to examine it by the touch," said he, "but you will all see that, by the time it was touched by sixty individuals, it would be likely to be injured, if not destroyed. So I concluded to label it *Tabu.* And it has occurred to me that this will be a convenient mode of apprising you generally that any article must not be handled. You know we sometimes have some apparatus exposed, which would be liable to injury from disturbance, where there are so many persons to touch it. I shall, in such a case, just mention that an article is Tabu, and you will understand that it is not only not to be *injured*, but not even *touched*."

A little delicate management of this sort will often have more influence over young persons than the most vehement scolding, or the most watchful and jealous precautions. The Tabu was always most scrupulously regarded, after this, whenever employed.

20. Mental Analysis.—Scene, a class in Arithmetic at recitation. The teacher gives them an example in addition, requesting them, when they have performed it, to rise. Some finish it very soon, others are very slow in accomplishing the work.

"I should like to ascertain," says the teacher, "how great is the difference of rapidity with which different members of the class work in addition. I will give you another example, and then notice by my watch the shortest and longest time required to do it."

The result of the experiment was that some members of the class were two or three times as long in doing it as others.

"Perhaps you think," said the teacher, "that this difference is altogether owing to difference of skill; but it is not. It is mainly owing to the different methods adopted by various individuals. I am going to describe some of these, and, as I describe them, I wish you would notice them carefully, and tell me which you practice.

"There are, then, three modes of adding up a column of figures, which I shall describe.

1. "I shall call the first *counting*. You take the first figure, and then add the next to it by counting up regularly. There are three distinct ways of doing this.

(a.) "Counting by your fingers." ("Yes, sir.") "You take the first figure—suppose it is seven—and the one above it, eight. Now you recollect that to add eight, you must count all the fingers of one hand, and all but two again. So you say 'seven — eight, nine, ten, eleven, twelve, thirteen, fourteen, fifteen.'"

"Yes, sir, yes, sir," said the scholars.

(b.) "The next mode of counting is to do it mentally, without using your fingers at all; but, as it is necessary for you to have some plan to secure your adding the right number, you divide the units into sets of two each. Thus you remember that eight consists of four twos, and you accordingly say, when adding eight to seven, 'Seven; eight, nine; ten, eleven; twelve, thirteen,' &c.

(c.) "The third mode is to add by threes in the same way. You recollect that eight consists of two threes and a two; so you say, 'Seven; eight, nine, ten; eleven, twelve, thirteen; fourteen, fifteen.'"

The teacher here stops to ascertain how many of the class are accustomed to add in either of these modes. It is a majority.

2. "The next general method is *calculating;* that is, you do not unite one number to another by the dull and tedious method of applying the units, one by one, as in the ways described under the preceding head, but you come to a result more rapidly by some mode of calculating. These modes are several.

(a.) "Doubling a number, and then adding or subtracting, as the case may require. For instance, in the example already specified, in order to add seven and eight, you say, 'Twice seven are fourteen, and one are fifteen'" ("Yes, sir, yes, sir"); "or, 'Twice eight are sixteen, and taking one off leaves fifteen." ("Yes, sir.")

(b.) "Another way of calculating is to skip about the column, adding those numbers which you can combine most easily, and then bringing in the rest as you best can. Thus, if you see three eights in one column, you say, 'Three times eight are twenty-four,' and then you try to bring in the other numbers. Often, in such cases, you forget what you have added and what you have not, and get confused ("Yes, sir"), or you omit something in your work, and consequently it is incorrect.

(c.) "If nines occur, you sometimes add ten, and then take off one, for it is very easy to add ten.

(d.) "Another method of calculating, which is, however, not very common, is this: to take our old case, adding eight to seven, you take as much from the eight to add to the seven as will be sufficient to make ten, and then it will be easy to add the rest. Thus you think in a minute that three from the eight will make the seven a ten, and then there will be five more to add, which will make fifteen. If the next number was seven, you would say five of it will make twenty, and then there will be two left, which will make twenty-two.' This mode, though it may seem more intricate than any of the others, is, in fact, more rapid than any of them, when one is a little accustomed to it.

"These are the four principal modes of calculating which occur to me. Pupils do not generally practice any of them exclusively, but occasionally resort to each, according to the circumstances of the particular case."

The teacher here stopped to inquire how many of the class were accustomed to add by calculating in either of these ways or in any simpler ways.

3. "There is one more mode which I shall describe: it is by *memory*. Before I explain this mode, I wish to ask you some questions, which I should like to have you answer as quick as you can.

"How much is four times five? Four *and* five?

"How much is seven times nine? Seven *and* nine?

"Eight times six? Eight *and* six?

"Nine times seven? Nine *and* seven?"

After asking a few questions of this kind, it was perceived that the pupils could tell much more readily what was the result when the numbers were to be multiplied than when they were to be added.

"The reason is," said the teacher, "because you committed the multiplication table to memory, and have not committed the addition table. Now many persons have committed the addition table, so that it is perfectly familiar to them, and when they see any two numbers, the amount which is produced when they are added together comes to mind in an instant. Adding in this way is the last of the three modes I was to describe.

"Now of these three methods the last is undoubtedly the best. If you once commit the addition table thoroughly, you have it fixed for life; whereas if you do not, you have to make the calculation over again every time, and thus lose a vast amount of labor. I have no doubt that there are some in this class who are in the habit of *counting*, who have ascertained that seven and eight, for instance, make fifteen, by counting up from seven to fifteen *hundreds of times*. Now how much better it would be to spend a little time in fixing the fact in the mind once for all, and then, when you come to the case, seven and eight are—say at once 'Fifteen,' instead of mumbling over and over again, hundreds of times, 'Seven, eight, nine, ten, eleven, twelve, thirteen, fourteen, fifteen.'

"The reason, then, that some of the class add so slowly, is not, probably, because they want skill and rapidity of execution, but because they work to a great disadvantage by working in the wrong way. I have often been surprised at the dexterity and speed with which some scholars can count with their fingers when adding, and yet they could not get through the sum very quick—at least they would have done it in half the time if the same effort had been made in traveling on a shorter road. We will therefore study the addition table now, in the class, before we go any farther."

21. TARDINESS.—When only a few scholars in a school are tardy, it may be their fault; but if a great many are so, it is the fault of the teacher or of the school. If a school is prosperous, and the children are going on well and happily in their studies, they will like their work in it; but we all come reluctantly to work which we are conscious we are not successfully performing.

There may be two boys in a school, both good boys; one, may be going on well in his classes, while the other, from the concurrence of some accidental train of circumstances, may be behindhand in his work, or wrongly classed, or so situated in other respects that his school duties perplex and harass him day by day. Now how different will be the feelings of these two boys in respect to coming to school. The one will be eager and prompt to reach his place and commence his duties, while the other will love much better to

loiter in idleness and liberty in the open air. Nor is he, under the circumstances of the case, to blame for this preference. There is no one, old or young, who likes or can like to do what he himself and all around him think that he does not do well. It is true the teacher can not rely wholly on the interest which his scholars take in their studies to make them punctual at school; but if he finds among them any very general disposition to be tardy, he ought to seek for the fault mainly in himself and not in them.

The foregoing narratives and examples, it is hoped, may induce some of the readers of this book to keep journals of their own experiments, and of the incidents which may, from time to time, come under their notice, illustrating the principles of education, or simply the characteristics and tendencies of the youthful mind. The business of teaching will excite interest and afford pleasure just in proportion to the degree in which it is conducted by operations of mind upon mind, and the means of making it most fully so are careful practice, based upon and regulated by the results of careful observation. Every teacher, then, should make observations and experiments upon mind a part of his daily duty, and nothing will more facilitate this than keeping a record of results. There can be no opportunity for studying human nature more favorable than the teacher enjoys. The materials are all before him; his very business, from day to day, brings him to act directly upon them; and the study of the powers and tendencies of the human mind is not only the most interesting and the noblest that can engage human attention, but every step of progress he makes in it imparts an interest and charm to what would otherwise be a weary toil. It at once relieves his labors, while it doubles their efficiency and success.

CHAPTER IX.

THE TEACHER'S FIRST DAY.

HE teacher enters upon the duties of his office by a much more sudden transition than is common in the other avocations and employments of life. In ordinary cases, business comes at first by slow degrees, and the beginner is introduced to the labors and responsibilities of his employment in a very gradual manner. The young teacher, however, enters by a single step into the very midst of his labors. Having, perhaps, never even heard a class recite before, he takes a short walk some winter morning, and suddenly finds himself instated at the desk, his fifty scholars around him, all looking him in the face, and waiting to be employed. Every thing comes upon him at once. He can do nothing until the day and the hour for opening the school arrives—then he has every thing to do.

Under these circumstances, it is not surprising that the young teacher should look forward with unusual solicitude to his first day in school, and he desires, ordinarily, special instructions in respect to this occasion. Some such special instructions we propose to give in this chapter. The experienced teacher may think some of them too minute and trivial. But he must remember that they are intended for the youngest beginner in the humblest school; and if he recalls to mind his own feverish solicitude on the morning when he went to take his first command in the district school, he will pardon the seeming minuteness of detail.

1. It will be well for the young teacher to take opportunity, between the time of his engaging his school and that of his commencing it, to acquire as much information in respect to it beforehand as possible, so as to be somewhat acquainted with the scene of his labors before entering upon it. Ascertain the names and the characters of the principal families in the district, their ideas and wishes in respect to the government of the school, the kind of management adopted by one or two of the last teachers, the difficulties they fell into, the nature of the complaints made against them, if any, and the families with whom difficulty has usually arisen. This information must, of course, be obtained in private conversation; a good deal of it must be, from its very nature, highly confidential; but it is very important that the teacher should be possessed of it. He will necessarily become possessed of it by degrees in the course of his administration, when, however, it may be too late to be of any service to him. But, by judicious and proper efforts to acquire it beforehand, he will enter upon the discharge of his duties with great advantage. It is like a navigator's becoming acquainted beforehand with the nature and the dangers of the sea over which he is about to sail.

Such inquiries as these will, in ordinary cases, bring to the teacher's knowledge, in most districts in our country, some cases of peculiarly troublesome scholars, or unreasonable and complaining parents; and stories of their unjustifiable conduct on former occasions will come to him exaggerated by the jealousy of rival neighbors. There is danger that his resentment may be roused a little, and that his mind will assume a hostile attitude at once toward such individuals, so that he will enter upon his work rather with a desire to seek a collision with them, or, at least, with secret feelings of defiance toward them—feelings which will lead to that kind of unbending perpendicularity in his demeanor toward them which will almost inevitably lead to a collision. Now this is wrong. There is, indeed, a point where firm resistance to unreasonable demands becomes a duty; but, as a general principle, it is most unquestionably true that it is the teacher's duty *to accommodate himself to the character and expectations of his employers*, not to face and brave them. Those italicized words *may be* understood to mean something which would be entirely wrong; but in the sense in which I mean to use them there can be no question that they indicate the proper path for one employed by others to do work *for them* in all cases to pursue. If, therefore, the teacher finds by his inquiries into the state of his district that there are some peculiar difficulties and dangers there, let him not cherish a disposition to face and resist them, but to avoid them. Let him go with an intention to soothe rather than to irritate feelings which have been wounded before, to comply with the wishes of all so far as he can, even if they are not entirely reasonable, and, while he endeavors to elevate the standard and correct the opinions prevailing among his employers by any means in his power, to aim at doing it gently, and in a tone and manner suitable to the relation he sustains—in a word, let him skillfully *avoid* the dangers of his navigation, not obstinately run his ship against a rock on purpose on the ground that the rock has no business to be there.

This is the spirit, then, with which these preliminary inquiries in regard to the patrons of the school ought to be made. We come now to a second point.

2. It will assist the young teacher very much in his first day's labors if he takes measures for seeing and conversing with some of the older or more intelligent scholars on the

day or evening before he begins his school, with a view of obtaining from them some acquaintance with the internal arrangements and customs of the school. The object of this is to obtain the same kind of information with respect to the interior of the school that was recommended in respect to the district under the former head. He may call upon a few families, especially those which furnish a large number of scholars for the school, and make as many minute inquiries of them as he can respecting all the interior arrangements to which they have been accustomed, what reading-books and other text-books have been used, what are the principal classes in all the several departments of instruction, and what is the system of discipline, and of rewards and punishments, to which the school has been accustomed.

If, in such conversations, the teacher should find a few intelligent and communicative scholars, he might learn a great deal about the past habits and condition of the school, which would be of great service to him. Not, by any means, that he will adopt and continue these methods as a matter of course, but only that a knowledge of them will render him very important aid in marking out his own course. The more minute and full the information of this sort is which he thus obtains, the better. If practicable, it would be well to make out a catalogue of all the principal classes, with the names of those individuals belonging to them who will probably attend the new school, and the order in which they were usually called upon to read or recite. The conversation which would be necessary to accomplish this would of itself be of great service. It would bring the teacher into an acquaintance with several important families and groups of children under the most favorable circumstances. The parents would see and be pleased with the kind of interest they would see the teacher taking in his new duties. The children would be pleased to be able to render their new instructor some service, and would go to the school-room on the next morning with a feeling of acquaintance with him, and a predisposition to be pleased. And if by chance any family should be thus called upon that had heretofore been captious or complaining, or disposed to be jealous of the higher importance or influence of other families, that spirit would be entirely softened and subdued by such an interview with their new instructor at their own fireside on the evening preceding the commencement of his labors. The great object, however, which the teacher would have in view in such inquiries should be the value of the information itself. As to the use which he will make of it, we shall speak hereafter.

3. It is desirable that the young teacher should meet his scholars first in an unofficial capacity. For this purpose, repair to the school-room on the first day at an early hour, so as to see and become acquainted with the scholars as they come in one by one. The intercourse between teacher and pupil should be like that between parents and children, where the utmost freedom is united with the most perfect respect. The father who is most firm and decisive in his family government can mingle most freely in the conversation and sports of his children without any derogation of his authority, or diminution of the respect they owe. Young teachers, however, are prone to forget this, and to imagine that they must assume an appearance of stern authority always, when in the presence of their scholars, if they wish to be respected or obeyed. This they call keeping up their dignity. Accordingly, they wait, on the morning of their induction into office, until their new subjects are all assembled, and then walk in with an air of the highest dignity, and with the step of a king; and sometimes a formidable instrument of discipline is carried in the hand to heighten the impression. Now there is no question that it is of great importance that scholars should have a high idea of the teacher's firmness and inflexible decision in maintaining his authority and repressing all disorder of every kind, but this impression should be cre-

ated by their seeing how he *acts* in the various emergencies which will spontaneously occur, and not by assuming airs of importance or dignity, feigned for effect. In other words, their respect for him should be based on *real traits* of character as they see them brought out into natural action, and not on appearances assumed for the occasion.

It seems to me, therefore, that it is best for the teacher first to meet his scholars with the air and tone of free and familiar intercourse, and he will find his opportunity more favorable for doing this if he goes early on the first morning of his labors, and converses freely with those whom he finds there, and with others as they come in. He may take an interest with them in all the little arrangements connected with the opening of the school—the building of the fire, the paths through the snow, the arrangements of seats; calling upon them for information or aid, asking their names, and, in a word, entering fully and freely into conversation with them, just as a parent, under similar circumstances, would do with his children. All the children thus addressed will be pleased with the gentleness and affability of the teacher. Even a rough and ill-natured boy, who has perhaps come to the school with the express determination of attempting to make mischief, will be completely disarmed by being asked politely to help the teacher arrange the fire, or alter the position of his desk. Thus, by means of the half hour during which the scholars are coming together, and of the visits made in the preceding evening, as described under the last head, the teacher will find, when he calls upon the children to take their seats, that he has made a very large number of them his personal friends. Many of these will have communicated their first impressions to the others, so that he will find himself possessed, at the outset, of that which is of vital consequence in the opening of any administration—a strong party in his favor.

4. The time for calling the school to order and commenc-

ing exercises of some sort will at length arrive, though if the work of making personal acquaintances is going on prosperously, it may perhaps be delayed a little beyond the usual hour. When, however, the time arrives, we would strongly recommend that the first service by which the regular duties of the school are commenced should be an act of religious worship. There are many reasons why the exercises of the school should every day be thus commenced, and there are special reasons for it on the first day.

There are very few districts where parents would have any objection to this. They might, indeed, in some cases, if the subject were to be brought up formally before them as a matter of doubt, anticipate some difficulties, or create imaginary ones, growing out of the supposed sensitiveness of contending sects; but if the teacher were, of his own accord, to commence the plain, faithful, and honest discharge of this duty as a matter of course, very few would think of making any objection to it, and almost all would be satisfied and pleased with its actual operation. If, however, the teacher should, in any case, have reason to believe that such a practice would be contrary to the wishes of his employers, it would, according to views we have presented in another chapter, be wrong for him to attempt to introduce it. He might, if he should see fit, make such an objection a reason for declining to take the school; but he ought not, if he takes it, to act counter to the known wishes of his employers in so important a point. But if, on the other hand, no such objections are made known to him, he need not raise the question himself at all, but take it for granted that in a Christian land there will be no objection to imploring the Divine protection and blessing at the opening of a daily school.

If this practice is adopted, it will have a most powerful influence upon the moral condition of the school. It must be so. Though many will be inattentive, and many utterly unconcerned, yet it is not possible to bring children, even in form, into the presence of God every day, and to utter in their hearing the petitions which they ought to present, without bringing a powerful element of moral influence to bear upon their hearts. The good will be made better; the conscientious more conscientious still; and the rude and savage will be subdued and softened by the daily attempt to lead them to the throne of their Creator. To secure this effect, the devotional service must be an honest one. There must be nothing feigned or hypocritical; no hackneyed phrases used without meaning, or intonations of assumed solemnity. It must be honest, heartfelt, simple prayer; the plain and direct expression of such sentiments as children ought to feel, and of such petitions as they ought to offer. We shall speak presently of the mode of avoiding some abuses to which this exercise is liable; but if these sources of abuse are avoided, and the duty is performed in that plain, simple, direct, and honest manner in which it certainly will be if it springs from the heart, it must have a great influence on the moral progress of the children, and, in fact, in all respects on the prosperity of the school.

But, then, independently of the *advantages* which may be expected to result from the practice of daily prayer in school, it would seem to be the imperious *duty* of the teacher to adopt it. So many human minds committed thus to the guidance of one, at a period when the character receives so easily and so permanently its shape and direction, and in a world of probation like this, is an occasion which seems to demand the open recognition of the hand of God on the part of any individual to whom such a trust is committed. The duty springs so directly out of the attitude in which the teacher and pupil stand in respect to each other, and the relation they together bear to the Supreme, that it would seem impossible for any one to hesitate to admit the duty, without denying altogether the existence of a God.

How vast the responsibility of *giving form and character to the human soul!* How mighty the influence of which the unformed minds of a group of children are susceptible! How much their daily teacher must inevitably exert upon them! If we admit the existence of God at all, and that he exerts any agency whatever in the moral world which he has produced, here seems to be one of the strongest cases in which his intervention should be sought. And then, when we reflect upon the influence which would be exerted upon the future religious character of this nation by having the millions of children training up in the schools accustomed, through all the years of early life, to being brought daily into the presence of the Supreme, with thanksgiving, confession, and prayer, it can hardly seem possible that the teacher who wishes to be faithful in his duties should hesitate in regard to this. Some teacher may perhaps say that he can not perform it because he is not a religious man—he makes no pretensions to piety. But this can surely be no reason. He *ought to be* a religious man, and his first prayer offered in school may be the first act by which he becomes so. Entering the service of Jehovah is a work which requires no preliminary steps. It is to be done at once by sincere confession, and an honest prayer for forgiveness for the past, and strength for time to come. A daily religious service in school may be, therefore, the outward act by which he, who has long lived without God, may return to his duty.

If, from such considerations, the teacher purposes to have a daily religious service in his school, he should by all means begin on the first day, and when he first calls his school to order. He should mention to his pupils the great and obvious duty of imploring God's guidance and blessing in all their ways, and then read a short portion of Scripture, with an occasional word or two of simple explanation, and offer, himself, a short and simple prayer. In some cases, teachers are disposed to postpone this duty a day or two, from timidity or other causes, hoping that, after becoming acquainted a little with the school, and having completed their more important arrangements, they shall find it easier to begin. But this is a great mistake. The longer the duty is postponed, the more difficult and trying it will be. And then the moral impressions will be altogether more strong and salutary if an act of solemn religious worship is made the first opening act of the school.

Where the teacher has not sufficient confidence that the general sense of propriety among his pupils will preserve good order and decorum during the exercise, it may be better for him to *read* a prayer selected from books of devotion, or prepared by himself expressly for the occasion. By this plan his school will be, during the exercise, under his own observation, as at other times. It may, in some schools where the number is small, or the prevailing habits of seriousness and order are good, be well to allow the older scholars to read the prayer in rotation, taking especial care that it does not degenerate into a mere reading exercise, but that it is understood, both by readers and hearers, to be a solemn act of religious worship. In a word, if the teacher is really honest and sincere in his wish to lead his pupils to the worship of God, he will find no serious difficulty in preventing the abuses and avoiding the dangers which some might fear, and in accomplishing vast good, both in promoting the prosperity of the school, and in the formation of the highest and best traits of individual character.

We have dwelt, perhaps, longer on this subject than we ought to have done in this place; but its importance, when viewed in its bearings on the thousands of children daily assembling in our district schools must be our apology. The embarrassments and difficulties arising from the extreme sensitiveness which exists among the various denominations of Christians in our land, threaten to interfere very seriously with giving a proper degree of religious instruction to the mass of the youthful population. But we must not, because we have no national *church*, cease to have a national *religion*. All our institutions ought to be so administered as openly to recognize the hand of God, and to seek his protection and blessing; and in regard to none is it more imperiously necessary than in respect to our common schools.

5. After the school is thus opened, the teacher will find himself brought to the great difficulty which embarrasses the beginning of his labors, namely, that of finding immediate employment at once for the thirty or forty children who all look up to him waiting for their orders. I say thirty or forty, for the young teacher's first school will usually be a small one. His object should be, in all ordinary cases, for the first few days, twofold: first, to revive and restore, in the main, the general routine of classes and exercises pursued by his predecessor in the same school; and, secondly, while doing this, to become as fully acquainted with his scholars as possible.

It is best, then, *ordinarily*, for the teacher to begin the school as his predecessor closed it, and make the transition to his own perhaps more improved method a gradual one. In some cases a different course is wise undoubtedly, as, for example, where a teacher is commencing a private school, on a previously well-digested plan of his own, or where one who has had experience, and has confidence in his power to bring his new pupils promptly and at once into the system of classification and instruction which he prefers. It is difficult, however, to do this, and requires a good deal of address and decision. It is far easier and safer, and in almost all cases better, in every respect, for a young teacher to revive and restore the former arrangements in the main, and take his departure from them. He may afterward make changes, as he may find them necessary or desirable, and even bring the school soon into a very different state from that in which he finds it; but it will generally be more pleasant for himself, and better for the school, to avoid the shock of a sudden and entire revolution.

The first thing, then, when the scholars are ready to be employed, is to set them at work in classes or upon lessons, as they would have been employed had the former teacher continued in charge of the school. To illustrate clearly how this may be done, we may give the following dialogue:

Teacher. Can any one of the boys inform me what was the first lesson that the former master used to hear in the morning?

The boys are silent, looking to one another.

Teacher. Did he hear *any* recitation immediately after school began?

Boys (faintly, and with hesitation). No, sir.

Teacher. How long was it before he began to hear lessons?

Several boys simultaneously. "About half an hour." "A little while." "Quarter of an hour."

"What did he do at this time?"

"Set copies," "Looked over sums," and various other answers are perhaps given.

The teacher makes a memorandum of this, and then inquires,

"And what lesson came after this?"

"Geography."

"All the boys in this school who studied Geography may rise."

A considerable number rise.

"Did you all recite together?"

"No, sir."

"There are two classes, then?"

"Yes, sir." "Yes, sir." "More than two."

"All who belong to the class that recites first in the morning may remain standing; the rest may sit."

The boys obey, and eight or ten of them remain standing. The teacher calls upon one of them to produce his book, and assigns them a lesson in regular course. He then requests some one of the number to write out, in the course of the day, a list of the class, and to bring it with him to the recitation the next morning.

"Are there any other scholars in the school who think it would be well for them to join this class?"

In answer to this question probably some new scholars might rise, or some hitherto belonging to other classes, who might be of suitable age and qualifications to be transferred. If these individuals should appear to be of the proper standing and character, they might at once be joined to the class in question, and directed to take the same lesson.

In the same manner, the other classes would pass in review before the teacher, and he would obtain a memorandum of the usual order of exercises, and in a short time set all his pupils at work preparing for the lessons of the next day. He would be much aided in this by the previous knowledge which he would have obtained by private conversation, as recommended under a former head. Some individual cases would require a little special attention, such as new scholars, small children, and others; but he would be able, before a great while, to look around him and see his whole school busy with the work he had assigned them, and his own time, for the rest of the morning, in a great degree at his own command.

I ought to say, however, that it is not probable that he would long continue these arrangements unaltered. In hearing the different classes recite, he would watch for opportunities for combining them, or discontinuing those where the number was small; he would alter the times of recitation, and group individual scholars into classes, so as to bring the school, in a very short time, into a condition corresponding more nearly with his own views. All this can be done very easily and pleasantly when the wheels are once in motion; for a school is like a ship in one respect—most easily steered in the right direction when under sail.

By this plan, also, the teacher obtains what is almost absolutely necessary at the commencement of his labors, time for *observation*. It is of the first importance that he should become acquainted, as early as possible, with the characters of the boys, especially to learn who those are which are most likely to be troublesome. There always will be a few who will require special watch and care, and generally there will be only a few. A great deal depends on finding these individuals out in good season, and bringing the pressure of a proper authority to bear upon them soon. By the plan I have recommended of not attempting to remodel the school wholly at once, the teacher obtains time for noticing the pupils, and learning something about their individual characters. In fact, so important is this, that it is the plan of some teachers, whenever they commence a new school, to let the boys have their own way, almost entirely, for a few days, in order to find out fully who the idle and mischievous are. This is, perhaps, going a little too far; but it is certainly desirable to enjoy as many opportunities for observation as can be secured on the first few days of the school.

6. Make it, then, a special object of attention, during the first day or two, to discover who the idle and mischievous individuals are. They will have generally seated themselves together in little knots; for, as they are aware that the new teacher does not know them, they will imagine that, though perhaps separated before, they can now slip together again without any trouble. It is best to avoid, if possible, an open collision with any of them at once, in order that they may be the better observed. Whenever, therefore, you see idleness or play, endeavor to remedy the evil for the time by giving the individual something special to do, or by some other measure, without, however, seeming to notice the misconduct. Continue thus adroitly to stop every thing disorderly, while, at the same time, you notice and remember where the tendencies to disorder exist.

By this means, the individuals who would cause most of the trouble and difficulty in the discipline of the school will soon betray themselves, and those whose fidelity and good behavior can be relied upon will also be known. The names of the former should be among the first that the teacher learns, and their characters should be among the first which he studies. The most prominent among them — those apparently most likely to make trouble — he should note particularly, and make inquiries out of school respecting them, their characters, and their education at home, so as to become acquainted with them as early and as fully as possible, for he must have this full acquaintance with them before he is prepared to commence any decided course of discipline with them. The teacher often does irreparable injury by rash action at the outset. He sees, for instance, a boy secretly eating an apple which he has concealed in his hand, and which he bites with his book before his mouth, or his head under the lid of his desk. It is perhaps the first day of the school, and the teacher thinks he had better make an example at the outset, and calls the boy out, knowing nothing about his general character, and inflicts some painful or degrading punishment before all the school. A little afterward, as he becomes gradually acquainted with the boy, he finds that he is of mild, gentle disposition, generally obedient and harmless, and that his offense was only an act of momentary thoughtlessness, arising from some circumstances of peculiar temptation at the time; a boy in the next seat, perhaps, had just before given him the apple. The teacher regrets, when too late, the hasty punishment. He perceives that instead of having the influence of salutary example upon the other boys, it must have shocked their sense of justice, and excited dislike toward a teacher so quick and severe, rather than of fear of doing wrong themselves. It would be safer to postpone such decided measures a little—to avoid all open collisions, if possible, for a few days. In such a case as the above, the boy might be kindly spoken to in an under tone, in such a way as to show both the teacher's sense of the impropriety of disorder, and also his desire to avoid giving pain to the boy. If it then turns out that the individual is ordinarily a well-disposed boy, all is right, and if he proves to be habitually disobedient and troublesome, the lenity and forbearance exercised at first will facilitate the effect aimed at by subsequent measures. Avoid, then, for the few first days, all open collision with any of your pupils, that you may have opportunity for minute and thorough observation.

And here the young teacher ought to be cautioned against a fault which beginners are very prone to fall into, that of forming unfavorable opinions of some of their pupils from their air and manner before they see any thing in their conduct which ought to be disapproved. A boy or girl comes to the desk to ask a question or make a request, and the teacher sees in the cast of countenance, or in the bearing or tone of the individual, something indicating a proud, or a sullen, or an ill-humored disposition, and conceives a prejudice, often entirely without foundation, which weeks perhaps do not wear away. Every experienced teacher can recollect numerous cases of this sort, and he learns, after a time, to suspend his judgment. Be cautious, therefore, on this point, and in the survey of your pupils which you make during the first few days of your school, trust to nothing but the most sure and unequivocal evidences of character, for many of your most docile and faithful pupils will be found among those whose appearance at first prepossessed you strongly against them.

One other caution ought also to be given. Do not judge too severely in respect to the ordinary cases of misconduct in school. The young teacher almost invariably does judge too severely. While engaged himself in hearing a recitation, or looking over a "sum," he hears a stifled laugh, and, looking up, sees the little offender struggling with the muscles of his countenance to restore their gravity. The teacher is vexed at the interruption, and severely rebukes or punishes the boy, when, after all, the offense, in a moral point of view, was an exceedingly light one—at least it might very probably have been so. In fact, a large proportion of the offenses against order committed in school are the mere momentary action of the natural buoyancy and life of childhood. This is no reason why they should be indulged, or why the order and regularity of the school should be sacrificed, but it should prevent their exciting feelings of anger or impatience, or very severe reprehension. While the teacher should take effectual measures for restraining all such irregularities, he should do it with the tone and manner which will show that he understands their true moral character, and deals with them, not as heinous sins, which deserve severe punishment, but as serious inconveniences, which he is compelled to repress.

There are often cases of real moral turpitude in school, such as where there is intentional, willful mischief, or disturbance, or habitual disobedience, and there may even be, in some cases, open rebellion. Now the teacher should show that he distinguishes these cases from such momentary acts of thoughtlessness as we have described, and a broad distinction ought to be made in the treatment of them. In a word, then, what we have been recommending under this head is, that the teacher should make it his special study, for his first few days in school, to acquire a knowledge of the characters of his pupils, to learn who are the thoughtless ones, who the mischievous, and who the disobedient and rebellious, and to do this with candid, moral discrimination, and with as little open collision with individuals as possible.

7. Another point to which the teacher ought to give his early attention is to separate the bad boys as soon as he can from one another. The idleness and irregularity of children in school often depends more on accidental circumstances than on character. Two boys may be individually harmless and well-disposed, and yet they may be of so mercurial a temperament that, together, the temptation to continual play

will be irresistible. Another case that more often happens is where one is actively and even intentionally bad, and is seated next to an innocent, but perhaps thoughtless boy, and contrives to keep him always in difficulty. Now remove the former away, where there are no very frail materials for him to act upon, and place the latter where he is exposed to no special temptation, and all would be well.

This is all very obvious, and known familiarly to all teachers who have had any experience. But beginners are not generally so aware of it at the outset as to make any direct and systematic efforts to examine the school with reference to its condition in this respect. It is usual to go on, leaving the boys to remain seated as chance or their own inclinations grouped them, and to endeavor to keep the peace among the various neighborhoods by close supervision, rebukes, and punishment. Now these difficulties may be very much diminished by looking a little into the arrangement of the boys at the outset, and so modifying it as to diminish the amount of temptation to which the individuals are exposed.

This should be done, however, cautiously, deliberately, and with good-nature, keeping the object of it a good deal out of view. It must be done cautiously and deliberately, for the first appearances are exceedingly fallacious in respect to the characters of the different children. You see, perhaps, some indications of play between two boys upon the same seat, and hastily conclude that they are disorderly boys, and must be separated. Something in the air and manner of one or both of them confirms this impression, and you take the necessary measures at once. You then find, when you become more fully acquainted with them, that the appearances which you observed were only momentary and accidental, and that they would have been as safe together as any two boys in the school. And perhaps you will even find that, by their new position, you have brought one or the other into circumstances of peculiar temptation. Wait, therefore, before you make such changes, till you have ascertained *actual character*, doing this, however, without any unnecessary delay.

In such removals, too, it is well, in many cases, to keep the motive and design of them as much as possible out of view; for by expressing suspicion of a boy, you injure his character in his own opinion and in that of others, and tend to make him reckless. Besides, if you remove a boy from a companion whom he likes, avowedly to prevent his playing, you offer him an inducement, if he is a bad boy, to continue to play in his new position for the purpose of thwarting you, or from the influence of resentment. It would be wrong, indeed, to use any subterfuge or duplicity of any kind to conceal your object, but you are not bound to explain it; and in the many changes which you will be compelled to make in the course of the first week for various purposes, you may include many of these without explaining particularly the design or intention of any of them.

In some instances, however, you may frankly state the whole case without danger, provided it is done in such a manner as not to make the boy feel that his character is seriously injured in your estimation. It must depend upon the tact and judgment of the teacher to determine upon the particular course to be pursued in the several cases, though he ought to keep these general principles in view in all.

In one instance, for example, he will see two boys together, James and Joseph we will call them, exhibiting a tendency to play, and after inquiring into their characters, he will find that they are good-natured, pleasant boys, and that he had better be frank with them on the subject. He calls one of them to his desk, and perhaps the following dialogue ensues:

"James, I am making some changes in the seats, and thought of removing you to another place. Have you any particular preference for that seat?"

The question is unexpected, and James hesitates. He wishes to sit next to Joseph, but doubts whether it is quite prudent to avow it; so he says, slowly and with hesitation,

"No, sir, I do not know that I have."

"If you have any reason, I wish you would tell me frankly, for I want you to have such a seat as will be pleasant to you."

James does not know what to say. Encouraged, however, by the good-humored tone and look which the master assumes, he says, timidly,

"Joseph and I thought we should like to sit together, if you are willing."

"Oh! you and Joseph are particular friends, then, I suppose?"

"Why, yes, sir."

"I am not surprised, then, that you want to sit together, though, to tell the truth, that is rather a reason why I should separate you."

"Why, sir?"

"Because I have observed that when two great friends are seated together, they are always more apt to whisper and play. Have you not observed it?"

"Why, yes, sir."

"You may go and ask Joseph to come here."

When the two boys make their appearance again, the teacher continues:

"Joseph, James tells me that you and he would like to sit together, and says you are particular friends; but I tell him," he adds, smiling, "that that is rather a reason for separating you. Now if I should put you both into different parts of the school, next to boys that you are not acquainted with, it would be a great deal easier for you to be still and studious than it is now. Do you not think so yourselves?"

The boys look at one another and smile.

"However, there is one way you can do. You can guard against the extra temptation by extra care; and, on the whole, as I believe you are pretty good boys, I will let you have your choice. You may stay as you are, and make extra exertion to be perfectly regular and studious, or I will find seats for you where it will be a great deal easier for you to be so. Which do you think you should rather do?"

The boys hesitate, look at one another, and presently say that they had rather sit together.

"Well," said the teacher, "it is immaterial to me whether you sit together or apart, if you are only good boys, so you may take your seats and try it a little while. If you find it too hard work to be studious and orderly together, I can make a change hereafter. I shall soon see."

Such a conversation will have many good effects. It will make the boys expect to be watched, without causing them to feel that their characters have suffered. It will stimulate them to greater exertion to avoid all misconduct, and it will prepare the way for separating them afterward without awakening feelings of resentment, if the experiment of their sitting together should fail.

Another case would be managed, perhaps, in a little different way, where the tendency to play was more decided. After speaking to the individuals mildly two or three times, you see them again at play. You ask them to wait that day after school and come to your desk.

They have, then, the rest of the day to think occasionally of the difficulty they have brought themselves into, and the anxiety and suspense which they will naturally feel will give you every advantage for speaking to them with effect; and if you should be engaged a few minutes with some other business after school, so that they should have to stand a little while in silent expectation, waiting for their turn, it would contribute to the permanence of the effect.

"Well, boys," at length you say, with a serious but frank tone of voice, "I saw you playing in a disorderly manner today, and, in the first place, I wish you to tell me honestly all about it. I am not going to punish you, but I wish you to be open and honest about it. What were you doing?"

The boys hesitate.

"George, what did you have in your hand?"

"A piece of paper."

"And what were you doing with it?"

George. William was trying to take it away from me.

"Was there any thing on it?"

"Yes, sir."

"What?"

George looks down, a little confused.

William. George had been drawing some pictures on it.

"I see each of you is ready to tell of the other's fault, but it would be much more honorable if each was open in acknowledging his own. Have I ever had to speak to you before for playing together in school?"

"Yes, sir, I believe you have," says one, looking down.

"More than once?"

"Yes, sir."

"More than twice?"

"I do not recollect exactly; I believe you have."

"Well, now, what do you think I ought to do next?"

The boys have nothing to say.

"Do you prefer sitting together, or are you willing to have me separate you?"

"We should rather sit together, sir, if you are willing," says George.

"I have no objection to your sitting together, if you could only resist the temptation to play. I want all the boys in the school to have pleasant seats."

There is a pause, the teacher hesitating what to do.

"Suppose, now, I were to make one more experiment, and let you try to be good boys in your present seat, would you really try?"

"Yes, sir," "Yes, sir, we will," are the replies.

"And if I should find that you still continue to play, and should have to separate you, will you move into your new seats pleasantly, and with good-humor, feeling that I have done right about it?"

"Yes, sir, we will."

Thus it will be seen that there may be cases where the teacher may make arrangements for separating his scholars, on an open and distinct understanding with them in respect to the cause of it. We have given these cases, not that exactly such ones will be very likely to occur, or that, when they do, the teacher is to manage them in exactly the way here described, but to exhibit more clearly to the reader than could be done by any general description, the spirit and tone which a teacher ought to assume toward his pupils. We wished to exhibit this in contrast with the harsh and impatient manner which teachers too often assume in such a case, as follows:

"John Williams and Samuel Smith, come here to me!" exclaims the master, in a harsh, impatient tone, in the midst of the exercises of the afternoon.

The scholars all look up from their work. The culprits slowly rise from their seats, and with a sullen air come down to the floor.

"You are playing, boys, all the time, and I will not have it. John, do you take your books, and go and sit out there by the window; and, Samuel, you come and sit here on this front seat; and if I catch you playing again, I shall certainly punish you severely."

The boys make the move with as much rattling and disturbance as is possible without furnishing proof of willful intention to make a noise; and when they get their new seats, and the teacher is again engaged upon his work, they exchange winks and nods, and in ten minutes are slyly cannonading each other with paper balls.

In regard to all the directions that have been given under this head, I ought to say again, before concluding it, that they are mainly applicable to the case of beginners and of small schools. The general principles are, it is true, of universal application, but it is only where a school is of moderate size that the details of position, in respect to individual scholars, can be minutely studied. More summary processes are necessary, I am aware, when the school is very large, and the time of the teacher is incessantly engaged.

8. In some districts in New England the young teacher will find one or more boys, generally among the larger ones, who will come to the school with the express determination to make a difficulty if they can. The best way is generally to face these individuals at once in the most direct and open manner, and, at the same time, with perfect good-humor and kindness of feeling and deportment toward them personally. An example or two will best illustrate what I mean.

A teacher heard a rapping noise repeatedly one day, just after he had commenced his labors, under such circumstances as to lead him to suppose it was designed. He did not appear to notice it, but remained after school until the scholars had all gone, and then made a thorough examination. He found, at length, a broken place in the plastering, where a *lath* was loose, and a string was tied to the end of it, and thence carried along the wall, under the benches, to the seat of a mischievous boy, and fastened to a nail. By pulling the string he could spring the lath, and then let it snap back to its place. He left every thing as it was, and the next day, while engaged in a lesson, he heard the noise again.

He rose from his seat.

The scholars all looked up from their books.

"Did you hear that noise?" said he.

"Yes, sir."

"Do you know what it is?"

"No, sir."

"Very well; I only wished to call your attention to it. I may perhaps speak of it again by-and-by."

He then resumed his exercise as if nothing had happened. The guilty boy was agitated and confused, and was utterly at a loss to know what to do. What could the teacher mean? Had he discovered the trick? and, if so, what was he going to do?

He grew more and more uneasy, and resolved that, at all events, it was best for him to retreat. Accordingly, at the next recess, as the teacher had anticipated, he went slyly to the lath, cut the string, then returned to his seat, and drew the line in, rolled it up, and put it in his pocket. The teacher, who was secretly watching him, observed the whole manœuvre.

At the close of the school, when the books were laid aside, and all was silence, he treated the affair thus:

"Do you remember the noise to which I called your attention early this afternoon?"

"Yes, sir."

"I will explain it to you now. One of the boys tied a string to a loose lath in the side of the room, and then, having the end of it at his seat, he was pulling it to make a noise to disturb us."

The scholars all looked astonished, and then began to turn round toward one another to see who the offender could be. The culprit began to tremble.

"He did it several times yesterday, and would have gone on doing it had I not spoken about it to-day. Do you think this was wrong or not?"

"Yes, sir;" "Wrong;" "Wrong," are the replies.

"What harm does it do?"

"It interrupts the school."

"Yes. Is there any other harm?"

The boys hesitate.

"It gives me trouble and pain. Should you not suppose it would?"

"Yes, sir."

"Have I ever treated any boy or girl in this school unjustly or unkindly?"

"No, sir;" "No, sir."

"Then why should any boy or girl wish to give me trouble or pain?"

There was a pause. The guilty individual expected that the next thing would be to call him out for punishment.

"Now what do you think I ought to do with such a boy?"

No answer.

"Perhaps I ought to punish him, but I am very unwilling to do that. I concluded to try another plan—to treat him with kindness and forbearance. So I called your attention to it this afternoon, to let him know that I was observing it, and to give him an opportunity to remove the string. And he did. He went, in the recess, and cut off the string. I shall not tell you his name, for I do not wish to injure his character. All I want is to have him a good boy."

A pause.

"I think I shall try this plan, for he must have some feelings of honor and gratitude, and if he has, he certainly will not try to give me pain or trouble again after this. And now I shall say no more about it, nor think any more about it; only, to prove that it is all as I say, if you look there under that window after school, you will see the lath with the end of the string round it, and, by pulling it, you can make it snap."

Another case, a little more serious in its character, is the following:

A teacher, having had some trouble with a rude and savage-looking boy, made some inquiry respecting him out of school, and incidentally learned that he had once or twice before openly rebelled against the authority of the school, and that he was now, in the recesses, actually preparing a club, with which he was threatening to defend himself if the teacher should attempt to punish him.

The next day, soon after the boys had gone out, he took his hat and followed them, and, turning round a corner of the school-house, found the boys standing around the young rebel, who was sitting upon a log, shaving the handle of the club smooth with his pocket-knife. He was startled at the unexpected appearance of the teacher, and the first impulse was to hide his club behind him; but it was too late, and, supposing that the teacher was ignorant of his designs, he went on sullenly with his work, feeling, however, greatly embarrassed.

"Pleasant day, boys," said the teacher. "This is a fine sunny nook for you to talk in.

"Seems to me, however, you ought to have a better seat than this old log," continued he, taking his seat at the same time by the side of the boy.

"Not so bad a seat, however, after all. What are you making, Joseph?"

Joseph mumbled out something inarticulate by way of reply.

"I have got a sharper knife," said he, drawing his penknife out of his pocket. And then, "Let me try it," he continued, gently taking the club out of Joseph's hand.

The boys looked surprised, some exchanged nods and winks, others turned away to conceal a laugh; but the teacher engaged in conversation with them, and soon put them all at their ease except poor Joseph, who could not tell how this strange interview was likely to end.

In the mean time, the teacher went on shaving the handle smooth and rounding the ends. "You want," said he, "a rasp or coarse file for the ends, and then you could finish it finely. But what are you making this formidable club for?"

Joseph was completely at a loss what to say. He began to show evident marks of embarrassment and confusion.

"I know what it is for; it is to defend yourself against me with. Is it not, boys?" said he, appealing to the others.

A faint "Yes, sir" or two was the reply.

"Well, now, Joseph, it will be a great deal better for us both to be friends than to be enemies. You had better throw this club away, and save yourself from punishment by being a good boy. Come, now," said he, handing him back his club, "throw it over into the field as far as you can, and we will all forget that you ever made it."

Joseph sat the picture of shame and confusion. Better feelings were struggling for admission, and the case was decided by a broad-faced, good-natured-looking boy, who stood by his side, saying almost involuntarily,

"Better throw it, Joe."

The club flew, end over end, into the field. Joseph returned to his allegiance, and never attempted to rise in rebellion again.

The ways by which boys engage in open, intentional disobedience are, of course, greatly varied, and the exact treatment will depend upon the features of the individual case; but the frankness, the openness, the plain dealing, and the kind and friendly tone which it is the object of the foregoing illustrations to exhibit, should characterize all.

9. We have already alluded to the importance of a delicate regard for the *characters* of the boys in all the measures of discipline adopted at the commencement of a school. This is, in fact, of the highest importance at all times, and is peculiarly so at the outset. A wound to the feelings is sometimes inflicted by a single transaction which produces a lasting injury to the character. Children are very sensitive to ridicule or disgrace, and some are most acutely so. A cutting reproof administered in public, or a punishment which exposes the individual to the gaze of others, will often burn far more deeply into the heart than the teacher imagines.

And it is often the cause of great and lasting injury, too.

By destroying the character of a pupil, you make him feel that he has nothing more to lose or gain, and destroy that kind of interest in his own moral condition which alone will allure him to virtuous conduct. To expose children to public ridicule or contempt tends either to make them sullen and despondent, or else to arouse their resentment and to make them reckless and desperate. Most persons remember through life some instances in their early childhood in which they were disgraced or ridiculed at school, and the permanence of the recollection is a test of the violence of the effect.

Be very careful, then, to avoid, especially at the commencement of the school, publicly exposing those who do wrong. Sometimes you may make the offense public, as in the case of the snapping of the lath, described under a former head, while you kindly conceal the name of the offender. Even if the school generally understand who he is, the injury of public exposure is almost altogether avoided, for the sense of disgrace does not come nearly so vividly home to the mind of a child from hearing occasional allusions to his offense by individuals among his playmates, as when he feels himself, at a particular time, the object of universal attention and dishonor. And then, besides, if the pupil perceives that the teacher is tender of his reputation, he will, by a feeling somewhere between imitation and sympathy, begin to feel a little tender of it too. Every exertion should be made, therefore, to lead children to value their character, and to help them to preserve it, and especially to avoid, at the beginning, every unnecessary sacrifice of it.

And yet there are cases where shame is the very best possible remedy for juvenile faults. If a boy, for example, is self-conceited, bold, and mischievous, with feelings somewhat callous, and an influence extensive and bad, an opportunity will sometimes occur to hold up his conduct to the just reprobation of the school with great advantage. By this means, if it is done in such a way as to *secure* the influence of the school on the right side, many good effects are sometimes attained. His pride and self-conceit are humbled, his bad influence receives a very decided check, and he is forced to draw back at once from the prominent stand he has occupied.

Richard Jones, for example, is a rude, coarse, self-conceited boy, often doing wrong both in school and out, and yet possessed of that peculiar influence which a bad boy often contrives to exert in school. The teacher, after watching some time for an opportunity to humble him, one day overhears a difficulty among the boys, and, looking out of the window, observes that he is taking away a sled from one of the little boys to slide down hill upon, having none of his own. The little boy resists as well as he can, and complains bitterly, but it is of no avail.

At the close of the school that day, the teacher commences conversation on the subject as follows:

"Boys, do you know what the difference is between stealing and robbery?"

"Yes, sir."

"What?"

The boys hesitate, and look at one another.

"Suppose a thief were to go into a man's store in the daytime, and take away something secretly, would it be stealing or robbery?"

"Stealing."

"Suppose he should meet him in the road, and take it away by force?"

"Then it would be robbery."

"Yes; when that which belongs to another is taken secretly, it is called stealing; when it is taken openly or with violence, it is called robbery. Which, now, do you think is the worst?"

"Robbery."

"Yes, for it is more barefaced and determined—then it gives a great deal more pain to the one who is injured. To-day I saw one of the boys in this school taking away another boy's sled, openly and with violence."

The boys all look round toward Richard.

"Was that of the nature of stealing or robbery?"

"Robbery," say the boys.

"Was it real robbery?"

They hesitate.

"If any of you think of any reason why it was not real robbery, you may name it."

"He gave the sled back to him," says one of the boys.

"Yes; and therefore, to describe the action correctly, we should not say Richard robbed a boy of his sled, but that he robbed him of his sled *for a time*, or he robbed him of the *use* of his sled. Still, in respect to the nature and the guilt of it, it was robbery.

"There is another thing which ought to be observed about it. Whose sled was it that Richard took away?"

"James Thompson's."

"James, you may stand up.

"Notice his size, boys. I should like to have Richard Jones stand up too, so that you might compare them; but I presume he feels very much ashamed of what he has done, and it would be very unpleasant for him to stand up. You will remember, however, how large he is. Now when I was a boy, it used to be considered dishonorable and cowardly for a large, strong boy to abuse a little one who can not defend himself. Is it considered so now?"

"Yes, sir."

"It ought to be, certainly; though, were it not for such a case as this, we should not have thought of considering Richard Jones a coward. It seems he did not dare to try to take away a sled from a boy who was as big as himself, but attacked little James, for he knew he was not strong enough to defend himself."

Now, in some such cases as this, great good may be done, both in respect to the individual and to the state of public sentiment in school, by openly exposing a boy's misconduct. The teacher must always take care, however, that the state of mind and character in the guilty individual is such that public exposure is adapted to work well as a remedy, and also that, in managing it, he carries the sympathies of the other boys with him. To secure this, he must avoid all harsh and exaggerated expressions or direct reproaches, and while he is mild, and gentle, and forbearing himself, lead the boys to understand and feel the nature of the sin which he exposes. The opportunities for doing this to advantage will, however, be rare. Generally it will be best to manage cases of discipline more privately, so as to protect the characters of those that offend.

The teacher should thus, in accordance with the directions we have given, commence his labors with careful circumspection, patience, frankness, and honest good-will toward every individual of his charge. He will find less difficulty at the outset than he would have expected, and soon have the satisfaction of perceiving that a mild but most efficient government is quietly and firmly established in the little kingdom over which he is called to reign.

THE END.

THE ADVENTURES OF A BROWNIE, as told to my Child. By the Author of "John Halifax, Gentleman." Illustrated. 16mo, Cloth, 90 cents.

GLADSTONE'S LIFE OF FARADAY. Michael Faraday. By J. H. GLADSTONE, Ph.D., F.R.S. 16mo, Cloth, $1 00.

BOURNE'S LONDON MERCHANTS. Famous London Merchants. A Book for Boys. By H. R. FOX BOURNE. With Portrait of George Peabody and 24 Illustrations. 16mo, Cloth, $1.

ABBOTT'S ROMANCE OF SPANISH HISTORY. The Romance of Spanish History. By JOHN S. C. ABBOTT. With Illustrations. 12mo, Cloth, $2 00.

ABBOTT'S FRANCONIA STORIES. Illustrations. Complete in 10 vols., 16mo, Cloth, 90 cents each. The volumes may be obtained separately; or complete, in neat case, $9 00:

Malleville.—Mary Bell.—Ellen Linn.—Wallace.—Beechnut. —Stuyvesant.—Agnes.—Mary Erskine.—Rodolphus.—Caroline.

ABBOTT'S LITTLE LEARNER SERIES. Harper's Picture-Books for the Nursery. Illustrated. In 5 vols., 90 cents each. The volumes complete in themselves, and sold separately; or the Set complete, in case, for $4 50:

Learning to Talk.—Learning to Think.—Learning to Read.—Learning about Common Things.—Learning about Right and Wrong.

ABBOTT'S MARCO PAUL'S VOYAGES AND TRAVELS IN THE PURSUIT OF KNOWLEDGE. Illustrated. Complete in 6 vols., 16mo, Cloth, 90 cents each. The Volumes may be obtained separately; or complete, in neat case, for $5 40:

In New York.—On the Erie Canal.—In the Forests of Maine. —In Vermont.—In Boston.—At the Springfield Armory.

ABBOTT'S STORIES OF RAINBOW AND LUCKY. Illustrated. 5 vols., 16mo, Cloth, 90 cents per vol. The volumes may be obtained separately; or complete, in neat case, for $4 50:

Hardie.—Rainbow's Journey.—Selling Lucky.—Up the River. —The Three Pines.

ABBOTTS' ILLUSTRATED HISTORIES. Illustrated with numerous Engravings. 16mo, Cloth, $1 20 per vol. The volumes may be obtained separately; or the Set complete, in box, for $38 40:

Cyrus the Great.—Darius the Great.—Xerxes.—Alexander the Great.—Romulus.—Hannibal.—Pyrrhus.—Julius Cæsar.—Cleopatra.—Nero.—Alfred the Great.—William the Conqueror. —Richard I.—Richard II.—Richard III.—Mary Queen of Scots.—Queen Elizabeth.—Charles I.—Charles II.—Josephine.—Marie Antoinette.—Madame Roland.—Henry IV.—Margaret of Anjou.—Peter the Great.—Genghis Khan.—King Philip.—Hernando Cortez.—Joseph Bonaparte.—Queen Hortense.—Louis XIV.—Louis Philippe.

GAIL HAMILTON'S LITTLE FOLK LIFE. Little Folk Life. A Book for Girls. By GAIL HAMILTON, Author of "Woman's Worth and Worthlessness." 16mo, Cloth, 90 cents.

ADVENTURES OF A YOUNG NATURALIST. By LUCIEN BIART. Edited and Adapted by PARKER GILLMORE. With 117 Illustrations. 12mo, Cloth, $1 75.

AIKIN'S EVENINGS AT HOME; or, The Juvenile Budget Opened. By Dr. AIKIN and Mrs. BARBAULD. With 34 Engravings by ADAMS. 12mo, Cloth, $1 50.

A CHILD'S HISTORY OF ENGLAND. By CHARLES DICKENS. 2 vols., 16mo, Cloth, $1 50.

A CHILD'S HISTORY OF THE UNITED STATES. By JOHN BONNER. 3 vols., 16mo, Cloth, $3 75.

A CHILD'S HISTORY OF ROME. By JOHN BONNER. With Illustrations. 2 vols., 16mo, Cloth, $2 50.

A CHILD'S HISTORY OF GREECE. By JOHN BONNER. With Illustrations. 2 vols., 16mo, Cloth, $2 50.

BAKER'S CAST UP BY THE SEA. Cast Up by the Sea. A Book for Young People. By Sir SAMUEL BAKER. With numerous Illustrations. 12mo, Cloth, 75 cents.

MUTINY OF THE BOUNTY. By Lady BELCHER. Illustrated. 12mo, Cloth, $1 50.

EDGAR'S BOYHOOD OF GREAT MEN. With Illustrations. 16mo, Cloth, $1 20.

EDGAR'S FOOTPRINTS OF FAMOUS MEN. With Illustrations. 16mo, Cloth, $1 20.

EDGAR'S HISTORY FOR BOYS; or, Annals of the Nations of Modern Europe. Illustrations. 16mo, Cloth, $1 20.

EDGAR'S SEA-KINGS AND NAVAL HEROES. A Book for Boys. Illustrated. 16mo, Cloth, $1 20.

EDGAR'S WARS OF THE ROSES. Illustrations. 16mo, Cloth, $1 20.

REID'S ODD PEOPLE. Being a Popular Description of Singular Races of Men. By Captain MAYNE REID. Illustrations. 16mo, Cloth, 75 cents.

MISS MULOCK'S OUR YEAR. A Child's Book in Prose and Verse. Illustrated by CLARENCE DOBELL. 16mo, Cloth, Gilt Edges, $1 00.

CHILDREN'S PICTURE-BOOKS. Square 4to, about 300 pages each, beautifully printed on Tinted Paper, with many Illustrations by WEIR, STEINLE, OVERBECK, VEIT, SCHNORR, HARVEY, and others. Bound in Cloth, Gilt, $1 50 a volume; or the Series complete, in neat case, $7 50:

The Children's Bible Picture-Book.—The Children's Picture Fable-Book.—The Children's Picture-Book of Quadrupeds and other Mammalia.—The Children's Picture-Book of the Sagacity of Animals.—The Children's Picture-Book of Birds.

HARPER'S BOYS' AND GIRLS' LIBRARY. 32 Volumes. Engravings. 18mo, Cloth. Sold separately at 75 cts. a volume:

Lives of the Apostles and Early Martyrs.—The Swiss Family Robinson, 2 vols. — Sunday Evenings, comprising Scripture Stories, 3 vols.—Mrs. Hofland's Son of a Genius.—Thatcher's Indian Traits, 2 vols.—Thatcher's Tales of the American Revolution.—Miss Eliza Robins's Tales from American History, 3 vols.—Mrs. Hofland's Young Crusoe; or, The Shipwrecked Boy.—Perils of the Sea.—Lives of Distinguished Females.—Mrs. Phelps's Caroline Westerley.—Mrs. Hughs's Ornaments Discovered.—The Clergyman's Orphan; the Infidel Reclaimed. —Uncle Philip's Natural History.—Uncle Philip's Evidences of Christianity.—Uncle Philip's History of Virginia.—Uncle Philip's American Forest.—Uncle Philip's History of New York, 2 vols.—Uncle Philip's Whale Fishery and the Polar Sea, 2 vols.—Uncle Philip's History of the Lost Colonies of Greenland.—Uncle Philip's History of Massachusetts, 2 vols.—Uncle Philip's History of New Hampshire, 2 vols.

HARPER'S STORY BOOKS. Narratives, Biographies, and Tales for the Young. By Jacob Abbott. With more than 1000 beautiful Engravings.

"Harper's Story Books" can be obtained complete in Twelve Volumes, each one containing Three Stories, at the price of $21 00; or in Thirty-six Thin Volumes, each containing One Story, at the price of $32 40. The volumes sold separately, the large ones at $1 75 each, the others at 90 cents each.

Volume I.—Bruno; Willie and the Mortgage; The Strait Gate.
" II.—The Little Louvre; Prank; Emma.
" III.—Virginia; Timboo and Joliba; Timboo and Fanny.
" IV.—The Harper Establishment; Franklin; The Studio.
" V.—The Story of Ancient History; The Story of English History; The Story of American History.
" VI.—John True; Elfred; The Museum.
" VII.—The Engineer; Rambles among the Alps; The Three Gold Dollars.
" VIII.—The Gibraltar Gallery; The Alcove; Dialogues.
" IX.—The Great Elm; Aunt Margaret; Vernon.
" X.—Carl and Jocko; Lapstone; Orkney the Peacemaker.
" XI.—Judge Justin; Minigo; Jasper.
" XII.—Congo; Viola; Little Paul.

Some of the Story Books are written particularly for Girls, and some for Boys; and the different volumes are adapted to various ages, so that the Series forms a complete Library of Story Books for Children of the Family and the Sunday-School.

HARPER'S FIRESIDE LIBRARY: expressly adapted to the Domestic Circle, Sunday-Schools, &c. Cloth, 75 cents each:

Alden's Alice Gordon.—Alden's Lawyer's Daughter.—Alden's Young Schoolmistress.—Burdett's Arthur Martin.—The Dying Robin.—Ellen Herbert; or, Family Changes.—Mayhew's Good Genius that turned every thing into Gold.—William the Cottager.—Mayhew's Magic of Kindness.

MAYHEW'S BOYHOOD OF MARTIN LUTHER; or, The Sufferings of the Little Beggar-Boy who afterward became the Great German Reformer. Beautifully Illustrated. 16mo, Cloth, $1 25.

MAYHEW'S PEASANT-BOY PHILOSOPHER. The Story of the Peasant-Boy Philosopher; or, "A Child Gathering Pebbles on the Sea-Shore." (Founded on the Early Life of Ferguson, the Shepherd-Boy Astronomer, and intended to show how a Poor Lad became acquainted with the Principles of Natural Science.) Illustrations. 16mo, Cloth, $1 25.

MAYHEW'S WONDERS OF SCIENCE; or, Young Humphrey Davy (the Cornish Apothecary's Boy, who taught himself Natural Philosophy, and eventually became President of the Royal Society). The Life of a Wonderful Boy written for Boys. Illustrations. 16mo, Cloth, $1 25.

MAYHEW'S YOUNG BENJAMIN FRANKLIN; or, the Right Road through Life. A Story to show how Young Benjamin Learned the Principles which Raised him from a Printer's Boy to the First Embassador of the American Republic. A Boy's Book on a Boy's own Subject. With Illustrations by JOHN GILBERT. 16mo, Cloth, $1 25.

FOLKS AND FAIRIES. Stories for Little Children. By LUCY RANDALL COMFORT. Illustrated. Square 4to, Cloth, $1 00.

MRS. MORTIMER'S READING WITHOUT TEARS; or, A Pleasant Mode of Learning to Read. Beautifully Illustrated. Small 4to, Cloth, $1 50.

MRS. MORTIMER'S LINES LEFT OUT; or, Some of the Histories left out in "Line upon Line." With Illustrations. 16mo, Cloth, 75 cents.

MRS. MORTIMER'S MORE ABOUT JESUS. With Illustrations and a Map. 16mo, Cloth, 75 cents.

MRS. MORTIMER'S STREAKS OF LIGHT; or, Fifty-two Facts from the Bible for Fifty-two Sundays of the Year. Illustrations. 16mo, Cloth, 75 cents.

HARRY'S LADDER TO LEARNING. With 250 Illustrations. Square 4to, Cloth, 75 cents.

HARRY'S SUMMER IN ASHCROFT. Illustrations. Square 4to, Cloth, 75 cents.

KINGSTON'S FRED MARKHAM IN RUSSIA; or, The Boy Travelers in the Land of the Czar. By W. H. G. KINGSTON. Illustrated. Small 4to, Cloth, Gilt, 75 cents.

THE ADVENTURES OF REUBEN DAVIDGER, Seventeen Years and Four Months Captive among the Dyaks of Borneo. By JAMES GREENWOOD. With Engravings. 8vo, Cloth, $1 75.

WILD SPORTS OF THE WORLD: A Book of Natural History and Adventure. By JAMES GREENWOOD, Author of "The True History of a Little Ragamuffin," "The Seven Curses of London," &c. With 147 Illustrations. Crown 8vo, Cloth, $2 50.

SELF-MADE MEN. By CHARLES C. B. SEYMOUR. Many Portraits. 12mo, 588 pages, Cloth, $1 75.

SMILES'S SELF-HELP; with Illustrations of Character and Conduct. By SAMUEL SMILES. 12mo, Cloth, $1 00.

SMILES'S CHARACTER. By SAMUEL SMILES. 12mo, Cloth, $1 50.

ROUND THE WORLD; Including a Residence in Victoria, and a Journey by Rail across North America. By a Boy. Edited by SAMUEL SMILES. Illustrations. 12mo, Cloth, $1 50.

THACKERAY'S ROSE AND THE RING; or, The History of Prince Giglio and Prince Bulbo. A Fireside Pantomime for Great and Small Children. By Mr. M. A. TITMARSH. Numerous Illustrations. Small 4to, Cloth, $1 00.

WOOD'S HOMES WITHOUT HANDS: being a Description of the Habitations of Animals, classed according to their Principle of Construction. By J. G. WOOD, M.A., F.L.S., Author of "Illustrated Natural History." With about 140 Illustrations. 8vo, Cloth, Beveled, $4 50.

A FRENCH COUNTRY FAMILY. Translated by the Author of "John Halifax" from the French of Madame DE WITT, *née* GUIZOT. Illustrations. 12mo, Cloth, $1 50.

MOTHERLESS. Translated by the Author of "John Halifax" from the French of Madame DE WITT, *née* GUIZOT. Illustrated. 12mo, Cloth, $1 50.

NINETEEN BEAUTIFUL YEARS; or, Sketches of a Girl's Life. Written by her Sister. With an Introduction by Rev. R. S. Foster, D.D. 16mo, Cloth, $1 00.

HOOKER'S CHILD'S BOOK OF NATURE. The Child's Book of Nature, for the Use of Families and Schools: intended to aid Mothers and Teachers in Training Children in the Observation of Nature. In Three Parts. Part I. Plants. Part II. Animals. Part III. Air, Water, Heat, Light, &c. By WORTHINGTON HOOKER, M.D. Engravings. The Three Parts, complete in One Volume, Small 4to, Cloth, $2 00; or, separately, 90 cents each.

MACÉ'S SERVANTS OF THE STOMACH. The Servants of the Stomach. By JEAN MACÉ. 12mo, Cloth, $1 75.

MACÉ'S HISTORY OF A MOUTHFUL OF BREAD, and its Effect on the Organization of Men and Animals. 12mo, Cloth, $1 75.

MISS WARNER'S THREE LITTLE SPADES. Illustrations. 16mo, Cloth, $1 00.

www.ingramcontent.com/pod-product-compliance
Lightning Source LLC
LaVergne TN
LVHW010151110826
845151LV00002B/490